THE SUNDAY TIMES
GUIDE TO
ENLIGHTENED EATING

Lis Leigh, a graduate of Somerville College, Oxford, is a television and radio producer specialising in scientific and consumer topics, and is a regular contributor to the *Sunday Times Magazine* on food. In autumn 1985, she wrote a four part investigative series on food additives as part of the Sunday Times Enlightened Eating campaign. She has always been someone for whom buying, preparing, eating and talking about food is a pleasure — and a pleasure to be shared with others.

THE SUNDAY TIMES

GUIDE TO

ENLIGHTENED EATING

LIS LEIGH
General Editor: Rose Shepherd

CENTURY

LONDON · MELBOURNE · AUCKLAND · JOHANNESBURG

First published in this edition in 1986 by
Century Hutchinson Ltd,
Brookmount House, 62-65 Chandos Place,
Covent Garden, London WC2N 4NW

Designed and produced by
Shuckburgh Reynolds Limited
289 Westbourne Grove, London W11 2QA

British Library Cataloguing in Publication Data
Leigh, Lis
    The Sunday times guide to enlightened
    eating.
    1. Nutrition
    I. Title
    641.1   TX353

ISBN 0-7126-1299-8
    ISBN 0-7126-1400-1 Pbk

Designer: Nigel Partridge

Typesetting by SX Composing Ltd,
Rayleigh, Essex
Printed and bound in Spain by
Printer Industria Grafica, SA, Barcelona D.L.B. 31078-1986

CONTENTS

ACKNOWLEDGEMENTS

I would like to thank the many people who have generously given of their time and expertise while I was writing this book. I am particularly indebted to the following:

British Nutrition Foundation
Professor D. M. Conning (Director General);
Dr. Richard Cottrell (Science Director);
nutritionists Gill Fine and Marnie Sommerville
Professor W. P. T. James, Director of Rowett Research Institute,
Aberdeen and Chairman of the NACNE Report

London Food Commission
Dr. Tim Lang; Tony Webb; Melanie Miller;
Izzy Cole-Hamilton

Dr. Louise Davies, Royal Free Hospital
Mr. Clive Wadey, Institution of Environmental Health Officers
Mrs. Shirley Bond (of the British Dietetic Assoc.)

My thanks, too, to the following organisations for
their co-operation

The Apple and Pear Development Council
National Dairy Council
Food from Britain
Fresh Fruit and Vegetable Information Bureau
Meat Promotion Executive
Sea Fish Industry Authority

PART ONE

FOOD AND NUTRITION

Why do we eat? Superficially, to satisfy hunger. But the primary reason is to keep going in health and in sickness, in action and in repose.

If there were a direct relationship between our physical requirements and what appetite dictates, there would be no need for this book. But while the body *does* know broadly what it wants, few of us are properly attuned to the signals it sends out.

Nutrition today is a matter for the intellect as much as for instinct, especially since, more than ever before, we are seeking precise answers to highly complex questions.

Recent nutritional research has concentrated on trying to determine how much an individual needs of all the various constituents of food, how they affect men and women, infants and adolescents, the mature and the elderly, with the aim of establishing three fundamental principles.

* The amount we should consume daily
* Which foods we should be eating
* The ideal balance of foods in the diet to maintain a healthy body

The Sunday Times Guide to Enlightened Eating aims to provide advice on eating enjoyably, and to eating healthily. In any food plan, there can be no absolutes, no diet which provides the magic key to total well being. But science has advanced sufficiently in the past 20 years to enable each of us, with a very basic knowledge of nutrition, to give our bodies a fighting chance of surviving into healthy old age.

Fashions in food

Surveys show that many of us are confused about the food we eat. This is hardly surprising when you consider the contradictory messages put out by advertisers, newspapers, magazines, "health" and slimming publications, doctors, scientists and government, or those earlier influences, ideas instilled by teachers, memories of school meals, the opinions and beliefs of parents and friends.

The past four decades have seen not one but several revolutions in the way we think about and treat our food. The prevailing wisdom has turned dizzyingly about and about, even as we have tried to assimilate altered living patterns and the advances of science.

You may have grown up with convenience and carry-out foods, and take for granted the latest technology, yet have been cut off from the inherited skills of food selection, storage and preparation, which were essential to anyone running a household in the days before packaged and pre-cooked food, fridges, freezers and microwaves. Or you may have learned all the traditional skills, but feel that technology has overtaken you.

Each new wave of influence creates patterns of desirable eating, as may be seen in this brief – and necessarily rather superficial – survey of predominant attitudes to food over four-and-a-half decades. Of course there is always an overlap of attitudes from one decade to the next, but the predominant assumptions will have the greatest influence on market forces and determine what we find in the shops.

The Forties

For those at home during the War the emphasis was on keeping up health and strength. In 1940, the new Ministry of Food stepped in to ensure fair distribution through rationing, to provide good nutrition for the masses, but it was 18 months before the shortages really began to bite. Then the civilian adult ration for a week included just 4oz bacon or ham, 1oz cheese, a shilling's worth of meat, 8oz fats (including no more than 2oz butter), 8oz sugar, 2oz tea, 2oz preserves. Eggs and milk were in short supply. Tinned luncheon meat, tinned fish and baked beans were the first foods to be put on "points" in December '41. There were few luxuries, but ingenious use was made of wholesome alternatives, and a little was found to go a long way. Cookery columnists gave sound advice on balanced diet, and dreamed up dishes based on offal, pulses and root vegetables. There was positive benefit to the nation's health from a regime with reduced animal protein, limited in sugar, high in fibre, and the public took a greater active interest than ever before in nutrition, cheerfully exchanging recipes for liver-and-oatmeal pudding, bread soup, lentil croquettes, carrot tart and Woolton pie (dishes which would not dismay dieticians today).

The Fifties

Prolonged rationing (until 1953) and world shortages meant that, when all foods were at last freely available, pleasure more than nutrition was the principle. Meats, fats, sugar, eggs and canned fruit and vegetables, manufactured sausages and pies, and above all sweets and chocolate were the rewards for years of austerity. In 1955, a lone voice bewailed the new "processed" and "chemicalised" foods (Doris Grant in *Dear Housewives*), but nobody cared to hear this message.

The Sixties

Incomes rose steeply, more women went out to work, and the new affluence brought new preoccupations. Less time in the kitchen, more time for enjoyment. Frozen food was wonderfood: sales rocketed. No one worried about food except the poor (the Child Poverty Action Group undermined Macmillan's never-had-it-so-good message) and except women, who were encouraged to believe that they ate too much. The craze for slimming meant bread, cakes and potatoes were eschewed in the quest for the Hollywood figure. The calorie became Public Enemy Number One.

The Seventies

Urban sprawl meant more people became town-dwellers, disposable income increased, as did the consumption of animal protein, sugar, fats, and every form of snack. Britain had the lowest fruit and vegetable consumption of any EEC country. With growing enthusiasm for foreign travel, and with the popularity of cheap ethnic restaurants, such exotic fare as instant chow mein, sweet-and-sour pork, ravioli, chilli con carne invaded the British kitchen. The minority hippy generation rejected meat and manufactured foods, but brown rice and vegetables represented a philosophy of life more than a theory of nutrition. Meanwhile, the majority spent more of the household budget on cars and cookers, in proportion to food. Towards the end of the decade came recession and mounting unemployment, yet sales of manufactured foods continued to boom. Scientists and doctors, if not the rest of us, were aware of the dangers in our diet.

The Eighties

Now food has supplanted sex as the fashionable subject for concern. Cooking has become "cuisine". For some, the pursuit of health has become a way of life, and tracksuited joggers stock up with muesli, yoghurt, brown rice and pulses, as they decry manufactured products, full of additives, and all "junk" food. Yet medical and nutritional reports show that most people still eat unhealthily. For the first time since the Forties, nutrition is a key issue.

The key reports

The growing number of us who give thought to food are continually swayed by conflicting theories and new health scares. The increasing polarisation of the debate does not help. The medical/scientific lobby and the "health" lobby have equally strong views as to what we should eat. Even though both groups refer to the same two key reports, the recommendations drawn from them are being interpreted – and sometimes misinterpreted – differently.

Let us look at the background and specific recommendations of these two most crucial reports on nutrition, that of NACNE (National Advisory Committee on Nutrition Education) and of COMA (the DHSS Committee on the Medical Aspects of Food Policy), to clear up at least one area of confusion.

In the Seventies, as we have seen, we began to experiment with unfamiliar cooking styles, having been introduced to them through cheap holiday travel or in high street Chinese, Indian, Greek and Italian restaurants and French-style bistros at home, which removed much of the ritual and expense from dining out. Manufacturers capitalised on the consumer's

heightened sense of adventure by introducing canned, packet and frozen versions of new-found foreign dishes. The excitement generated by food had little to do with what was good for us.

The medical profession, however, had another perspective. There was widespread concern among experts that the increasing incidence of heart disease in the West was directly related to diet. With no outside factors such as war or extreme economic depression, which might have required the government to step in, to promote public awareness of nutrition, the "anything goes" attitude prevailed both in Europe and in America. Besides, governments are able to legislate or advise on health, only against a

The British discovery in the Seventies of foreign cuisine was to prove a gastronomic mixed blessing

background of generally accepted scientific findings. However, as the disturbing data on heart disease accumulated, it became clear that, somehow or other, people had to be helped to understand what they were eating, and to change some shopping and cooking habits.

The NACNE Report

In 1979, a working party was set up in Britain by the British Nutrition Foundation and the Health Education Council to bring together available evidence on the relevance of diet to health and disease, which would form a guideline for organisations directly or indirectly concerned with health education. Back in 1973, Sir Keith Joseph, then Secretary of State for Social Services, had voiced the urgent need for "a point of reference that would provide simple and accurate information on nutrition". The sources consulted were principally reports by the DHSS, the Royal College of Physicians, the British Cardiac Society, and the World Health Organisation. The array of subjects covered was comprehensive, ranging from body weight, diet balance, the importance of fibre, the role of sugar, salt and fat in disease, to the special needs of certain sections of the population.

In September 1983, 10 years after Sir Keith Joseph's urgent request, the NACNE Report was finally published, and then only mainly thanks to journalistic pressure. Though the thinking behind the Report was familiar to nutritionists, the specification of foods to be increased or decreased in the nation's diet, as well as the quantifying of recommended intakes, was a radical departure. And the political implications were controversial.

If the nation had to change its diet, ran the arguments, how was this to be brought about? By legislation? Surely fundamental democratic freedoms were at stake here? Why should a group of doctors and nutritionists dictate how we eat, and who could prove them right? In any case, "ordinary people" would not be able to understand the message, so why be so alarmist? How could you put into practice the dietary reforms recommended? Force manufacturers to produce "healthy" fare? Make farmers grow more "healthy" produce? A lot of people, particularly some food producers, hoped the Report would be left on the shelf.

The COMA Report

In the event, the advice of the NACNE Report was not ignored. And the importance of establishing nutritional guidelines was further strengthened by the appearance of another report, on Diet and Cardiovascular Disease, published in 1984 by the DHSS Committee on the Medical Aspects of Food Policy. NACNE had paved the way for the discussion on the pursuance of a healthier diet, but the COMA Report represented the official voice of medicine.

Some people want to know why a group of doctors and nutritionists should dictate what the nation eats

Henceforth, any policy on nutrition (formulated by the DHSS in consultation with the Ministry of Agriculture, Food and Fisheries) would have to take COMA into account.

Problems were to arise (and are still unresolved) when the demands of farming policy, governed by the EEC, as well as the influence of powerful conglomerate manufacturers, came into conflict with those negative recommendations contained in both reports, particularly concerning the advice to cut down on fats, sugar and salt. Advertising has more than ever become a weapon, in the bid to establish counter messages of reassurance.

The message of the NACNE Report was basically this: cut down on fats; cut down on sugar; cut down on salt; eat more fibre. But by how much? It would clearly be impracticable to set up government-funded nutrition advisory centres, where balanced food plans could be worked out for each individual, so a general and universal guideline had to be set down. COMA and NACNE were broadly in agreement, though there were significant differences. NACNE considered that about 15 years would be needed to implement the drastic changes it considered desirable in public attitudes, agricultural policies, manufacturing techniques and government and EEC regulations, so it gave two diet strategies, one for the Eighties, one for the long term. The main specific recommendations of the Reports are as follows.

Fats NACNE: the nation should reduce total fat intake from an average 42 per cent to 34 per cent of daily energy needs short term; to 30 per cent long term. COMA: individuals should reduce total fat intake to 35 per cent of daily energy needs.

Sugar NACNE: reduce average sucrose intake by 10 per cent, from 38kg a year to 34kg short term; to 20kg long term. COMA: the intake of simple sugars (sucrose, glucose, fructose) should not be increased.

Salt NACNE: reduce salt intake from the present average 12g a day by 1g a day short term; by 3g a day long term. COMA: the intake of common salt should not be increased further, and consideration should be given to ways of decreasing it.

Fibre NACNE: increase dietary fibre from 20g a day to 25g short term; to 30g long term. COMA: sees advantages in compensating for reduced fat intake with increased fibre-rich carbohydrates (eg, bread, cereals, fruit, vegetables), provided this can be achieved without increasing total intake of common salt or simple sugars.

A survey published in early 1986 (D'Arcy Masius Benton & Bowles: *Health Study*) showed that "housewives" had taken certain of these recommendations to heart. Half the population was making a determined effort to change its diet. But a *Which?* report, published at around the same time, suggested that, in terms of total nutrition, deficiencies were now probable. The "Cut Down" message had been misinterpreted to the detriment of such components as fibre and certain vital nutrients in diet.

Our aim, with this book, is to make the nutritional message both clearer and less dogmatic. Nutritional guidelines do and will change, as more evidence becomes available about the role of diet in preventive medicine, in allergy and in disease. For now, however, the NACNE and COMA proposals, taken generally, and – since food is after all to be enjoyed – taken occasionally with a pinch of salt, can only improve our diet.

Food for energy

Food is fuel. It provides the energy which enables the body to function, the heart to pump, the lungs to take in oxygen, muscles to maintain tension.The process of utilising energy, in which a complex series of chemical changes takes place, is known as "metabolism".

Energy is obtained in two ways: first by the food taken in daily; second, by drawing on reserves of animal starch (glycogen) or fat stored in the body.

It is the energy and nutrients obtained from food which enable the body to function efficiently. A convenient measure for the heat produced by energy is the kilocalorie (commonly referred to simply as "calorie"). In Europe, the kiloJoule is preferred: 1 kilocalorie (kcal) equals 4.184 kiloJoules (kJ).

Our energy needs can be assessed in terms of total kilocalories (see table, below). The amount we must eat to provide this energy can be calculated by measuring the kilocalories in food. The composition of food is usually analysed per 100 grams, but the portion values listed in calorie counters, available from newsagents and bookshops, are more helpful. In the ideal meal plan, the kilocalories in our diet will match the kilocalories needed for the body's activities, but this alone is not enough. The mixture of foods must also provide the right nutrients. (And remember that "energy" in the food context refers strictly to its biological function; it has only so much to do with feeling energetic.)

Nearly all foods provide energy; not all supply significant nutrients. The term "empty calories" has been coined to describe foods of high energy and minimal nutrient value.

Where the energy goes

The energy provided by food is converted in the body to satisfy four separate needs. First, it gives mechanical energy for activities. Second, it gives chemical energy for body tissue.

These recommendations for daily intake of kilocalories according to age and sex may be subject to amendment in the light of continuing researches, but they serve as a rough guide to energy requirements

RECOMMENDED DAILY INTAKE OF KILOCALORIES (DHSS, 1979)			
MALE		**FEMALE**	
Under 12 months	780	Under 12 months	720
1 year	1200	1 year	1100
2	1400	2	1300
3 to 4	1560	3 to 4	1500
5 to 6	1740	5 to 6	1680
7 to 8	1980	7 to 8	1900
9 to 11	2280	9 to 11	2050
12 to 14	2640	12 to 14	2150
15 to 17	2880	15 to 17	2150
18 to 34		18 to 54	
sedentary	2510	most occupations	2150
moderately active	2900	very active	2500
very active	3350	55 to 74	1900
35 to 64		75 and over	1680
sedentary	2400		
moderately active	2750	Pregnant	2400
very active	3350	Lactating	2750
65 to 74	2400		
75 and over	2150		

ACCEPTABLE WEIGHTS FOR MEN AND WOMEN
From Royal College of Physicians' Report on Obesity, 1983

HEIGHT (barefoot)		WEIGHT (without clothes)		HEIGHT (barefoot)		WEIGHT (without clothes)	
ft in	cm	lb	kg	ft in	cm	lb	kg
MALE				FEMALE			
5 5	165	121-152	55-69	5 0	152	96-125	44-57
5 6	168	124-156	56-71	5 1	155	99-128	45-58
5 7	170	128-161	58-73	5 2	157	102-131	46-59
5 8	173	132-166	60-75	5 3	160	105-134	48-61
5 9	175	136-170	62-77	5 4	162	108-138	49-62
5 10	178	140-174	64-79	5 5	165	111-142	51-65
5 11	180	144-179	65-80	5 6	168	114-146	52-66
6 0	183	148-184	67-83	5 7	170	118-150	53-67
6 1	185	152-189	69-86	5 8	173	122-154	55-69
6 2	188	156-194	71-88	5 9	175	126-158	58-72
6 3	191	160-199	73-90	5 10	178	130-163	59-74

*Obesity can seriously undermine your health. If your weight falls
outside the range considered to be acceptable for your height (see
above) consider either reducing your food intake or increasing your
energy expenditure, or adjusting both*

Third, it gives heat for bodily warmth. Fourth, it is needed by children for growth and repair. The energy for these needs is released by means of digestion and absorption, two stages of metabolism. Metabolism entails a series of chemical reactions which allow the elements in nutrients to reach and be used by the appropriate cells in the body, and waste products to be eliminated. Each step is controlled by enzymes, proteins which act as catalysts in bio-chemical reactions, sometimes assisted by vitamins.

Some principles of energy requirements hold true. Growing children, relative to their body weight, need more than adults. Those with more lean muscle tissue have greater energy needs, so that (usually) men require more than women.

The official estimates of energy needs make necessarily fairly crude distinctions between girls and boys, men and women of different age groups, since it would be impossible to take into account the variations of activity in – and out of – one's job. They are also likely, in the future, as research goes on, to be subject to amendment, but they do provide a rough guide.

When people habitually eat more food than their bodies require, the excess energy is accumulated as fat. Any food is, in this sense, "fattening". But foods which have a concentrated energy-releasing potential (ie, those with a high kilocalorie content) will tend to accumulate more body fat than the same quantities of food of lower energy value. The comparative energy release of carbohydrate, protein and fat, per gram, is:

Carbohydrate 4 kcal
Protein 4 kcal
Fat 9 kcal

Simply, fat supplies more than twice the energy of protein or carbohydrate. And the energy value of food depends on the amount of fat, protein and carbohydrate it comprises.

Basal metabolism

We all know people who are able to eat large quantities of food without putting on weight – and others who complain that they pile on the pounds while following an apparently low-energy diet. One possible explanation is that basal metabolism (the energy expenditure of a person who is relaxed and comfortable in the morning, soon after waking and 14 hours after the last meal) varies from one individual to the next. It also varies with age, usually slowing down with the decades. And gender differences and body size have to be taken into the reckoning, too. Body size, in itself, is not a reliable indicator of how much energy is needed: what matters most is the lean body weight, excluding body fat. A rugby player who is the same height and weight as a deskbound executive will have a far greater lean body weight, and thus more substantial energy requirements, even while resting.

For the sake of convenience, it is assumed that we each have an *average* basal metabolic rate for our weight and gender. Thus a man weighing 70kg is deemed to need 1785 kilocalories, and a woman weighing 54kg to need 1465 kilocalories, just to keep the body warm and functioning. Beyond this, activity burns up additional kilocalories, according to how strenuous it is, and of what duration. There is, again, some variation from person to person, but here is a rough guide to the energy you might expend at different activities.

APPROXIMATE ENERGY EXPENDITURE IN DIFFERENT ACTIVITIES

(Note: This is necessarily a rough guide, since expenditure of kilocalories depends on gender, age, body size and composition, climate, and of course how hard you work or play at whatever you are doing. Figures are based on an hypothetical man weighing 65kg and an hypothetical woman weighing 55kg. Where they are given per hour, no allowance has been made for rests. Where an activity would be hard to sustain over a period, kilocalories per minute are given.)

MAN	kcals per hour	WOMAN	kcals per hour
In bed asleep	65	In bed asleep	54
Sitting quietly	84	Sitting quietly	70
Standing quietly	105	Standing quietly	84
Walking moderately fast	240	Walking moderately fast	180
Sedentary work	108	Office work	95
Domestic work		Domestic work	
light	125	cooking	100
moderate	185	light cleaning	150
more energetic (polishing etc)	255	more energetic (polishing etc)	210
Carpentry	240	Light industrial work	
Mechanical (motor repairs)	245	in bakery	140
Driving (lorry)	100	electrical industry	115
Decorating	190	laundry	195
Bricklaying	240	Recreational	
Recreational		sedentary	120
light (snooker, bowls, golf)	150	light (snooker, bowls, croquet)	120-240
moderate (riding, swimming, tennis)	150-300	moderate (riding, swimming, dancing)	240-360
energetic (rowing, soccer etc)	450	heavy (athletics, rowing etc)	over 340
very strenuous	over 600		

STANDARD BASAL METABOLIC RATES OF MALES AND FEMALES AT DIFFERENT WEIGHTS
(kilocalories needed per 24 hours just to keep ticking over)

WEIGHT IN KG	MALE	FEMALE	WEIGHT IN KG	MALE	FEMALE
3	150	136	36	1270	1173
4	210	205	38	1305	1207
5	270	274	40	1340	1241
6	330	336	42	1370	1274
7	390	395	44	1400	1306
8	445	448	46	1430	1338
9	495	496	48	1460	1369
10	545	541	50	1485	1399
11	590	582	52	1505	1429
12	625	620	54	1555	1465
13	665	655	56	1580	1487
14	700	687	58	1600	1516
15	725	718	60	1630	1544
16	750	747	62	1660	1572
17	780	775	64	1690	1599
18	810	802	66	1725	1626
19	840	827	68	1765	1653
20	870	852	70	1785	1679
22	910	898	72	1815	1705
24	980	942	74	1815	1731
26	1070	984	76	1870	1756
28	1100	1025	78	1900	1781
30	1140	1063	80	1930	1805
32	1190	1101	82	1960	1830
34	1230	1137	84	2000	1855

''Basal metabolism'' refers to the amount of energy needed by the body for such functions as breathing, heartbeat, the maintenance of temperature, brain activity etc. These needs vary from person to person and are influenced by such factors as age and the proportion of lean tissue to fat in the body, but the above tables will give some guide to how many kilocalories you require simply to keep ticking over

The most important factor in determining energy requirements – and the most difficult to gauge – is the degree of activity engaged in. The table opposite indicates the number of kilocalories you might expect to use at work or play (including those needed for basic bodily functions), but individual variations are to be expected

Food, as we know, does not just supply energy, but also gives essential nutrients for the growth, maintenance and repair of cells, and certain elements in its structure help with the regulation of these activities. The health-giving aspects of food are sometimes neglected in the everyday business of eating, but it is important to remember that carbohydrates, fats, proteins, vitamins and minerals are all essential. Although it is possible to stay alive on bread and water, denying the body those vital nutrients contained in other foods will sooner or later cause sickness and degeneration.

The human body is a complex machine in which every part is interdependent. Unlike simpler forms of animal and vegetable life, we must have a wide range of foods to sustain and balance our chemical processes. This is why nutritionists' primary message will always be: for health as well as enjoyment, follow a balanced and varied diet.

Although this idea is straightforward, it cannot be properly grasped without some understanding of the way the primary elements of food behave inside the body.

Fats

In everyday parlance, fat is associated with obesity or grease. But in relation to food, these associations can be misleading. Fatty foods can contribute to fat storage in the body – but so can other foods. Some fat is obviously greasy, but some cannot readily be identified. Butter, margarine, lard, oils and animal fats are all greasy in use; less obvious is the fat in milk, cheese, fish, nuts, lean meat and some vegetables.

One difference between oils and fats is that oils are liquid at room temperature. But the most significant distinction between fatty substances, in whatever form, lies in the mixture of chemical components. Although animal and vegetable fats can contain the fat-soluble vitamins A, D, E and K (as well as cholesterol), the primary constituents are the triglycerides, each of which is a combination of fatty acids reacting differently in the atmosphere and in the body. The many combinations of fatty acids divide chemically into two main groups, which have considerable relevance to health. They are: saturated and unsaturated fatty acids. Although these are found in combination, it is their relative proportion which counts in evaluating the benefit to the human body.

Saturated fatty acids are the more stable, and predominate in hard cooking fats such as lard, butter, hard cheeses and block margarine.

Unsaturated fatty acids are divided into polyunsaturated and mono-unsaturated. This group contains acids which cannot be made in the body, but which have been found to have important implications to health.

All fats provide the body with energy (9 kcal per gram), and some carry fat-soluble vitamins which are stored in the tissue under the skin when surplus to body requirements.

Healthguide: The major threat to health is thought to lie in the over-consumption of saturated fats, because of the way they can raise the cholesterol level in the blood. High levels of cholesterol in the bloodstream can lead to it being deposited in the arteries, including those which supply the heart. The constriction and hardening of the arteries is a forerunner of heart disease, leading to angina or clotting which may precipitate a heart attack. An estimated 90 per cent of the population of the UK, at the age of 40, have diseased arteries, and with 160,000 deaths each year from heart disease Britain is near the top of the statistics.

Cholesterol belongs to the same chemical group as fat, and is present in small quantities in

The oils shown here are far higher in unsaturated than in saturated fatty acids. Of those used for cooking, safflower oil is highest in polyunsaturates, but it is unsuitable for deep frying since it is unstable at high temperature. Olive oil and peanut/groundnut oil are largely monounsaturated. Almond oil, hazelnut, walnut and sesame oils are best used as flavourings being both distinctive in taste and expensive to buy

KEY
1. Grapeseed oil
2. Rapeseed oil
3. Sunflower oil
4. Extra virgin olive oil
5. Groundnut oil
6. Hazelnut oil
7. Corn oil
8. Safflower oil
9. Soya oil
10. Almond oil
11. Vegetable oil
12. Walnut oil
13. Sesame oil
14. Toasted sesame oil

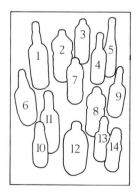

all foods of animal origin. It is also found in the human body, in blood plasma and cell membranes. It is needed for the production of bile and is present in all body cells, and what the body does not obtain from diet, it manufactures.

In fact, 80 per cent of cholesterol is produced by the body, and there is no conclusive evidence to show that that supplied *directly* by diet contributes to the cholesterol loading in the body. The only significant sources of cholesterol are eggs, offal and fish roe, and then only a proportion of it is absorbed.

All fats are important for energy and are valuable sources of vitamins, particularly A and D. But the balance of saturates with unsaturates is crucial. Of the fats we obtain from foods and cooking, more than half should be unsaturated (ie, mono- and polyunsaturated).

While not all the causes of cholesterol deposits are known (and stress and lack of exercise may be factors), it has been demonstrated that diets high in polyunsaturates, particularly those high in linoleic acid, can reduce them. This does not mean that polyunsaturates should be consumed in quantities as some kind of magic antidote to the harmful effects of saturated fats. To reduce cholesterol levels in the body, you have to reduce your intake of all fats, and particularly of saturated ones.

The COMA Report made the following recommendations for changing fat consumption in the average diet (note, these do not apply to children under five).

The COMA Report sees advantages in compensating for reduced fat intake with increased consumption of fibre-rich carbohydrates such as are shown here. This should be achieved without increasing consumption of common salt or simple sugars. It is now known that some types of fibre are absorbed during digestion. Insoluble fibre such as is found in wheatbran has greater implications to bowel function

SOME FIBRE-RICH FOODS
1. *Porridge oats*
2. *Weetabix*
3. *Shredded Wheat*
4. *Bran*
5. *Haricot beans*
6. *Peanuts*
7. *Hazelnuts*
8. *Brown rice*
9. *Raisins*
10. *Peas*
11. *Runner beans*
12. *Carrots*
13. *Spinach*
14. *Potatoes*
15. *Leeks*

RULE OF THUMB

Reduce your fat intake by cutting your consumption of cakes, biscuits, pastries and puddings, lard, suet, butter and hard margarine. Eat more oily fish like herrings and mackerel (high in polyunsaturates). Remove visible fat from meat, and remove skin from poultry before or after cooking as appropriate. Use reduced-fat alternatives where possible (skimmed milk, low-fat yoghurt, sorbets instead of ice cream). Favour low-fat cheeses. Grill, poach or steam instead of frying where possible, and, when you do fry, remember, the hotter the frying medium, the less fat is absorbed by food. Don't par-boil potatoes for roasting as this makes them absorb more fat. Cut chips thickly. Use oils higher in mono- and polyunsaturates for cooking and for salad dressing. Be careful of anything labelled simply "vegetable oil", which could contain saturated fats, although nowadays rapeseed oil is commonly used, and this is low in saturates.

---

* Saturated fats should be cut by one quarter.
* The energy derived from *all* fats should be no more than 35 per cent of total dietary energy.
* More than half of all fats (20 per cent of total energy consumption) should be mono-unsaturated and polyunsaturated.

Fats to reduce Cut back on lard, suet, butter and hard margarine. Many bought cakes and biscuits rely heavily on coconut oil and palm oil, which are both saturated fats. Beef, lamb and pork fat should be trimmed from meat (it is now becoming more possible to buy lean cuts). Use a reduced-fat alternative when one is available (low-fat yoghurt, sorbets instead of ice cream). High-fat cheeses (see page 85) should be eaten in moderation, and cheese-lovers should avoid using butter or margarine on the accompanying bread or biscuits.

Milk is an essential part of our diet, an important source of calcium as well as of protein, vitamins and minerals. But when reducing total fat intake, it is advisable to use the skimmed or semi-skimmed variety, even though there is some loss of fat-soluble vitamins A and D (and skimmed milk should not be given to children under five). Note that some dried whiteners for use in tea and coffee are high in saturated fats, which appear on the label as "hydrogenated vegetable fat", so go for those made from skimmed milk.

There is no denying that, for many people, having a variety of cheeses, cooking occasionally with butter and cream, eating fried fish and chips and hamburgers, and home-baking cakes and pastries, is very much a part of enjoying food. Few nutritionists would suggest banning all such indulgences, except where medically required, but they should not be eaten with abandon, and should not form the staple of any sensible meal plan.

Fats to use in cooking The following are recommended as being higher in unsaturated than in saturated fats: olive oil, corn oil, safflower oil, sunflower oil, grapeseed oil, peanut or groundnut oil, rapeseed oil, soya bean oil, sesame oil, mustard seed oil, walnut oil, almond oil. Some oil is labelled "vegetable oil", but this might be blended with palm or coconut oil, which are mainly saturated fats, and could well be lower in polyunsaturates than unblended varieties.

Eat more fish Oily varieties like mackerel, herring, sardines and pilchards, trout and salmon are prime sources of polyunsaturated fats.

Caution If you are drastically cutting down on fat-rich dairy produce and fatty meat, you will also be cutting down on essential nutrients. Vary your diet by eating fish, poultry, game, liver and kidneys, low-fat dairy produce, pulses, cereals and vegetables.

The message on fat, remember, is "cut down", not "cut out". The recommended proportion in diet is 30/35 per cent (NACNE long term/COMA), measured in kilocalories, not by weight. Of this 35 per cent, says COMA, 20 should come from unsaturated fat, and only 15 from saturated. NACNE sets a long term goal of 10 per cent of total energy to derive from saturated, and 20 per cent from unsaturated fats.

Carbohydrates

The name refers to their chemical structure: they contain carbon, hydrogen and oxygen. The hydrogen and oxygen are in the proportion of two to one, just as they are in water, hence "hydrate". Carbohydrates include sugars of various kinds, starches, and those substances termed "unavailable", such as cellulose, pectins and gums, which pass through the body, mainly without being absorbed, and which are commonly known as fibre or roughage.

Sugars There are several types. Common table sugar is called sucrose and is a combination of fructose and glucose, of which fructose is the sweeter. All three are frequently listed on labels. Sucrose is produced from sugar cane and sugar beet as well as being found in most fruits and vegetables. Fructose is found in fruits and honey. Glucose (or dextrose) is a basic unit of a starch molecule, is found in fruit juice, and is one of the components of lactose, which is a constituent of milk. Other sugars are xylitol (from wood), sorbitol (from glucose) and mannitol (from seaweed).

Starches Monosaccharides are basic sugars structured in single units (eg, glucose, fructose, galactose), but when two elements join they form disaccharides (eg, sucrose, lactose, maltose). In the same family of carbohydrates are starches, made up of multiple units of glucose (polysaccharides).

Starches are found in the seeds and roots of plants, particularly in cereals such as wheat, rice and maize, and in such vegetables as potatoes and peas. Cereals contain about 70 per cent starch, chestnuts 30 per cent, potatoes 20 per cent, pulses between 10 and 15 per cent. Cornflour is almost 100 per cent starch.

Until recently, starch was widely considered to be a food "baddie", particularly by slimmers, but medical and nutritional views are now stressing its importance.

Sugar and starch sometimes convert to one another in plants. The starch in unripe apples and bananas gradually converts to sugar during ripening. The sugar in young peas and maize gradually converts to starch.

Fibre The unavailable carbohydrates which on the whole the body does not absorb are known collectively as fibre (roughage). These are also polysaccharides. Recent research has found that some types of fibres are absorbed, and a distinction is now made between soluble and insoluble fibre. Both have a beneficial but differing effect on digestive processes. Soluble fibre (eg, found in oats, apples and other fruit and

---

RULE OF THUMB

Eat more fibre-rich foods, which are essential for adding bulk. Prime sources are wholemeal flour (in bread, pastry and pasta), brown rice, cereals, pulses (peas and beans, fresh and dried), nuts, dried fruit. Other fresh fruit and vegetables supply some fibre, notably potatoes, carrots, parsnips, turnips, swedes, spinach, cabbage, celery, tomatoes, apples, bananas, pears, oranges ... All these foods supply significant quantities of other valuable nutrients.

vegetables) breaks down more quickly than insoluble fibre, and is associated with the lowering of blood cholesterol. Insoluble fibre (eg, found in wheatbran) has a greater implication to bowel functioning.

Healthguide Some forms of carbohydrate are better foods than others. Each gram of starch or sugar produces 4kcal. The difference is that, unless they are in fruits, vegetables or milk, there is no additional benefit to the body. In a healthy diet, most carbohydrate should be derived from unrefined foods (brown rice, pulses, wholemeal flour, cereals), and fresh fruit and vegetables; and more energy should be obtained from starches rich in fibre than from refined carbohydrates.

Sugar has two big minuses. It is a major factor in dental decay, and it can contribute, in the form of "empty calories", to weight problems, in themselves a cause of further risks, such as gall stones, high blood pressure, and arthritis.

Emotively, brown sugar might sound more acceptable (less refined; must be all right), and honey still more so, but both have minimal amounts of nutrients (vitamins and minerals). Concentrated solutions of sugar, syrups, treacles and molasses may have traces of calcium and iron, but far less than other foods such as milk and liver.

Sugar is a major ingredient in many manufactured foods, where it is used, not only to lend "mouth appeal", but also to bring out other flavours and to act as a preservative. As its use is common even in savoury foods, people relying heavily on manufactured products should be aware of the sugar content (see page 75).

Insoluble fibre assists peristalsis (the passage of faeces along the colon, the large intestine), thus avoiding the unpleasantness of constipation, and preventing waste products from lingering in the body. The consequences of habitual constipation might be serious. Diverticulitis results from the muscles in the wall of the colon having such difficulty in moving hard faeces, characteristic of constipation, that they tighten into painful spasm. Irritable bowel syndrome, inflammation of parts of the bowel, is another distressing complaint arising out of strained bowel muscle.

Constipation is also thought to play a part in the development of appendicitis, piles and hiatus hernia. Laxatives are not the best solution. It is far better to make a habit of eating high-fibre foods which produce soft, bulky, water-retentive stools which pass easily through the large intestine.

The NACNE Report recommends the daily

RULE OF THUMB

Most of us will need to cut sugar intake. A sweet tooth is very much a matter of conditioning, usually in childhood. Learn to love unsweetened tea and coffee, and favour mineral water and natural fruit juice to squashes and fizz. Eat fresh fruit instead of sugary puddings, and experiment with traditional recipes, since many work well with substantially reduced sugar content. Avoid ice cream, jam (both "sugar reduced" and regular), cakes, biscuits, tinned fruit in syrup, squashes, sweet sherry and liqueurs, and, obviously, confectionery. (It's hard to prevent children from eating sweets but the practice should be confined to certain times of day such as after a meal. It is the constant eating of sweet things which causes decay since the saliva has no chance to combat acid.) Eat savoury biscuits rather than sweet (but remember, crisps and certain other snack foods, because they are high in salt and fat, are not a good substitute for confectionery). Always read the labels on manufactured foods to determine sugar content, and turn to page 75 for advice on "hidden" sugars.

---

consumption of 30g fibre, in the long term. As both soluble and insoluble fibre are increasingly considered to be an essential element of diet, it is important to obtain fibres from a variety of food sources – just adding bran to a low-fibre diet won't do.

Although it has not been conclusively proved as yet that fibre prevents bowel cancer, research seems to be backing up the present emphasis on the benefits of fibre. It is very likely that, if you change to a diet high in a wide variety of fibre sources, you will feel better.

Proteins

These are found in all living cells, and, as well as providing energy, they play the vital roles of enabling body tissue to grow or to repair itself. The proteins in foods are broken down during digestion, and re-formed into body proteins, which are constantly being replaced.

The basic units of protein are called amino acids, and these occur in different combinations. There are 22 known amino acids, and nine are essential in diet since they cannot be synthesised by the body or are insufficiently synthesised.

The most valuable in diet are the complete proteins (usually from animal products). These

---

RULE OF THUMB

Vary the meat in your diet. As well as red meat, eat poultry and game, fish, liver and kidneys. Add plenty of vegetables to stews, casseroles, etc.

In the average diet at present, some 64 per cent of protein derives from animal sources; 21 per cent from cereals, the rest from pulses and other vegetables. To increase dietary fibre and reduce consumption of saturated fats, the balance should be tipped in favour of cereals and pulses. These should be eaten in combination, to supply complementary amino acids (the basic units of protein, of which eight are essential to good nutrition) of high biological value.

Some examples of this principle from different countries are: baked beans on toast; Indian dhal (lentils) and rice; the Jamaican dish of pigeon peas and rice; the Cuban *moros y cristianos* (Moors and Christians), black beans and white rice; Greek houmus and pitta bread.

In many familiar dishes, animal protein is extended by combining with pulses or cereals (eg, beans in chilli con carne; rice in kedgeree; pasta with meat sauce).

---

are described as being of a "high biological value", and their structure — perhaps not surprisingly — contains the right amount and proportions of amino acids for building proteins in the body.

Proteins derived from plants may lack several essential amino acids. However, eaten together, foods with complementary amino acids will be as valuable as the single-source animal protein. Many popular dishes supply this combination, so that, say, baked beans on toast is as good a protein source as eggs. The combination of amino acids is of particular concern to vegans, who, if they are to obtain the maximum nutritional benefit, should eat a wide variety of vegetable foods.

Our Western diet is high in protein, much of it deriving from meat, which can be an expensive source (nuts and pulses are far cheaper). Any excess which is not needed for growth and tissue regeneration converts to energy, which may be stored as fat.

Healthguide The healthy adult is now thought to need about 40g to 50g of protein a day to function properly — and most nutritionists believe that more is necessary to combat minor illnesses. Certainly, pregnant and lactating women require extra. So do growing children.

Activity is also a factor, and women generally need less protein than do men.

Some recommendations for daily protein intake (DHSS, 1979)

Aged 5-6 years: boys 43g, girls 42g
Aged 12-14 years: boys 66g, girls 53g
Moderately active men (aged 35-64) 69g
Most women, unless very active (aged 18-54) 54g
Pregnant women 60g
Lactating women 69g

The latest WHO/FAO estimates suggest these figures are rather high — they are certainly on the high side if you are overweight.

Vitamins

As recently as 1912, researchers established (particularly in studies of scurvy, beriberi and pellegra, now known to be "deficiency diseases"), that the main constituents of food — proteins, fats, carbohydrates and mineral salts — were not in themselves sufficient to keep the body healthy.

Casimir Funk, a Pole working at the Lister Institute, decided to name certain newly isolated substances "vitamines" (vital amines). When the amine origin proved erroneous in the majority of cases, a British biochemist, Jack Drummond, suggested dropping the 'e', and the name vitamins was adopted in 1920.

As more was learned about vitamins, the original classifications were modified, and some were dropped, which is why there are gaps in vitamin numbers (eg. B_3, B_4 and B_5 are no longer recognised). Only recently has the chemical structure of all the vitamins become known, and scientists now prefer to give them names rather than numbers — which can lead to confusion on food labels.

CLASSIFICATION OF VITAMINS
Vitamin A (retinol)
Vitamin B_1 (thiamin)
Vitamin B_2 (riboflavin)
Vitamin B_6 (pyridoxine)
Vitamin B_{12} (cyanocobalamin)
Nicotinic acid
Folic acid
Pantothenic acid
Biotin
Vitamin C (ascorbic acid)
Vitamin D (cholecalciferol)
Vitamin E (tocopherol)
Vitamin K

Vitamins are organic compounds which are essential for the body's growth and continuing health. They cannot generally be made by the body (but see notes on vitamin D, and on vegans and vitamin B12), so they must come from food. They are needed only in minute quantities, yet their effects are dramatic.

Different vitamins behave differently in the body. Some are soluble in water, others in fat. Some are destroyed during processing or cooking, or by exposure to light. In general the body will excrete any water-soluble vitamins surplus to requirements, but it is now thought that it may be harmful to take large excesses of vitamin supplements (whose value, anyway, for healthy eaters, is being questioned), whether water- or fat-soluble. Ideally, you should be aware of the presence of vitamins in particular foods, and know which are the prime sources especially if you are suspected of suffering from deficiency. Treat any "miracle" products with scepticism. (The use of vitamins in cosmetics and hair products is also, while not harmful, of questionable benefit.)

Vitamin A (retinol)

This fat-soluble vitamin occurs in animal food, in lambs' liver and fish oils. There are lower amounts in cheese, butter, and in margarine (to which it is added by law). Contained in milk, and in some fruit and vegetables, are yellowy-orange substances called "carotenes" which, in the body, partly convert to retinol. The most efficient of these is beta-carotene. Vitamin A is extremely important in maintaining healthy skin tissue and protecting against infection, particularly in the eyes and lungs. Deficiency causes night blindness (hence the old story that carrots help you see in the dark) and inflamed eyes, and inhibits growth in children. Because it is fat-soluble, retinol is not lost in cooking, except in frying and roasting at over 100°C. Recommended daily intake for a moderately active man and for most women aged 18-54, is 750 micrograms. As an excess is not excreted, but stored in the human liver, and as the British diet supplies on average twice the recommended intake, it is dangerous to take supplements except on the advice of a doctor. Heavy over-consumption of vitamin A can cause loss of appetite, itchy, dry skin, headaches. Vitamin A deficiency is rare in Britain, but common in the Middle East and India, where it is the most usual cause of blindness. Consuming large amounts of carotene, which is converted to vitamin A, will affect skin colour, turning it yellow, but is not dangerous unless taken to extremes.

B-vitamins

All the vitamins in this group are water-soluble, and are usually found in conjunction with proteins. Their function is to ensure efficient operation of the body's enzyme system, so that energy can be released and protein synthesised. A deficiency of any in the B group retards tissue growth and affects the skin, digestive glands, bone marrow and nerve functioning. In the processing of manufactured foods, many important B vitamins are reduced — canning, freezing and dehydrating are particularly destructive — B vitamins are frequently added to such products.

Vitamin B1 (thiamin) This is responsible for assisting several metabolic reactions, and is important for releasing energy from carbohydrates, completing the oxidation of glucose, important for the brain and nervous system. A lack of this vitamin in children can retard growth; in adults, a lack can cause appetite loss, fatigue, digestive problems and irritability. Vitamin B1 appears in a variety of foods, especially animal ones. Good sources are offal, pork, eggs, vegetables and fruit. Highest concentrations are found in yeast (and yeast extract, eg, Marmite), fortified breakfast cereals and unrefined flour, and rice. In the preparation of white flour and white rice, most of the B1 is removed, and in white flour and bread it is added by law during manufacture, to make good the loss. Recommended daily intake for a moderately active man is 1.2mg; for most

(continued on page 28)

Those vitamins which are water soluble and susceptible to heat may be destroyed by boiling

GOOD SOURCES OF VITAMINS AND MINERALS

•• Prime source	Vitamin A (retinol)	Vitamin B1 (thiamin)	Vitamin B2 (riboflavin)	Vitamin B6 (pyridoxine)	Vitamin B12 (cobalamin)	Niacin	Folic acid	Vitamin C	Iron	Calcium
MEAT										
Bacon		•	•			•				
Beef		•	•	•	•	•			•	
Black pudding									••	•
Chicken			•	•		•				
Ham		•			•	•				
Kidneys	••	••	••	••	••	••		•	••	
Lamb			•			•				
Liver	••	••	••	••	••	••	•	•	••	
Pork		•	•	•		•				
Turkey						•				
Veal			•							
FISH										
Haddock					•					
Halibut				•						
Herring			•		••	•				•
Mackerel			••	••		•			•	
Pilchard			•		••	•			•	•
Prawns						•			•	•
Salmon (tinned)										•
Sardine			••		••	•			•	•
Tuna				•					•	
Tuna in brine						••				
CEREALS										
Barley		•								
Bread – brown		•								
Bread – wholewheat				•					•	
Cornflakes		••	••			••			••	
Muesli		•	•			•			•	
Oatmeal		•								
Porridge oats		••				•			•	
Rice						•				
Rice bran				•						
Weetabix		••	••			••			••	
Wheatgerm		•								
Wholemeal flour		•				•				

	Vitamin A (retinol)	Vitamin B₁ (thiamin)	Vitamin B₂ (riboflavin)	Vitamin B₆ (pyridoxine)	Vitamin B₁₂ (cobalamin)	Niacin	Folic acid	Vitamin C	Iron	Calcium
VEGETABLES										
Acorn squash							•			
Asparagus	•	•	•	•		•	•			
Aubergines								•		
Beetroot								•		
Broccoli	•		•				•			•
Brussels			•				•			
Cabbage	•							•		•
Carrots	••							•		•
Cauliflower							•	•	•	
Celery								•		
Collard greens										•
Corn-on-the-cob		•		•		•				
Courgette								•		
Cucumber								•		
Endive							•			
Escarole							•			
Green peppers								••		
Kale				•			•			
Lettuce	•							•		
Mustard greens	•		•				•	•	•	•
Mushrooms			•			•		•		
Okra							•			
Onion								•		
Papaya	•							•		
Parsnips								•		
Peas		•				•		•		
Potatoes		•		•		•		•		
roast	•									
sweet	••							•		
Pumpkin	•									
Seaweed										••
Spinach	•		•	•		•	•		••	•
Tomatoes	•							•		
Tomato juice				•						
Turnips								•		
Watercress	•							•		

GOOD SOURCES OF VITAMINS AND MINERALS (continued)

•• Prime source

	Vitamin A (retinol)	Vitamin B₁ (thiamin)	Vitamin B₂ (riboflavin)	Vitamin B₆ (pyridoxine)	Vitamin B₁₂ (cobalamin)	Niacin	Folic acid	Vitamin C	Iron	Calcium
FRUIT										
Acerola								••		
Apples								•		
Apricots								•		
dried	••	•	•			•			••	
Avocado				•		•				
Bananas				••				•		
Blackcurrants								••		
Cherries								•		
Coconuts						•			•	
Dates						•				
Figs						•				
dried									••	•
Gooseberries								•		
Grapefruit								•		
Kumquats								•		
Lemon								•		
Limes								•		
Mango	•							•		
Melon	•							•		
Nectarines	•									
Oranges								•		•
Pineapple								•		
Prunes	•	•				•			•	•
Pumpkin	•									
Raisins				•						
Raspberries								•		
Squash	•									
Strawberries								•	•	
Tangerines								•		•
Watermelon	•									
DAIRY PRODUCE										
Butter	••									
Cheese	•		••			•				••
cottage				•						
Swiss					•					
Cream	•									•

	Vitamin A (retinol)	Vitamin B₁ (thiamin)	Vitamin B₂ (riboflavin)	Vitamin B₆ (pyridoxine)	Vitamin B₁₂ (cobalamin)	Niacin	Folic acid	Vitamin C	Iron	Calcium
Eggs	•		••		•				•	
Margarine	••									
Milk	•		•	•	•			•		••
Yoghurt			•				•	•		••
BEANS & PULSES										
Beans										
black eye				•			•			
kidney		•	•				•		••	•
lima		•					•			•
navy				•						
runner			•				•	•		•
soya		•		•					•	
white		•								•
Chick peas				•						
Lentils				•			•		•	
NUTS										
Almonds		•	•				•	•	•	•
Brazils		•								
Cashews		•								
Filberts							•			
Peanuts		•				••		•	•	
Pecan		•					•			
Pecan butter						••				
Walnuts				•			•			
MISCELLANEOUS										
Brewer's yeast		•	•	•						
Marmite		•	•			••				
Molasses									•	

Use the tables above and on the previous pages to
check that you are getting some of each vitamin and
mineral listed. It is clearly impossible to measure your
intake of vitamins and minerals with any accuracy. A
varied and balanced diet should provide all you need
and ensure no deficiencies. Vitamin supplements are
helpful in special circumstances, such as pregnancy
or for those suffering from food allergies, and should
be taken in consultation with a doctor or nutritionist.

women aged 18-54, 0.9mg. All B vitamins are susceptible to loss during cooking in water; use as little liquid as possible, and incorporate the resulting stock in sauces or gravy.

Vitamin B2 (riboflavin) Necessary for the release of energy from nutrients. Deficiency is rare, but symptoms may include slow growth in children; inflamed and greasy facial skin; reddened eyes; sores in the mouth; itchy genitals. Recommended daily intake for a moderately active man is 1.6mg; for most women aged 18-54, 1.3mg. Most important sources are milk, liver, kidneys, mackerel, beef, fortified breakfast cereal. B2 is destroyed by light, so milk should not be left outside (it loses nearly half its B2 content after four hours' exposure to sunlight, and some fluorescent light can destroy it completely in a short time).

Vitamin B6 (pyridoxine) This converts in the body to help with the metabolism of amino acids. Most foods contain some B6. It is widely found in a varied diet, but particularly in liver, kidneys, mackerel, cheese, eggs and breakfast cereals. An average diet will provide 1-2mg per day. It is important for babies, and some may need large amounts because of a defect in metabolism. The use of oral contraceptives (and some drugs) can lead to deficiency. B6 supplements have been found helpful by women suffering from morning sickness, premenstrual tension and menopausal syndrome, but not all doctors are convinced of its efficacy. Supplements should not be taken continually, or in excess, as this can lead to lack of co-ordination and impairment of sensation. B6 is

Bring the milk indoors as soon as possible. On the doorstep in sunlight it is rapidly depleted of vitamin B2

susceptible to light, heat and processing, and 75 per cent is lost in the milling of grain.

Vitamin B12 (cyanocobalamin) The most potent of the B vitamins, this appears only in animal foods, particularly in liver, kidneys, pilchards, sardines and herrings, but also to a lesser extent in other fish and milk. It is important in helping to produce red blood cells in the bone marrow, and for maintaining the health of nerve tracts in the spinal cord. Deficiency of B12 can cause pernicious anaemia and degeneration of the spinal cord. Occasionally, there are cases of people suffering from anaemia who are unable to absorb B12 from their diet. This is remedied through injections or oral supplements. General dietary deficiency is rare, although vegans may need supplements, as B12 is not present in vegetable foods. There is, however, medical evidence suggesting that, in a strict vegan diet, this vitamin is produced by bacteria in the intestine. B12 is stable during heating, and there should be sufficient in a balanced diet, especially if this occasionally includes liver.

Niacin This term embraces two B vitamins, nicotinic acid and nicotinamide, both of which play a key role in metabolism. Nicotinic acid can be made in the body from the amino acid (trytophan) present in protein-rich foods, but it cannot be absorbed directly by the body, although it is found in some natural foods. Amounts of nicotinic acid and nicotinamide available to the body are termed niacin or nicotinic acid equivalents. Recommended daily intake for a moderately active man is 18mg; for most women 18-54, 15mg. Liver, kidneys, tuna in oil and breakfast cereals are good sources. (Some is added to white flour.) As it is water-soluble, boiling will result in loss, so use as little water as possible and incorporate stock in gravy or sauces.

Folic acid (or folate) Helps in several ways, principally with cell division, in conjunction with vitamin B12. Deficiency is a contributory factor in anaemia but is rarely found with the Western diet, except possibly during pregnancy, and in some older people on a restricted diet, and during the prolonged administration of oral contraceptives and certain anti-epileptic drugs. It is found in many foods, notably liver, oysters, spinach and other green vegetables, but is rapidly lost in cooking.

Pantothenic acid (vitamin B5) Present in almost all foods. Contributes to the energy release from fats and carbohydrates. As a deficiency in rats was found to produce grey hairs, it was thought by some that the taking of supplements would prevent greying – but this has not been so.

Biotin Produced by micro-organisms in the human intestine. Performs an essential function in the metabolism of fat. As it is found in a wide variety of foods, and is needed in tiny amounts, deficiency in the Western diet is unrecorded.

Vitamin C (ascorbic acid)

The first vitamin to be discovered in the search for a means to prevent scurvy. It is vital for the maintenance and repair of connective tissue, particularly skin, for the growth of cartilage, and for the healing of wounds and burns. Deficiency is characterised by bleeding gums, loss of teeth, swollen joints, wounds failing to heal, and, in chronic cases, death. Scurvy is almost unknown today, but lack of vitamin C is claimed by some to play a part in cancer and other ills including the common cold. The precise amounts needed for an everyday intake, for disease prevention, or during illness, are still debated. People on a poor or restricted diet, lacking in fruit and vegetables, may be slightly deficient. The recommended daily intake for men and women is 30mg (60mg for pregnant or lactating women). American Linus Pauling considers this is far too low, and suggests 2-3g. Many people believe that 1g or more a day helps to combat the effects of a cold. As vitamin C is not stored in the body, but rapidly excreted, it was believed until recently that large amounts were not harmful – but there is now some evidence to the contrary. Vitamin C is found in fresh fruit and vegetables, especially blackcurrants, but levels fluctuate considerably. The highest values will occur early in the growing season, and as the freezing of fruit and vegetables is done at this time, frozen versions can contain more vitamin C than the fresh, particularly if the latter are past their prime. This is a good reason for buying all fruit and vegetables in the best possible condition, from greengrocers and supermarkets with a high turnover. Vitamin C is water soluble and susceptible to heat, so fierce or prolonged boiling can destroy it. It is also destroyed by contact with alkalis, iron and copper. Furthermore, since it is an anti-oxidant, it combines with oxygen in the atmosphere, and ceases to be active. Some food-processing techniques can deplete this fragile vitamin. So attention must be paid in buying, storing and preparing, according to these rules:
* Buy fruit and vegetables as fresh as possible.
* Do not leave in sunlight, or keep cooked vegetables on warming-trays (C levels will drop rapidly if you do).
* Prepare fruit and vegetables immediately before cooking. Wash quickly in running water; don't soak. Use minimal cooking water, steam and cover where possible, and heat for the minimum period necessary.
* Use aluminium rather than copper or iron cooking utensils.
* Acid salad dressings (made with lemon or vinegar) help to prevent enzymes from reducing vitamin C.

Vitamin D (cholecalciferol or calciferol)

This is responsible for maintaining the level of calcium (and phosphorus) in the blood, important for creating strong bones and teeth, particularly in children. Ultra-violet rays acting on a substance in the skin (a derivative of cholesterol), stimulate it to produce vitamin D, which travels through the bloodstream to the gut and bones. Adults tend to acquire sufficient vitamin D for their needs from exposure to sunlight, but children, the housebound and elderly, and pregnant or lactating women need a limited quantity from diet. It is present in a few foods, principally in fish liver oils and dairy products, but is also synthesised and added to infant foods and margarine. Vitamin D deficiency can lead to decalcification of the bones, causing rickets (deformity of the leg bones) in children, osteomalacia in adults. Vitamin D is highly potent, and needed in small quantities, even by children. The recommended daily intake for everyone except infants under one year is 10 micrograms. Too much is dangerous, and can be harmful to the kidneys.

Vitamin E (tocopherol)

Found in a wide variety of foods, especially vegetable oils, cereals and eggs. The exact working of vitamin E, a group which comprises eight different tocopherols, is not known, but it is thought to have importance in cell metabolism. Ills directly attributable to deficiency are rare in adults, although lack of vitamin E in infants and children can result in anaemia. One of the tocopherols, alpha tocopherol, is a powerful anti-oxidant, and is used as a food additive to prevent rancidity in vegetable oils. Most nutritionists believe that healthy adults can obtain enough vitamin E, needed in very small quantities, from diet. However, supplements have been used medically in the treatment of a wide range of diseases, including muscular dystrophy and heart disease, and in cases of infertility and miscarriage, sometimes on the basis of experiments into vitamin E deprivation in laboratory rats, rabbits and chickens. There is not necessarily an analogy with human beings, of course, and no conclusive results have so far been achieved. Some face creams include vitamin E, supposedly to inhibit wrinkles, and it is promoted to improve sexual performance, but there is no evidence that it confers any benefit.

Vitamin K

This was named as the coagulation vitamin by a Dane, Henrik Dam, just before the Second World War. The function of vitamin K, as with many others, was discovered by observing the effect of diet on animals. It is essential for forming blood-clotting proteins, and is injected to prevent uncontrollable bleeding in operations, especially on a blocked bile duct, when vitamin K absorption is low. Like vitamin E, K is widely available in the normal diet, and, being

Be sceptical of claims that vitamin E cream will prevent wrinkles, or pills improve sexual stamina

fat-soluble, is not significantly lost in cooking. Deficiency is very rare, but can occur in young babies.

Vitamin therapy – is there a case for it?

The body needs only specific amounts of vitamins. A lack of one or other may, in time, cause symptoms of deficiency, but it does not follow that an amount over and above that already in existence and sufficient for the body's needs, will be beneficial. Take vitamin A. This is important for enabling eyes to cope with low levels of light, and a continuing deficiency can be one of the causes of night blindness. In parts of Asia and the Middle East, the diet is so lacking in vitamin A that it can lead to total blindness in children . A supplement will strengthen eyesight only if weakness is due specifically to vitamin A deficiency, but taking extra will have no effect on naturally weak eyes. There is no direct relationship between good eyesight, in this sense, and vitamin A. Indeed, not only would an excess of vitamin A have no effect on the eyes, but it would also be dangerous to the body. A reference to the recommended daily intake (in this case, a mere 750 micrograms a day for adults) confirms that only minute quantities of the vitamin are needed. Vitamins take part in complex chemical reactions in the body, and exist in a delicate state of balance one with the other. To "overdose" with one particular vitamin can upset this balance.

Obviously, circumstances occur in which the body is under stress (because of rapid growth or illness), when it is unable to obtain enough of certain vitamins from the diet. This can happen with pregnant and lactating women, people on special diets, with those who refuse to eat or who are allergic to certain important foods. A doctor or nutritionist must be consulted so that any necessary vitamin supplements can be determined and monitored.

At the risk of being repetitious, it cannot be too strongly emphasised, that a weekly meal-plan containing a wide variety of foods, particularly fresh fruit and vegetables, meat and fish, is the best way to obtain valuable vitamins.

Minerals

All proteins and vitamins contain elements of carbon, hydrogen, oxygen and nitrogen. Foods also contain minerals, inorganic elements of which some 25 are present in highly varying proportions, in the human body. Some are more important than others and play an essential part in teeth and bone construction, cell manufacture, in balancing the composition of body fluid and enabling enzymes to release and utilise energy.

Minerals required in small quantities are known as trace elements.

Some minerals, such as aluminium, lead, mercury and strontium, found in the body, are absorbed from the soil by plants and thus enter the food chain. These have not been shown to be essential to health, and can be toxic in large amounts.

Two minerals known to play an important part in nutrition are iron and calcium.

Iron This has two functions related to the body's use of oxygen. It contributes to haemoglobin, that part of the red blood cells responsible for carrying oxygen from the lungs to the tissues. It is involved in oxidation in processes in body cells. Iron deficiency results in anaemia, characterised by tiredness and pallor. It is a recognised deficiency disease in Britain, and particularly afflicts young women and the elderly.

The recommended daily intake of iron for a moderately active man is 10mg; for women of 18-54, 12mg. Severe blood loss will considerably deplete the body's iron reserves, and women and girls, particularly those who experience heavy menstrual bleeding, need to watch iron intake and will need more than the recommended 12mg. Rapid growth also depletes iron, and pregnant women and adolescents need more than others; babies over six months should obtain what they need through a diet of meat, liver, eggs and vegetables.

The best iron source is liver, which needs to be eaten only once a week, as iron is stored by the body. Iron is contained in other foods, but it is not equally well absorbed by the body. For instance, spinach, rhubarb and cereals, although they contain iron, also contain acids with which it forms insoluble compounds, so it is prevented from entering the bloodstream. Also, tannins (in tea, for example) decrease iron absorption. Vegetarians who do not eat many iron-rich foods should compensate by including plenty of vitamin C foods in their diet, as this assists the absorption of iron.

Calcium This plays a key role in the building and maintenance of bone structure; teeth and nails; in blood clotting; in nerve functioning; in the contraction of the heart and other muscles, and is important for enzyme activity. Most of the calcium in the body is contained in the bones and teeth, with only one per cent being found in tissues and blood. Some calcium is recycled from that already present in the body, but most must be supplied by diet. However, it must be

remembered that calcium contained in food is useless inside the body unless adequate vitamin D is also present, either synthesised by the skin, or from diet. The most significant sources of calcium in the diet are milk, yoghurt, and hard cheese. Some is found in breakfast cereals and white bread. Calcium carbonate, a form of chalk, is added to white bread by a law dating back to the last War, when it was introduced to ensure that the population received enough calcium at a time of low milk and cheese production. There have been moves recently to rescind the law, but in the end it was retained since people who do not like milk or who exist on very low incomes, are still at risk from insufficient calcium.

More calcium is needed for body growth than for body maintenance. Children and adolescents need it for their growing bones; pregnant women need it for the growing foetus; lactating mothers need it for the growing baby.

Supplements of calcium do *not*, as might be expected, have any effect on the teeth or nails. Less calcium is needed than was previously thought, and the recommended daily intake for men and women is 500mg, increasing to 1200mg for women beyond six months of pregnancy, or breastfeeding. This extra can be provided by one pint of milk a day.

Sodium chloride Common household salt contains about 40 per cent sodium, and chlorine. When dissolved in water, these minerals separate into two ions, chloride and sodium, fulfilling different functions in the body. Chloride helps to maintain the electrolyte balance of the body, to transmit nerve impulses and, in forming hydrochloric acid in the stomach, to aid digestion.

Sodium is necessary for the correct volume and pressure of the blood, and also ensures constant water balance in the body. Further functions include a key role in the contraction of the heart and other muscles, and in the transmission of nerve impulses. Sodium is an important component in blood and in all the body fluids, as well as in the bones.

Most salt in our diet, apart from that which we add, comes from manufactured food where it is used as a preservative or to enhance flavour. The greatest concentration is found in bacon, smoked fish, yeast extract, soy sauce, sausages, salami and corned beef, in bread, crisps, and some breakfast cereals, in cheeses, especially smoked or blue cheeses, Feta, Parmesan.

Cooking and table salt are manufactured from a brine obtained by mining rock salt deposits. Table salt has added magnesium carbonate to

---

RULE OF THUMB

Try cooking vegetables without salt, choose unsalted butter and use it sparingly, rely on herbs and spices for more pungent flavour, and serve no more than one salty dish, such as bacon, smoked cheese or smoked fish, in a meal. Head for salt-free brands in supermarkets. Salt substitutes are both expensive and unpalatable.

---

make it flow smoothly. "Sea" and "rock" salt differ only in the number of trace minerals they contain; otherwise, they are chemically identical to ordinary salt.

Potassium chloride, a saline residue from rock salt, and potassium sulphate, are used in some manufactured foods as a salt substitute.

Although salt is vital for the body, few people in Britain suffer from a deficiency. Excessive losses through perspiration can occur in miners, steel workers or athletes, for example, and are also a hazard in hot climates. Symptoms of salt deficiency include a fall in blood pressure, loss of appetite, muscle cramps, fatigue and vomiting. In such circumstances, a high salt – as well as water – intake is necessary. To a certain extent, however, the body is able to compensate for deficiency by reducing urine excretion and the salt content of perspiration.

There is a possibility that people who are genetically susceptible to high blood pressure will benefit from a reduced salt intake, even though there is no evidence that restricting salt *prevents* hypertension. It is any way true that most people eat more salt than necessary.

The NACNE report recommends cutting back on salt by 3g a day, given the assumption that average salt intake in this country is 9-12g. An advisable daily salt intake is therefore around 6g, including that in manufactured foods. This represents about one-and-a-quarter teaspoons. To achieve this, most people will have to stop adding salt at table, avoid bacon, tinned fish and meats, manufactured sauces, cakes and biscuits, as well as salted nuts and other snacks. This is a tall order for most, but thanks to consumer pressure, manufacturers are starting to introduce salt-free ranges. This is a welcome innovation from the taste point of view alone as salt – and sugar – is often the dominant flavour.

Phosphorus This is a valuable and abundant mineral in the body – an average adult male will have about 700g. It is involved with the enzyme which helps with the absorption of glucose in the small intestine, and with the cell metabolism of glucose, fat and protein.

Lecithin (a fat) is one important compound of phosphorus. It is involved in the formation of membranes of cells, including the covering of nerve fibres, and in carrying fat around the body. Lecithin is often added to margarine and other products as an emulsifier and anti-spattering agent (see page 89).

Phosphorus is widely available in the human diet, and is sometimes added to certain meats (as polyphosphate) for its water-retaining properties.

Human beings do not suffer from phosphorus deficiency.

Potassium This mineral complements sodium and helps to regulate the functioning of the body cells, and is found in a variety of fruit and vegetables, in beef, fish, poultry, bread, cheese and other foods. Human deficiency is unknown, except in space travellers (astronauts have to take additional potassium because, without gravity, it tends to "leak" from the cells and get lost in excretion) and in cases of malnutrition, intractable diarrhoea and uncontrolled use of laxatives and diuretics (sufferers from bulimia nervosa are in danger of depleting potassium supplies by purging and vomiting).

Iodine This has a very specific function: to contribute to the two hormones in the thyroid gland which are involved in body metabolism. An iodine deficiency can cause goitre, in which the thyroid gland in the neck swells. Although it is rare in this country, goitre is still common in mountain areas like the Alps and Andes, and the use of iodised table salt is advisable where the complaint is prevalent. Because iodine derivatives are used in animal feed, an adequate supply is ensured by the consumption of milk, meat and eggs. Iodine is present in many other foods such as vegetables and cereals, but in small and varying quantities, according to levels in the soil. It is, however, significant in saltwater fish and seafood (cod contains 146mg per 100g; cabbage around 5.2mg per 100g).

Fluorine Controversy continues about the exact role of fluorine in the body, but it is known to counteract dental decay caused by sugars and cooked starch. Fluorine is present in tea, the principal source is drinking water. Water supplies contain varying amounts, which is why further fluoridation has been deemed necessary to bring all levels up to one part per million. There are those who object to this addition, which they see as "enforced mass medication"; others protest on taste and health grounds, given the uncertainty of the effects of fluoride, and would prefer to ensure dental protection by using fluoride toothpaste.

Trace minerals Several minerals such as cobalt, copper, magnesium, selenium and zinc, are known to be essential in the diet, in minute amounts. Because research into trace minerals is still being conducted, there is often no firm basis on which to establish or refute the claims of certain health products. Prolonged use of mineral supplements may be dangerous, and could create an imbalance in the body.

Water

Although essential to life and the main component of all living cells, water is strictly speaking not a nutrient. Some vegetables, such as lettuce and cabbage, have a water content of over 90 per cent and low energy content, while even in highly nutritious foods such as milk and eggs, there is over 70 per cent water.

All biochemical reactions in the body require water, and it is important to obtain enough daily, to ensure the regular and proper functioning of the kidneys in disposing of waste, to enable the body temperature to be regulated through the sweat glands, and to act as a "carrier" for foods to be metabolised. As the body loses water in sweat, and through breathing and in excretion, it must be replaced so as to maintain the correct fluid balance.

The recommended daily intake is about 1½ litres and it can come from tea, coffee, soft drinks, etc, although, particularly in the latter case, sugar content should be borne in mind and mineral water should be the preferred tipple. Slimming diets which recommend limiting liquid intake are not advisable.

Liquid intake should be increased when fluid losses are higher than normal, such as in heavy pespiration, during physical labour; fever, vomiting and diarrhoea.

PART TWO

FRESH FOOD

Fruit and vegetables

Never before has such a rich variety of fruit and vegetables been within our reach at greengrocers and ethnic stores, from markets and supermarkets. The appearance of a host of strange-looking species – and a greater choice of old favourites – has happened so swiftly that many of us are at a loss to know how to select, store or cook them. We hope this guide will make it easier to be adventurous, as well as offering some ideas on how fresh fruit and vegetables can be included in a healthy diet.

In spite of the choice and abundance of fruit and vegetables in the shops, however, the freshest produce, with the best flavour, is still that which you grow yourself or buy directly from a genuine farm shop, especially one where you can pick your own produce. Although modern packing and distribution methods have greatly improved overall quality, the fresh food fanatic will be only too aware of the loss of flavour which can be the price paid for appearance (immaculate specimens, uniform in shape, prettily packaged).

For town-dwellers, a conscientious, imaginative, knowledgeable greengrocer should be as valued as a first-class butcher or fishmonger. He or she will select, wherever possible, from the best of locally grown produce, knowing that any potatoes or celery with soil still clinging to them, or that misshapen fruit or vegetables, may actually be preferable to the pressure-cleaned, packaged, uniform alternatives, which are bred for easy cultivation and abundant yield, rather than for subtlety and richness of flavour. Complaints from consumers about floppy, watery lettuces, tasteless tomatoes, scarcity of British apples and the disappearance of traditional varieties, are at last having effect. Some fruits, such as bullaces and damsons, which had almost disappeared, now stand a chance of making a comeback. The more we know about how fruit and vegetables should taste, and about what might be available, the more we can pressurise shops and supermarkets to extend their ranges. So keep badgering. After all, it was demand from consumers, concerned about the use of chemicals or seeking better flavour, which led Safeway to take a lead in selling organic produce, first in selected stores, then countrywide. Other supermarkets are bound to follow.

The best greengrocers – those who stock a wide selection of home-produced and imported fruit and vegetables in prime condition, who are prepared to offer something different and who throw out any tired specimens – deserve the enthusiastic support of the customer

The only problem is that there are not enough organic farms in Britain to meet the demands of consumers – but with time this will change.

If you buy fruit and vegetables sometimes from a supermarket, sometimes from a greengrocer or a street market, you should approach each a little differently.

The greengrocer
Fruit and vegetables stocked will depend on the majority needs of the neighbourhood. A greengrocer in a racially mixed area will generally carry a wide variety of produce. Greengrocers who offer only the basics are unlikely to extend their range unless the customers demand it. Some are reluctant to stock anything unfamiliar or expensive as, with such perishable merchandise, the profits can too easily end up in the dustbin. A top-class greengrocer will throw away anything even slightly tired, will select only grade-one produce and will not store anything chilled – but this policy will almost certainly be reflected in prices, especially in hot weather.

The market
A great source of cheap fruit and vegetables to be eaten the same day, or very soon after. Rock-bottom prices can indicate near over-ripeness, bruising, or size variations (many fruit and vegetables have official gradings) which would not be acceptable to greengrocers. The price for top-quality produce will be slightly lower than at the greengrocer's. Look for bargains at the end of the day in highly perishable produce, and get to know the best stalls where they do not slip in the odd reject.

The supermarket
Happily, most are giving increasing space to fresh fruit and vegetables, but they are very dependent on imported produce, and stock a relatively low proportion of home-grown varieties. This should change over the next few years, with the current encouragement to British growers. Supermarkets sell fruit and vegetables on freshness and attractiveness, and rely on high-volume, fast turnover. Some major chains make stipulations about specific varieties to be cultivated, as well as dictating picking and storing methods to foreign growers able to supply the required quantities. This means high standards of hygiene, freshness and appearance. It also means you will pay more and will sometimes forgo flavour and variety. The rather tasteless but immaculate, imported, trimmed, self-blanching celery, which is preferred to the far more aromatic, if stringier British variety, is but one example. Inevitably, the customer pays for convenience (selected goods, cleaned and wrapped), air freight and rapid, chilled transportation (the "chill chain" operating from immediate low-temperature storage after harvesting anywhere in the world, all the way down the line to supermarket delivery). The price is higher; flavour is lost.

Organic produce
Organically-grown fruit and vegetables can vary greatly in quality, freshness, and in strict adherence to chemical-free standards. The best earns the Soil Association symbol, which denotes the produce has not been treated with manufactured chemicals for at least two years, has been grown in soil enriched according to recommended methods, and is free from growth regulators and post-harvest chemical treatment. Standards are ensured by regular inspections by the Soil Association. Although more growers would like to farm organically, less than one per cent of arable land in the UK is farmed to such standards. So, for the present, organic produce is expensive, not always of good quality, and subject to poor

distribution. It is for us to decide if greater freedom from chemical residue outweighs in importance, a possible vitamin loss from delayed distribution, and damage from weather and insects to which such produce is vulnerable. It could be argued that, with our present need for more home-produced fruit and vegetables, and fewer imports, it would be more practical to campaign for tighter controls and minimal use of chemicals.

One day, growers will find a way to make organic produce economically competitive. Safeway, who have to charge between 10 and 20 per cent more for the organically grown fruit and vegetables which they have started, subject to seasonal availability, to supply, express the hope that an increase in both supply and demand will lead to lower prices.

If you happen to live in an area where fruit and vegetables are grown, you may well have a local farm shop which sells direct from field or orchard. You may even have the pleasure of picking produce for yourself. Growers are starting to cater for families, many providing picnic areas and the perfect excuse for townies to make a day trip to the country. The Farm Shop and Pick Your Own Association will give information about these outlets nationwide. They have 400 members, plus contacts with non-member growers. Write to them at Hunger Lane, Mugginton, Derbyshire DE6 4PL, or telephone 0332 360991.

Keep an eye open for the Foodmark Quality symbol. This was introduced in 1984 so that the very best British produce could receive an endorsement and be instantly recognised by consumers. The scheme is administered by Food from Britain, which lays down exacting criteria for standards in growth and all stages of production. Standards are further maintained by a team of independent shopping monitors, as well as a procedure for consumer complaints. Any British food producer, including organic farmers, can apply to be included in this scheme, which at present covers the following: apples and pears, celery, iceberg lettuce, leeks, carrots, plums, tomatoes, freshly pressed juice. Onions will be included shortly. Other foods now in the scheme are: canned fruit and vegetables; bacon; English, Scottish, Welsh and Northern Ireland cheese; turkey; chicken; Welsh lamb; Scottish beef and lamb; Scottish salmon. Soon to be finalised is a mark for sugar, table cereals, trout and quality British preserves. If you buy food with the Quality symbol, but think it could be improved, or if you have trouble in tracking it down, contact Food from Britain, 301-334 Market Towers, 1 Nine Elms Lane, London SW8 5NQ, telephone 01-720 2144. One of the main reasons for this organisation's existence is to help the consumer, and comments are welcome from shoppers.

The only way we can communicate what we feel about our food, is to insist and at times to complain. For the reticent, this might mean making a special effort (we are notoriously over-polite shoppers). And it is just as important to give praise when expectations are fulfilled.

The following two "case histories" explain how produce can be manipulated to meet the demands for high yields and uniformity of shape and size.

Whatever happened to the tomato?

The tomatoes on sale in Britain never quite seem to live up to memories of the plump, juicy, aromatic varieties eaten abroad. It is true that this highly seasonal vegetable is now available all year round, and supermarkets stock cleanly packaged, orange-coloured specimens of

Seek out produce which bears the Foodmark Quality symbol (left), an endorsement of the best of British goods, and the Soil Association symbol (right), which indicates that produce has been grown in accordance with strict standards

RULE OF THUMB

Include plenty of fresh fruit and vegetables in your daily diet, to ensure adequate supplies of vitamin C and folates, and to provide valuable dietary fibre. Slimmers in particular can benefit from a meal plan rich in fruit and vegetables, since these have a low fat and high water content, supplying bulk and essential nutrients at a relatively low cost in kilocalories.

uniform size, but, sadly, they are no longer a pleasure to eat. Many gardeners who grow their own have contempt for any shop-bought tomatoes. The story of the Tasteless Tomato is but one example of the corruption of our superb native crops. How and why has it happened?

To start with we need to track down the decision-makers, those dictating the criteria for "the perfect tomato". The EEC, as one might expect, has a say. Under its regulations, all tomatoes must be graded in four classes: extra, and classes 1 to 3, according to size, shape, absence of cracks in the skin. Probably the main determining influence on the eating qualities of tomatoes comes from Holland. Most tomatoes grown commercially come from Dutch seed houses who conduct trials on different varieties and decide which hybrids to promote for British growers. One major British tomato producer confessed to us, "Flavour is definitely not the most important factor for us." His first priority, he admitted, had to be high yield.

The commercial tomato grower is dependent on his major customers, the dominant high street retailers, who account for 50-60 per cent of the market. Over the past five years, their demands have been Number One priority for growers, with the wholesale market taking second place. The major specification is size: tomatoes have to come strictly within a grading of between 45 and 57 millimetres. One or two supermarkets will not allow even a 10mm latitude, conceding 5mm maximum variation. They also specify the precise degree of ripening, a "backward condition" shown by a flush of orange or green, so that a decent shelf-life can be maintained.

Bio-technologists and chemical manufacturers have rushed to the aid of the hard-pressed grower. The problems which bedevil the home gardener – unpredictable climate, greenfly, whitefly, erratic ripening, as well as size variation and irregular cropping – can be controlled. Something like a production line can be set up, with tomatoes as the end product, neatly packaged, of the right size and colour, chilled on site to prevent deterioration, ready to be rushed off in temperature-controlled lorries to supermarkets nationwide.

Most tomatoes are force-grown under glass, with two main cropping seasons, March to May, and July to August. Early croppers need a lot of heat, and the high fuel costs are passed on to the customer. The later crop is cheaper as less heat is needed. It is primarily the use of heat which allows tomatoes to develop with unnatural rapidity, while their size can be largely dictated by the control of water intake.

To further regulate size and to ensure a high yield, many tomatoes are grown under glass, without soil, in a sterile environment either on rockwoll, which looks like glass fibre, or in concrete channels. The nutrients required for growth, nitrogen, phosphates and potash, cannot themselves ensure healthy tomatoes, so in the sterile glasshouse, trace elements found naturally in soil, such as boron, iron and manganese, must be added by introducing them directly on the plants' roots in measured doses. By precisely spacing the plants and controlling the exact proportions of nutrients, it is possible to turn out tomatoes of more-or-less equal size, with a heavy yield per plant. The greenhouses are really growth-laboratories, where humans must wear sterile clothing. Greenflies and white flies can enter through air vents. The former are checked by spraying, while tiny wasps are introduced to eat the latter.

Blight is eliminated through the development of resistant species. The only element outside human control is sunshine to lend an orange blush.

However, perhaps encouragingly, tomatoes do not always behave as expected, and they are still less predictable than anything made by machine.

After years of the tasteless tomato, the message is at long last getting through that flavour might matter, and the supermarkets are responding. Small, bright red, sweet and juicy cherry tomatoes in our stores are the first sign of a shift in priority. They are not popular with growers because their yield is less than half that of other varieties now produced, and they are more trouble to pick. Nevertheless, if they are to remain competitive, growers must embrace the flavour concept and must rely on the Dutch seed houses to come up with a hybrid which will marry the sweetness of the traditional cherry tomato, Gardener's Delight, with the size and keeping qualities of existing hybrids. This they should do in the next two or three years.

Few producers would deny, if pressed, that tomatoes grown in soil, in unheated glasshouses, and allowed to ripen naturally, are the best-tasting specimens, although yields will be low. Cold-house tomatoes now account for just 10 per cent of the market. Organically grown ones are likely to have been produced in this way, and will taste superior.

. . . and the apple?

The invasion of our greengrocers and fruiterers by the French Golden Delicious apple a few years ago caused widespread anger and resentment. Happily, some of the best of our native varieties have won back a good share of the market, but the way in which those tasteless, pappy, imported apples gained such dominance provides an insight into the forces at work with fresh produce.

Uncharacteristically, the French decided to develop an apple whose most desirable qualities would be appearance and size. No thought was given to flavour, and this bright green, heavy-cropping, weighty apple came into existence through rootstock trials. It was destined for the South of France, the region chosen for the Golden Delicious orchards, and could cope well with hot sunshine. All right, the skin might be thick, but the colour was good, and the variety was capable of yielding 1500 bushels an acre, compared with about 800 bushels for the British Cox.

British greengrocers were glad to have such a plentiful supply of apples which looked pretty on display, and at first few people challenged the notion that size and uniformity equalled quality. Some might have grumbled that you couldn't find a decent apple any more, and wondered what had happened to the wonderful range of home-produced apples we used to enjoy, but the public went on buying Golden Delicious because they were there.

Eventually, though, shoppers started to ask for something better, and growers realised that there was a demand for the subtler, thinner-skinned, smaller but more aromatic British apples. They responded, and there are now several dessert varieties to be found in shops and supermarkets: Discovery, Worcester Pearmain, Cox, Egremont Russet, Spartan and Ida Red – with the unbeatable Bramley for cooking. Even so, what has become of the hundreds of other varieties grown in this country, and why are apples still so tasteless on occasion?

The apple does not adapt to today's fast pace of supply and demand. It takes three years for a tree to crop, and five before its yield is sufficient to be profitable. A large commercial grower cannot afford to take a gamble in the hope that the variety he chooses will be popular. Not only must it sell to the public, but it must also be acceptable to the major retailers, and the yield must be sufficient to ensure supply for a three-week period. Lesser-known apple varieties are not produced in quantity, but can be found in shops close to where they are grown. If growers were encouraged by demand for, say, Beauty of Bath, it would be possible, with time, for them to step up the yield with more intensive techniques, such as developing smaller, less bushy trees which can be planted close together and will receive more sun. The outlook for the gradual return of many more varieties looks quite bright, and consumer research shows that we are willing to pay substantially more for apples with real flavour and good texture, even if they are irregular in shape.

From October to January there is a range of good, freshly picked British apple varieties, but for the rest of the time, the apples which must still appear on the supermarket shelves to satisfy the demand for "all year" availability, will be out-of-season ones, or imports from South Africa, France, Italy or Spain, and will not compare in taste or texture with home-grown, freshly-picked varieties, in spite of new preservation techniques and swifter distribution. If you have noticed that an apple bought in April is pappy and bland, here's why. Apples picked in season are stored in bins inside sheds at low temperature. The oxygen level is reduced by means of a chemical, so that the apples "breathe" more slowly through their skins, rather like a hibernating animal, and development is halted. Once packed, graded and sent on their way in a normal temperature to the retailer, the maturing cycle continues, but the apples deteriorate rapidly. When taken home and kept at room temperature, they quickly stale.

Since Britain joined the EEC we expect and demand greater choice with all foods, and apples are no exception. In the name of choice and availability, we have tended cheerfully to lower our standards. Growers recognise that consumer habits can be trained over the years by the major retailers, but they are also encouraged by, for instance, the Real Ale campaign to believe that more and more we will insist on Real Apples. When our pressure on supermarkets is perceived as sufficiently strong and representative, there usually follows a change of policy. So take your supermarket apples back if they let you down, and suggest that they stock some traditional varieties from our rich heritage. It is estimated that around 600 are to be found in Britain.

Exotic and unusual vegetables

Adventurous greengrocers and supermarkets are offering an increasing variety of unfamiliar imported and home-grown vegetables. Here are just a few you will find alongside your old favourites.

Aubergine (eggplant) Handsome, shiny purple vegetable which features in Asian, Middle Eastern and Mediterranean cookery, and is finding increasing popularity here. Best June-September. Can be oblong or squat but should feel heavy and solid, with tight, glossy, unblemished skin. No need to peel. Slice, sprinkle with salt and leave in a colander so bitter juices drain off. Delicious fried, grilled with a sprinkling of cinnamon, and in ratatouille (the vegetable stew of Provence) and moussaka.

Callaloo (dasheen, patra) The strong-flavoured leaves of this plant, sometimes called West Indian kale, are a feature in Indian and Caribbean cooking, and can be used like cabbage.

Celeriac Related to celery, but grown for its turnip-like root rather than its inedible stalk. Has recently made a comeback in greengrocers.

Popularly used for a salad in France, peeled, cut in julienne strips, blanched and dressed with *remoulade* sauce. Delicious in a purée with other root vegetables.

Chanterelle (girolle, egg mushroom) Firm-fleshed fungus found in woods from summer until midwinter, has a delicious, faintly peppery flavour and requires longer cooking than more fragile varieties.

Choi sum Brassica with spinach-like leaves, yellow flowers and juicy stalks which vary from white to light green and taste faintly of asparagus when cooked. Choose specimens in flower and prepare like broccoli (the leaves are best steamed; the stalks can be eaten separately, with a little butter).

Chow chow (chayote, christophene) Pale green, pear-shaped vegetable with ribbed skin, imported from the Caribbean and South America. Rinse and peel both layers of skin. Cut in half lengthways and remove core and seeds. Flesh can be diced and steamed or stir-fried with other vegetables. Or boil unpeeled for 10 minutes, cut in half, remove flesh, mix with stuffing ingredients, replace in shell and bake.

Eddoes (dasheen, baddo) Rough, brown, hairy vegetable with large lateral tubers growing from central corm. Imported from the Caribbean. Wash, peel, slice and cook in the same way as potatoes. Mashed eddoes are slightly mealier than potatoes and benefit from seasoning with nutmeg.

Gai lan (Chinese kale) Distantly resembles spring greens. Has white flowers and succulent white stalk, dark green oval leaves, reminiscent of calabrese. Choose flowering specimens, pull away fibrous stalks before cutting off leaves, and use like broccoli.

Horseradish The bottled sauce to accompany roast beef and smoked fish is familiar to all of us. It is also possible to buy the tapering horseradish root, which should be trimmed of its hairy rootlets, scrubbed or scraped and grated (discard the woody core), then added to soups or salads, or mixed with soured cream or yoghurt to serve as a relish.

Kohlrabi Hybrid developed from cabbage, bred for its swollen stem, although young leaves are edible too. Worth trying for its delicate, slightly nutty flavour. Can be steamed whole, in the skin (first trim off roots). When cooked, skin can be removed, and flesh served on its own, or with sauce or melted butter. Also good steamed, cooled, served as a salad with vinaigrette or mayonnaise.

Kuchai (Chinese chives) Available from oriental grocers and some supermarkets, usually sold in bunches. These are coarser than our own chives and have white flower heads and a strong, garlicky flavour. Add to soups, salads, meat and fish dishes, or chop a little into scrambled eggs.

Lemon grass Lemon-scented grass with bulbous base, usually sold in small bundles in oriental stores and some supermarkets. Used in South East Asia to impart flavour to curries and other dishes, it has a lemon taste with gingery undertones.

Lotus root Underwater root of lotus, available from Chinese stores in summer. Cavities run the length of the root, which looks attractive cut in cross-sections. Seek out unblemished specimens which should be scrubbed, peeled and plunged into water with a little lemon juice to prevent discoloration. Slice across thinly and cook in boiling salted water (cooking times vary considerably, according to age). Use in curries, Chinese or Japanese dishes, or cut into fine slivers and fry like potato crisps.

Mooli (icicle radish, rettich) A relation of and similar to white Continental radish, but longer and more tusk-like. Milder in taste than red radish, but used in the same way. Peel and chop for salads; shred into soup for texture. The tops of young mooli can be cooked like spinach.

Mousserons These tiny fungi should be washed and trimmed and need gentle cooking. Will add distinction to meat and fish dishes.

Okra (ladies' fingers) A "mucilaginous and aromatic bean", originating from the Caribbean. Good for thickening stews and soups. Widely used in Indian and Caribbean cooking, and a traditional feature in South American gumbo (fish stew). Rinse and scrape ridges if they appear rough. Plunge into an inch or so of boiling water and cook until tender (about five minutes). To lose the gluey juices, soak in 4 fl oz vinegar and ½ litre water for 45-60 minutes, sliced, before cooking. Leave okra whole with stalk cap intact to contain juice. Overcooking can contribute to stickiness.

Pak choi Small, leafy bunches known as Chinese cabbage but unlike cabbage in flavour. Sometimes has a small, yellow branched flower. Raw, tastes similar to kai lan; cooked it has a mild broccoli flavour. The stalks take longer than the leaves to cook; strip off leaves, diagonally slice stalks and steam. Leaves may also be eaten raw.

Pleurotte (oyster mushroom, abalone mushroom) These ear-shaped mushrooms are now grown commercially both here and on the Continent. May be pink, grey, fawn, brown, cream or yellow (like those in our picture). Store in the salad drawer. Trim off tough stalk ends, slice and use in stir fries or in any dish in place of ordinary mushrooms.

Salsify (including scorzonera, black salsify) Root vegetable, white- or black-skinned. Also known as "vegetable oyster", which describes its flavour. Mostly imported from Belgium and France. Scrape salsify roots and cook in salted water with some lemon juice to prevent discoloration. Scorzonera should be scraped, not peeled, or gently scrubbed under running water. Cook it in salted boiling water or in water and milk for up to 30 minutes. Cooked and cooled, combines well with other root vegetables in salad. Also a good accompaniment to grilled meat and roast poultry.

Squash We are seeing many different varieties of squash in our shops today. Most familiar is the golden nugget squash, which should be peeled then steamed or boiled or can be stuffed and baked like marrow. Custard squash is a summer variety which, too, can be steamed, boiled or stuffed and baked. Butternut squash (see photograph) is pear-shaped and should be sliced and stewed or boiled or served with sauce.

41

Sweet potato (known, confusingly, as yam in America) Tuber with pinky-red skin; flesh pale pink to orange. Originally from South America, but imported mainly from the Caribbean, where it is sometimes made into puddings or syrupy sweetmeats. Prepare like ordinary potatoes: scrub or peel then boil or bake. They have a wonderful rich, chestnut flavour which goes well with gammon, game and poultry. White sweet potatoes are smaller than red, with yellow flesh, and are drier with fluffier texture.

Swiss chard (varieties include seakale, beet, spinach beet, ruby chard). A kind of beetroot which has been developed for its stalk and leaves. It is spinach-like with substantial leaves and thick stems. Wash, drain, steam or boil in minimal water and chop thoroughly. In France, stems and leaves are served as separate vegetables.

Vine leaves *Dolmas* or *dolmades* (stuffed vine leaves) are popular in the Middle East. The leaves are widely available in sealed packs from supermarkets, and may occasionally be found fresh. Before use, pour boiling water over the leaves and let them stand for 15 minutes. Rinse and drain several times and use to wrap little parcels of your favourite filling (for instance, a mixture of par-boiled rice, pine nuts, raisins, tomato and garlic). Gently steam or poach.

Water asparagus Spindly stalk with small asparagus tip, requires the gentlest of steaming since it is very delicate.

Yam Edible tuber growing in many shapes and varieties, ranging in size from that of a large potato to around 100lb. Flesh can be white, browny-pink or yellow, with flavour more akin to potato than to sweet potato. Remove tough bark, then bake, boil, steam or roast with herbs and spices.

Exotic and unusual salad vegetables

Not so very long ago, ''salad'' meant floppy lettuce, tomato, cucumber, with the possible addition of beetroot and spring onions, and the inevitable glob of bottled salad cream.

Today, we have become more adventurous – and have a far greater choice of vegetables with which to construct refreshing and nutritious mixed salads.

Beansprouts The young shoots of mung beans are easy to grow at home in a jar of water or a sprout-tray, and are also widely sold. A good alternative to lettuce for winter salads, and believed by some to be among the most health-giving vegetables. Other sprouts sometimes found in supermarkets and health food shops include lentil and soya bean.

Chicory Refreshing salad vegetable with slightly bitter taste which complements sweeter ingredients such as orange. Shop-bought chicory is usually more bitter than home-grown because it has been exposed to light (if it is kept in the dark until harvesting, it is much less so). Look for plump tightly-furled, conical heads with white leaves showing yellow or green at the tips.

Chinese leaves (Chinese cabbage or pak choi) Brassica, now grown commercially in the UK. Raw leaves are superior to forced lettuce for winter salads. Remove and discard tough outer leaves. Wash and shred.

Corn salad (lob lollie, lamb's lettuce, mâche) Has long been popular for salads in Europe. Gets its name because it grows wild in cornfields. Wash thoroughly to remove grit. Has a bitter and not highly distinguished flavour, but is available all winter, when home-grown salad leaves are rare.

Dandelion Like broccoli and kale, these leaves are a good source of protein, iron and calcium. They also supply more vitamin A than carrots, as well as liberal quantities of vitamins B_1, B_2 and C. The cultivated varieties, which are thick-leaved and blanched, are superior to those which grow wild.

Endive Resembles a dishevelled lettuce, with coarse, serrated leaves, dark green on the outside, straggling around a compact series of finer, more yellow foliage. Batavia is a thicker-leaved variety. Lends crispness, texture and a touch of bitterness to a mixed salad. Remove dark green outer leaves. Wash thoroughly. Particularly good with mustardy vinaigrette or in a Greek salad with black olives and feta cheese. Can also be cooked like spinach, or braised.

Land cress Can be substituted for watercress and used as a garnish or to add flavour to salads. Also, like watercress, makes a delicious soup.

Lettuce Main varieties are: crisp, firm-hearted cabbage lettuce such as Webb's Wonder or Cos; the softer-leaved round lettuce; the curled or leaf lettuce with jagged leaves. One of the best in winter is crunchy Iceberg.

Nasturtium Closely related to watercress, and just as nutritious, although it is a more familiar sight in the herbaceous border than in the salad drawer. Both the leaves and the flowers have been used in salads for centuries. Pick young, tender leaves and wash well to remove black fly. Mix with shredded lettuce. Use flower heads for garnish.

Paupier Similar in taste and appearance to corn salad but with larger leaves.

Purslane This small, fleshy herb has fattish stalks and rounded, dull green leaves. It is rich in mineral salts and combines well with other salad leaves. In the Middle East it is used as an ingredient of fattoush, a salad of toasted pitta bread torn into shreds and tossed with lettuce, cucumber, peppers and onion in a garlicky dressing.

Radicchio (red chicory) More closely resembles a lettuce than chicory, with deep red leaves and white ribs, wrapped tightly around a firm heart. The flavour is, however, bitter, like that of white chicory. Radicchio is now widely sold here, and, though expensive, a very little in a salad will add a splash of colour and variety.

Rocket From the watercress family and much used in French cooking. A good source of iron and other minerals, and of vitamin C. Assertive flavour.

Salad burnet Has a cool taste reminiscent of cucumber. Add a few leaves to sandwiches or to the salad bowl.

Seaweed A good source of iodine and now finding favour as a salad vegetable in the proliferating Japanese restaurants here, as well as in *nouvelle cuisine*. Dried varieties, available from some health shops and oriental stores, should be soaked for 20 minutes before use.

Sorrel Has the highest potassium content of all green vegetables; also rich in vitamin C. This tufted perennial has "bunny ear" leaves and a slightly acid flavour faintly reminiscent of gooseberry. Good in sauces, especially with fish. Use young leaves sparingly in salads or shredded in an omelette. An essential ingredient of the French *potage sante*.

Watercress The most refreshing and welcome salad greenery. Grown in pure spring water, mainly in Hampshire. The National Farmer's Union have their own standards to ensure cultivated watercress is of the highest quality. Always look for a grower's label. Wash well, dry and use in salads, as a garnish, or to make delicious soup. Also goes well with eggs (in omelettes and quiches) and in a sauce with chicken, salmon or white fish.

Exotic and unusual fruit

With fruit, as with vegetables, the choice has never been so wide or so enticing. Here are some which you may not have tried.

Blueberry Recently brought into cultivation here, our appetites having been whetted by the frozen variety. Best in tarts and pies; good for jam. A little lemon juice helps bring out the flavour.

Cranberry Small, tart berry fruit. The American

RULE OF THUMB

Be selective when buying fresh fruit and vegetables. Remember that produce in prime condition will be richer in essential nutrients than that which is past its best. Raw fruit and vegetables will also be more nutritious than cooked. Prolonged, fierce boiling will destroy water-soluble vitamins. Prepare vegetables immediately before cooking and put straight into a little water which has been brought to the boil to drive off some of the dissolved oxygen responsible for loss of vitamin C.

---

variety is superior to our native ones. Best cooked. They need only 10 minutes of gentle stewing before they pop (any longer and they become bitter). Make a delicious sauce to accompany game and poultry, as well as an unusual flavouring for jellies and sorbets.

Fig A ripe, succulent fig is a delight far removed from the dried versions. They are imported from Cyprus, France, Greece, Turkey and Brazil, are fragile so need careful handling, and may be white, green, purple or black. Outside skin should peel off easily (although it is edible), exposing the pinky, seed-filled flesh. Figs are especially good with smoked foods (eg Parma ham) and strong cheeses. Or serve them as a dessert with creamy Greek yoghurt, or marinated in sweetish sherry.

Guava More than 50 varieties of this exotic fruit are known. All are round or pear-shaped and a yellowy-green with tough skin. We import from Brazil and the Caribbean. Guavas are sweet with a delicious scent and a slightly musky flavour which many find more acceptable in jams and jellies and ice cream. But do try them fresh with low-fat cheese or yoghurt. Cut in half crossways and scoop out pinky-white flesh and edible seeds.

Kiwi fruit (Chinese gooseberry) Resembles a hairy, brown egg, and feels a little soft when ripe. Peel off thin skin to reveal bright green flesh (a potato peeler is useful for this), then slice in rounds to show pattern of black seeds. One kiwi fruit lends a muted but refreshing taste and beautiful emerald colour to garnish meats, fish and desserts.

Kumquat Resembles a tiny, elongated orange (the name comes from *kum kwat*, Cantonese for golden orange). Kumquats are tart and aromatic, with edible skin and a flavour approaching that of tangerine. Rinse and eat whole or cook and use as a garnish for poultry, pork or pâtés. A little goes a long way.

Lime As well as marrying happily with cocktails, limes can give a different flavour to fruit salads, yoghurts, soufflés and cakes. Use sparingly and try as a marinade for fish.

Lychee Looks more like a nut than a fruit, with knobbly reddish-brown shell, which peels off to reveal fragrant, translucent flesh surrounding a large, shiny seed. Kenneth Lo, the Chinese cookery writer and restaurateur, uses lychees with pork, an imaginative and surprising combination. They mix well in tropical fruit salads.

Mango One of the oldest and most prized of tropical fruits, now readily obtainable here in a variety of shapes and sizes – round, oval, elongated, pear-shaped. All mangoes are green when unripe, but on ripening the skin colour can vary from green to a wonderful, rich pink. To eat the same day, a mango should be slightly soft. They can be ripened at home and a pronounced perfume will tell you when they are ready to eat. Cut through horizontally and gently ease flesh away from stone, or score outside in quarters and scoop out flesh.

Mangosteen Small, round fruit with leathery outer skin and superb, translucent white flesh which divides into five or seven segments. The flavour is said to be reminiscent of strawberries, peach or grape. To open, hold in the palm of the hand and twist off half the shell.

Papaya (paw paw) Pear-shaped fruit with smooth skin, green at first but yellow when ripe. Flesh is orangey-pink, studded with dark seeds, and has a texture akin to mango, though less stringy. Slightly scented, very sweet and musky. Use in tropical fruit salad or eat on its own with lime juice or even salt and pepper to add tang. Cut in half lengthways and scoop out seeds. Unripe papayas can be treated as a vegetable and boiled, or stuffed like a marrow and baked. Juice contains an enzyme which breaks down animal tissue and is useful for tenderising meat.

Pomegranate The appearance of this fruit, with its glistening red pulp surrounding an abundance of seeds set in golden rind, far outshines the taste. The best way to approach a pomegranate is to squeeze the juice from the pips through muslin, taking care not to crush them because they are bitter. The sweet aroma works well in jellies and sorbets. In Italy they use the juice to baste turkey. Grenadine syrup, an essential in some cocktails, is made from pomegranate juice.

Pomelo Largest of the citrus fruits and similar in appearance to grapefruit, although slightly pear-shaped. Flesh is firm, coarse, may be pale yellow, cream or pink, and tastes less bitter than grapefruit. Add segments to salads or cut across and eat like grapefruit.

Prickly pear Fruit of the cactus plant with spiny skin, and fresh, floral-scented flesh which tastes faintly of melon. Use a knife and fork to peel the fruit; prickly pears live up to their name.

Quince Sadly, quince has disappeared from our traditional repertoire, although it is still grown by gardeners. Quinces are yellow with a rough skin and yellow flesh which becomes pink when cooked. Size depends on variety, and the fruits resemble apples or pears. Best cooked, particularly in jams and jellies (the pips contain gum with powerful setting properties). Good for imparting flavour to cooked apples and as an ingredient in apple pie.

Rambutan About the same size and colour as a lychee, but very hairy. The flesh, too, is reminiscent of lychees, but lacks the fragrance. Cut open over a bowl to catch the juice.

Sapodilla The skin of this small round or egg-shaped fruit is brown and unappealing, but it encloses delicious flesh, sweet, granular and melting, which has been compared to pear or banana. They should feel slightly soft to the touch; hard fruit will ripen at room temperature. The seeds have little hooks and should not be swallowed; discard them before eating.

Sharon fruit Really an improved persimmon (an often uninviting fruit, as it can be very acid and full of pips), this bright orange tomato-like variety was developed in Israel to be seedless and to lack astringency. Rinse and eat whole or slice across and add to fruit salad. Puréed, can be used as a topping for sponge cake.

Star fruit (star apple, carambola) Until recently this Brazilian fruit (which is also grown in Israel) proved too fragile to travel. Now, thanks to improved transportation, it is being imported. It is pale, shiny yellow-green and tapered, and has a sweet-sour flavour. Remove pointed top and bottom, then cut away ribbed edges with scissors. Slice across to produce the star-shaped sections. Skin is edible. Makes an attractive and unusual decoration for sweet and savoury dishes.

Tamarillo (tree tomato) An egg-shaped fruit from Peru, grown commercially in New Zealand and Kenya. Skin varies from deep red to yellow (the paler the skin, the sweeter the flesh). Like the tomato, which it resembles in taste, this is a fruit which may be used in salads or desserts, or grilled with meat and fish.

Ugli fruit A cross between tangerine, orange and grapefruit. Pinkish yellow flesh is sweeter than grapefruit, sharper than tangerine, and is good for salads. Juice is lovely in salad dressing with soured cream or yoghurt.

Storing fresh fruit

Apples like a constant cool temperature, and should be kept in a basket or wooden (not cardboard) box in a dark, frost-free place with a water-container nearby to keep the atmosphere moist. As few people have cellars, and many have central-heating, the best compromise for short-term storage is to put apples in polythene bags with a couple of small holes for air circulation, and to keep in the salad drawer.

Apricots should be kept at room temperature and eaten as soon as possible.

Bananas hate cold so don't put in the fridge.

Blackberries, raspberries etc should be kept in a cool place. Pick out and discard any damaged fruit. Eat as soon as possible.

Blackcurrants and redcurrants may be kept in the fridge for a few days. Sort through and remove damaged fruit.

Cherries should be eaten the same day if ripe and soft; others will keep a few days in the fridge.

Dates can be kept in the fridge for a few days. Take out half an hour before serving.

Gooseberries are best kept covered in the fridge, where, if they're hard and unripe they will keep for up to three weeks, with some loss of flavour.

Grapes should be kept in the salad drawer. Snip off any damaged ones. Firm-skinned fruit last up to a week at room temperature.

Melons will keep a couple of days, somewhere dark and cool, but not in the fridge where flavour will be impaired.

Peaches when just ripe can be kept a little while at room temperature. When slightly unripe, leave somewhere warm to ripen. Green-tinged fruit will not ripen. Smooth-skinned *nectarines* as hard as apples will be ready to eat in a couple of days.

Pears when under-ripe should be stored in a warm, draught-free place for two or three days. When fully ripe, transfer to a cool place or they will become "sleepy" (like cottonwool).

Pineapples should be kept at room temperature.

Plums should be eaten as soon as they are ripe; keep hard, under-ripe ones in a warmish place until ready.

Rhubarb is best used as soon as possible, but will keep a day or two in a cool, dry place. Revive tired stalks by standing them in cold water for about an hour.

Storing fresh vegetables

Aubergines will keep for two or three days in the salad drawer.

Beans (broad, French, runner) should be kept in a cool, dry place and used as soon as possible.

Beansprouts, if bought packaged, will be good if kept for no longer than 24 hours in a cool place.

Beetroots, once cooked, will keep for only a few days, in the fridge or in a cool place. Raw, they can be stored somewhere dark, cool and airy until needed.

Broccoli should be eaten as soon as possible but can be kept for a day or two in a cool place.

Brussels sprouts will last for about three days in the fridge; discard outer leaves, wash sprouts and store in polythene bags.

Cabbages of the green variety will keep only a day or two, stored in the fridge. Curly Savoys will last for a week somewhere cool and airy, while hard white and red cabbages, kept the same way, will last for several days.

Carrots, unwashed, will keep for five or six days in a cool, dark, airy place. Do not store in polythene as this induces rot.

Cauliflowers should ideally be eaten at once, but will keep for a day or two, wrapped in clingfilm or foil in the salad drawer.

Celeriac should be stored somewhere cool, dark and airy.

Celery, pre-packed in a polythene sleeve, will keep well in the fridge. Otherwise, wash, trim leaves and wrap before chilling.

Chicory can be stored in the salad drawer for not more than a day or two.

Chinese leaves keep well and will remain crisp for up to a week in the salad drawer. Wash and dry, and place in a polythene bag.

Courgettes, washed and dried, will keep for a few days in the salad drawer.

Cucumbers are increasingly sold sheathed in polythene to keep them fresh, and will keep for several days in the salad drawer of the fridge. An unwrapped section of cucumber can be left to stand, cut end upwards, in a glass of cold water, away from warmth and light.

Endive will keep for a couple of days in the salad drawer.

Kale should be kept somewhere cool and eaten as soon as possible. Wrapped kale from supermarkets will last for a few days in the salad drawer.

Kohlrabi will keep for a few days in the salad drawer or somewhere cool. Leaves should be used as soon as possible.

Leeks can be kept for a few days somewhere cool, dark and airy, or in the salad drawer.

Continued on page 52

Shown here are just a few of the innumerable varieties of vegetable to be found in our shops today. Until quite recently, only ethnic stores and specialist greengrocers offered the customer a choice of more exotic produce. And the fact that supermarkets, street markets and high street shops are increasingly prepared to stock new and unfamiliar fare, is a reflection of a growing awarenes and curiosity among shoppers. The greater the interest we express, the more choice we will be offered.

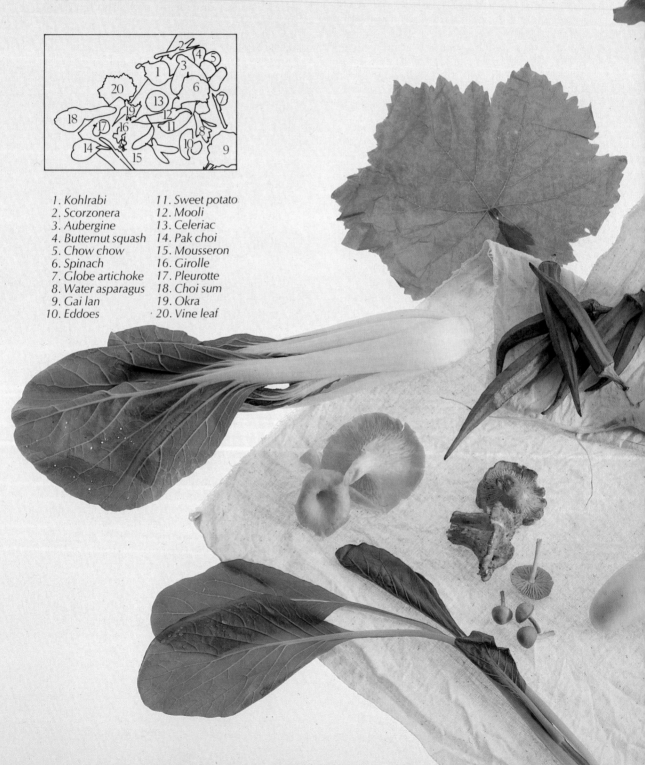

1. Kohlrabi
2. Scorzonera
3. Aubergine
4. Butternut squash
5. Chow chow
6. Spinach
7. Globe artichoke
8. Water asparagus
9. Gai lan
10. Eddoes
11. Sweet potato
12. Mooli
13. Celeriac
14. Pak choi
15. Mousseron
16. Girolle
17. Pleurotte
18. Choi sum
19. Okra
20. Vine leaf

Once upon a time, salad meant a couple of limp lettuce leaves, a few wedges of tomato and a round or two of cucumber. But today a wide range of leaves and shoots are available to add variety in both taste and texture to the salad bowl at any time of year. The more enterprising of us can sprout our own seeds for extra crunch, or raid the herbaceous border for nasturtium leaves and colourful flowers. Even weeds like sorrel and the humble dandelion can be cultivated for the table.

1. Webb's lettuce
2. Nasturtium flower
3. Endive
4. Cos lettuce
5. Seaweeds
6. Chicory
7. Watercress
8. Lamb's lettuce
9. Cress
10. Baby turnips
11. Radicchio
12. Paupier
13. Sorrel
14 as 18
15. Chinese leaves
16. Soya beansprouts
17. Mung beansprouts
18. Oak leaf lettuce

Fruits are often surprising. You cannot always guess from the look of them, quite how they will taste. Who would imagine that the wizened passion fruit would have so tantalising a fragrance or flavour? Or that the unprepossessing sapodilla would have granular, almost sugary flesh? Who would expect to find, within the papery "Chinese lantern" calyx of the Cape gooseberry, a delicious, sweet-sharp berry reminiscent in taste of a blackberry? And what of the tamarillo, with its overtones of tomato? The mesage is, as ever, to be adventurous. If your fruiterer offers something new, be sure to buy it and try it. It is almost certain to be a treat.

1. Mango
2. Blueberries
3. Papaya
4. Prickly pear
5. Guava
6. Figs
7. Kumquats
8. Mangosteen
9. Lychees
10. Tamarillo
11. Lime
12. Kiwi fruit
13. Cape gooseberries
14. Sapodilla
15. Cranberries
16. Passion fruit
17. Star fruit

Lettuce keeps quite well, stored in a polythene bag in the salad drawer, or wrapped in newspaper and left somewhere cool. Icebergs are the longest-lasting.

Mange tout will keep for a few days in a cool, airy place, but are best eaten on the day of purchase.

Mushrooms should not be washed until needed. They can be kept in a paper bag in the salad drawer for up to two days. Button mushrooms for salads should be perfectly fresh; use the same day.

Onions, if they show no signs of sprouting, can be kept for some time in a cool, dry place.

Parsnips, if earth-covered, are best for keeping and will last several days. Washed and packaged ones should be used.

Peas can be kept for a day or two if shelled, placed in a polythene bag and kept in the fridge.

Peppers, particularly green ones, will last up to a week in the salad drawer. If they've been cut, wrap them in foil.

Potatoes, when new, should be kept no more than a day or two somewhere cool, dark and airy. If you buy main-crop potatoes in a sack, empty them out at home to make sure they are dry and that none is sprouting or damaged. Remove bad specimens and place the rest in a new sack. If bought loose, dry out damp or muddy ones by covering with sacking or layers of newspaper. Main-crop potatoes should be stored off the ground in a dark, cool, dry place, free from frost. Never store near anything strong-smelling which can taint them. Check frequently for sprouting; rub off any sprouts to prevent potatoes softening. Never store in polythene bags but keep in paper bags or loose in a vegetable rack out of the light.

Pumpkins, once cut, should be used fairly soon. Store in a cool place. Whole pumpkins will keep well for several weeks somewhere cool and dry.

Radishes will keep for a couple of days in the salad drawer.

Spinach should be kept cool until needed and is best used the same day.

Swedes will keep for up to two months in a cool, dark, dry atmosphere.

Sweetcorn must be fresh; eat on the day of purchase if possible. Store somewhere cool until ready to cook.

Tomatoes, if ripe, will keep for a day or so in the salad drawer. Ripen green tomatoes by placing one ripe one in the paper bag with the others, and place in a drawer, where it should help the rest to ripen. Very green tomatoes will often ripen on a sunny window sill.

Turnips should be kept in a cool, dark, dry, airy place for up to a week.

Watercress should be washed very thoroughly, drained and dried, then put in a container in the salad drawer for up to 24 hours.

Meat

The current exhortation to eat more fresh fruit, vegetables, pulses and cereals, has led some people to assume that meat must be "bad for you". On the contrary, it supplies many nutrients, such as protein containing the essential amino acids in a directly assimilable form, and vitamins A and B plus iron. Although some meats can have a relatively high fat content, this can be minimised by trimming, by favouring lean cuts and by low-fat or no-fat cooking techniques. For most people, meat is an essential part of the diet.

Within living memory, cattle used to be taken by train to the heart of London and herded along the streets to the slaughter-houses. And many country butchers, even now, select living animals from local farmers to provide quality meat. However, meat is increasingly sold in supermarkets, cut up in portions and pre-packaged, hygienic and brightly coloured. As with many other foods, the shopper is becoming insulated against the realities of production, and many of us would prefer not to acknowledge that cattle, sheep, pigs, poultry and even game are raised to be slaughtered. But it is only fair to recognise the contribution of the many farmers who take the utmost care in raising and breeding livestock, those responsible for the stringent specifications of good practice in transportation and slaughter, as well as the skill of a good butcher in providing a wide range of meat.

The question of quality

It is not easy for an untrained eye to recognise a good piece of meat, and there are misconceptions about colour. If meat is bright red, this indicates only that it has just been cut by the butcher, or that the carcase has not been hung long enough. It is not a sign that the meat will be tender or have good flavour. About 20 minutes after meat is cut, the pigment in it, myoglobin, turns bright red through exposure to air. A little later, it darkens to a more browny colour, but this does not affect the quality. The variation in colour of, for example, mince in a butcher's shop, will tell you only whether or not the meat has just been minced. In supermarkets, special packaging has been developed to keep meat bright red, on the assumption that consumers see this as a sign of freshness.

A good butcher will give guidance to the shopper bewildered by an increasing choice of cuts of meat

Some of the fat content of meat is clearly visible, and the unseen fat in a lean cut is not as high as is sometimes assumed. The fat content of 100g each of lean meat is as follows:

Roast beef (topside) 4.4g fat
Roast leg of lamb 8.1g fat
Roast leg of pork 6.9g fat

The most difficult quality to assess is tenderness. The use of different feeds today means that it is rarely possible to judge tenderness from light or dark pigment, as dark red meat does not signify an older, tougher animal. In general, long, thick muscle fibres (the grain of the meat) with a lot of thick, connective tissue (gristle) mean tougher meat unsuitable for grilling or roasting. Lighter coloured meat with a fine grain could mean a young, tender animal – but bear in mind that the most active parts of the animal, like the neck and legs, will show a coarser grain, regardless of age.

With any animal, the hindquarters have less connective tissue, as they are under less strain; such cuts are suitable for faster cooking methods and fiercer heat, while other cuts need slower, moister cooking. The older the animal, the longer the cooking time needed to dissolve the connective tissue. It is essential to know which cut you buy, so you can decide on the best cooking method to bring out flavour and tenderness.

Beef Great Britain now produces almost all the beef it needs for home consumption. Continental breeds such as Charolais and Limousin, as well as the traditional Hereford and Aberdeen Angus, are raised for fleshy, lean carcases.

The price of beef depends on the number of joints and cuts a butcher can obtain from a carcase after trimming. The consumer always has to pay more for leaner meat, the hindquarter cuts, and it is from these that the butcher makes the most profit.

Beef is cut according to traditional cooking methods. When you try recipes from countries with different traditions of butchery, it is advisable to ask your butcher for the nearest equivalent cut. Some supermarkets have begun to stock Continental cuts to keep up with more adventurous cooking styles. Butchers often lag behind domestic cooking trends, but they are starting to provide special, leaner cuts in line with health recommendations to reduce fat consumption.

The prime cuts of beef, although expensive, are ideal for people with little time for cooking. Rump, fillet and sirloin steaks can all be grilled in 10 minutes or so, depending on how rare you like them. From the economy and health point of view, a small piece of top-quality meat accompanied by at least two vegetables, will be highly nutritious and cost about the same as many ready-made convenience dishes which rarely contain such high-quality ingredients. A grilled rump steak, trimmed of fat, will provide 168 kcal per 100g (8oz/225g supplies 384 kcal; 6oz/170g supplies 288 kcal), 6g fat, 28.6g protein, a whole range of B vitamins, vitamin E, as well as a wealth of mineral salts.

The lowest part of the back, from which fillet cuts originate, is the tenderest. If that, above flavour, is your priority, and if you can afford them, fillet, medallion, tournedos and Châteaubriand steaks will be your choice.

Entrecôte steaks are cut from next to the fillet.

The sirloin, just above the fillet area, provides more richly flavoured meat found in T-bone, rump and porterhouse steaks.

Flash-fry steaks are very thin, lean cuts which have been mechanically tenderised so that they can be cooked quickly at high temperature.

For roasting, you should go for wing ribs, sirloin or top rump.

Cuts such as brisket, topside, silverside, are often sold for roasting, but are more tender if pot-roasted (cooked in a covered pot, with vegetables) or braised. Both methods need less fat than roasting. Silverside and brisket, salted or not, can be boiled.

CUTS OF MEAT

BEEF

1. Leg
2. Topside
3. Silverside
4. Top rump or thick flank
5. Rump
6. Sirloin
7. Flank
8. Ribs
9. Chuck and blade
10. Neck and clod
11. Brisket
12. Shin

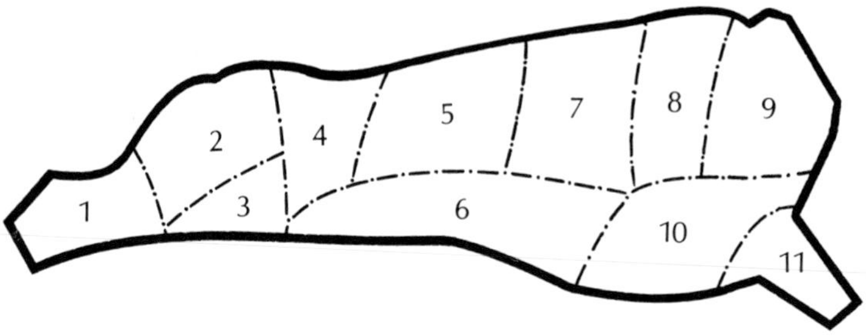

LAMB

1. Leg
2. Loin
3. Best end neck
4. Breast
5. Middle neck
6. Scrag
7. Shoulder

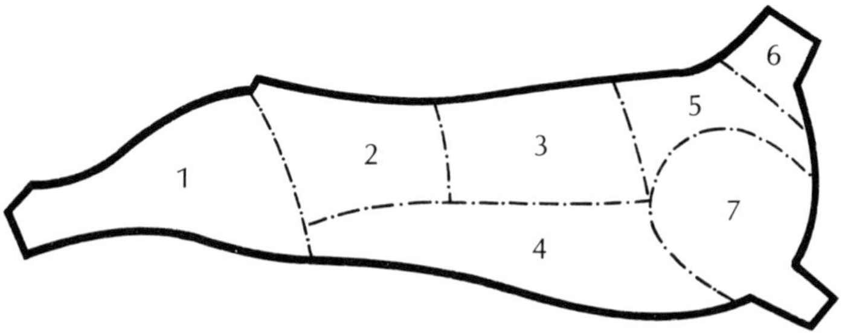

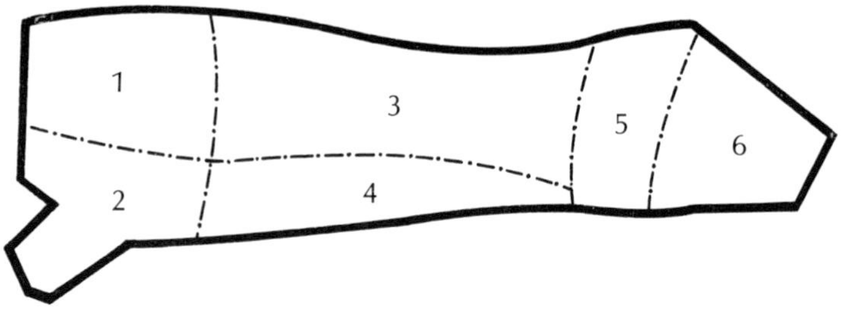

PORK

1. Shoulder
2. Hand and spring
3. Loin
4. Belly
5 and 6. Leg

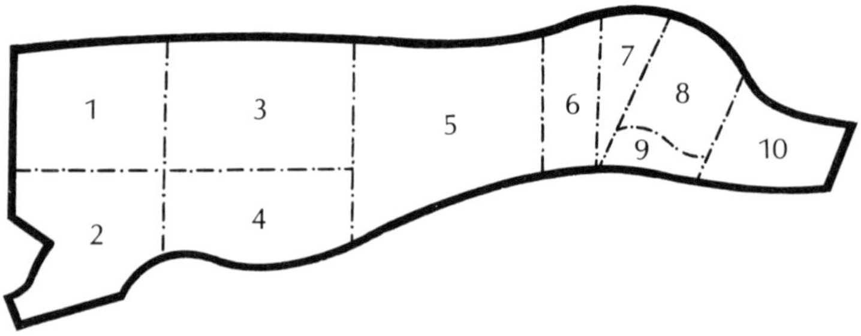

BACON

1. Prime collar
2. Prime forehock
3. Prime back
4. Prime streaky
5. Prime middle or throughcut
6. Long back
7. Corner gammon
8. Middle gammon
9. Gammon slipper
10. Gammon hock

Cheaper braising steaks for casseroles, meat pies and curries include chuck and blade, which are fairly lean. The cheapest cuts definitely need long, slow cooking: neck, clod, shin (the top part of the front legs) and leg (top of the hind legs), which have the advantage of not needing to be browned in fat beforehand.

Mince is usually prepared by the butcher from the flank section, and is suitable for meat sauces like bolognese. For meatballs and hamburgers, you should ask your butcher to mince a better-quality cut for you (here a food processor comes into its own: not all butchers will specially mince a small quantity of meat).

Veal Veal is the meat from a young calf fattened on a diet of reconstituted, skimmed milk powder with additional fat, minerals and vitamins. It has never been in great demand in Britain, perhaps because its flavour pales beside that of beef. It is, however, popular in restaurants, eg, in schnitzels, escalopes, slices or medallions served with white sauce or stewed. One advantage of veal is that, although it is expensive, it is quick to cook (but horribly tough if overcooked), contains little fat, and combines well with the delicately flavoured vegetables, ideal for summer cooking. Veal should appear lean, moist (not wet), with pale pink flesh.

For roasting choose shoulder, loin (oyster) or breast cuts.

Veal escalopes can be cut from rump, top rump (topside and silverside).

For pies and casseroles, choose neck, clod or shin cuts.

Shin of veal, when you find it, is used cut into sections to make the northern Italian stew, *osso bucco*, in which the bone marrow imparts a delectable flavour.

A veal cutlet (fried, coated with egg and breadcrumbs) contains 215 kcal per 100g; supplies 31.4g protein, 8.1g fat.

Lamb The first British lamb appears in spring from mild lowland areas, followed by lamb from hill farms in colder parts, with the peak-time being early summer. New-season New Zealand lamb arrives in early spring when British lamb is scarce and expensive to produce, but we import far less than we used to.

Lamb can vary enormously in fat content, according to age, feed and breed, and carcases are classified accordingly, with the top grade

With any animal, cuts from the hindquarters, which are under less strain, will be more tender and thus suitable for faster, fiercer cooking. Cuts from the forequarters will benefit from slow, moist cooking methods to dissolve connective tissue

awarded to the leanest meat. Apart from the traditional cuts, butchers are today using different methods, in response to demands for leaner meat for quick cooking, so a greater variety of joints and steaks can be bought.

The best quality lamb has fine grained, pinky-brown flesh, with white fat. Later in the summer, the meat is liable to become darker. Most of the traditional cuts are suitable for roasting or grilling. Leg, either on the bone or off it, rolled, is the prime roasting joint. It is often sold by the half as the knuckle or fillet portion. Shoulder, also for roasting, but rather fatty, is best bought off the bone, rolled, as it is tricky to carve. On the bone, it is sold either whole, or by the blade and knuckle half.

Best end of neck, a row of six or seven rib bones, known as rack of lamb, is excellent roasted. When two racks are put together, this becomes the splendid crown roast or guard of honour. Another special-occasion joint is the large saddle of lamb, the whole loin from both sides of the animal left intact. Chump and loin chops can also be roasted in one piece. Breast of lamb is another roasting cut, often sold rolled and stuffed, but it is extremely fatty.

Loin, chump and best end of neck can be cut as chops for grilling.

The smaller chops, scrag and middle neck, are suitable for stewing and braising (especially good with vegetables and dried haricot beans).

The new cuts of lamb mean it can be sold in smaller quantities. Butchers now supply joints trimmed of fat, boned and rolled; boneless loin and leg steaks; lean cubes and mince. Thus the meat becomes more suitable than traditional cuts for kebabs, for stir-frying and braising. A loin chop contains 222 kcal per 100g (grilled, with fat cut off); it supplies 12.3g fat, 27.7g protein; vitamins and minerals.

Mutton, which used to be a standard ingredient in the great British stew, and which is the meat from two- to three-year-old sheep, is no longer produced in quantity. Demand has lessened, and the large carcase requires of the butcher time, attention and space, if it is to give tender meat. Nonetheless, many interesting recipes depend on the special flavour of mutton, which can be bought from Halal butchers.

Pork Pork has gained steadily in popularity over the past 20 years, particularly in southern England, and again butchers are starting to provide leaner, more versatile cuts.

Pork needs a little more care and attention than beef or lamb. Be strict about handling the raw meat; wash your hands with great thoroughness before and after. Wrap it and keep it in a container separate from other foods, especially cooked ones. It needs thorough cooking and it is not to be eaten rare. When roasting a joint, you can avoid adding extra fat by using foil or by a roasting bag.

Fresh pork should feel firm, look pale pink, contain little gristle and have compact, white fat. Any bones should be pinky-blue.

Cuts of pork vary in different parts of the country, according to regional cooking styles, but these are the basic cuts.

For roasting: the large neck end, often boned, stuffed and rolled. This is also sold divided into spare rib (quite distinct from the spare ribs used in Chinese cooking, which come from the belly) and blade bone. Leg of pork, like lamb, is sold whole or divided into fillet and knuckle, of which the fillet is of prime quality for roasting. Loin is a lean joint which may include the kidneys. The tenderloin, the most prized part of all, underneath the loin backbone, is equivalent to a beef fillet in leanness and tenderness, and is sometimes rolled as a roasting joint.

Although they can be roasted, hand and spring, from the front of the carcase, are better pot-roasted or casseroled, as are neck end and blade bone.

Chops from the neck end, blade bone, are suitable for grilling, but the meatiest chops are loin and chump.

Traditionally, we like crisp and brown pork crackling, but this should be only a very occasional treat because of the very high saturated fat content. If you must fry pork, select a thinnish chop and use a non-stick pan, adding no fat.

New boned, leaner, smaller cuts of pork include topside leg steaks, shoulder steaks and double loin steaks. These cuts are excellent quickly grilled, stir-fried or used in curries.

A pork chop (grilled, fat removed) contains 226 kcal per 100g; supplies 19.1g protein, 10.7g fat.

Bacon Bacon is a cured form of pork which can be either unsmoked (green) or smoked. The most widely used curing technique is the Wiltshire Cure, in which sides of pork are injected with a special pickling brine, then put into large tanks for a few days and covered with a salt solution. The meat is then drained and brought to maturity in a cool cellar for a week or so. Green bacon has a pale rind and deep pink flesh. If the process continues with smoking, the rind turns golden brown, the flesh browny red.

There is a quick method for producing bacon, which involves injecting the curing solution (often containing sugar and spices) into the muscles, when it can be ready after two to three days. This bacon usually ends up in a vacuum pack as sweet, mild, or tender cure.

Sodium nitrite is used in regulated amounts to give bacon its pink colour, to add flavour, and most importantly to inhibit the growth of harmful bacteria.

A hind leg of pork, when cured, is known as gammon and may be green or smoked. It is cured in brine along with bacon from the body of the pig. Ham, also from the hind leg, is removed from the side of pork before salting, and cured according to local methods. Manufacturers produce hams such as York and Bradenham, according to their own recipes. Cures are given names such as Old Smokey or Virginia.

Many butchers advise you, when cooking bacon or gammon joints, to soak them for a few hours, then to boil, and finally to roast to impart colour and flavour. Soaking will reduce salt, but may also reduce flavour. Prime collar, prime forehock, middle gammon and gammon hock are suitable for this method. Keep the boiling stock, it makes delicious soup, especially with pulses or lentils.

For grilling or fatless frying, the best rashers come from prime back, and are lean and meaty. The middle or throughcut is the long rasher, with back and streaky in the same piece. Prime back and long back are shorter cuts. Prime streaky is the cheapest, most fatty cut, useful as an ingredient for other dishes, for example in making pâtés, quiches or stuffing, rather than on its own.

An average back bacon rasher, grilled, with fat removed, contains 292 kcal per 100g. Fried, including lean and fat, it contains 465 kcal.

Poultry

Chicken To satisfy an overwhelming demand for chicken (we each eat on average 6oz per week), they have to be intensively reared. Although this is not a pleasant thought (we would prefer to imagine a few chickens scratching around in the farmyard), conditions have improved somewhat in the past few years. EEC and poultry meat hygiene regulations ensure veterinary and hygiene inspections, and producers maintain that correct housing and feeding are essential to keep the birds calm and to enable them to gain weight.

Most chickens produced are termed "broilers", and weigh up to 5lb. This has nothing to do with "boilers", applied to old birds suitable for lengthy simmering. Poussins are tiny chickens; capons (fattened, castrated cockbirds) are now illegal under EEC rules, and have been replaced by large roasting chickens, available chiefly at Christmas time and often still referred to, erroneously, as capons.

Without doubt, the best quality is in a fresh chicken seen hanging in a butcher's shop, waiting to be cleaned on purchase. Hanging develops flavour, and the trimmings and giblets are valuable for chicken stock, basis of so many recipes.

When selecting a freshly plucked chicken, look out for a plump, white breast, smooth, pliable legs, and a pliable beak and breastbone. When birds are sold with the innards wrapped inside them, remember to take them out before cooking.

Although chicken portions are ready-packed and therefore ideal for quick and easy everyday cooking, it is well worth being reminded, once in a while, of the real thing. A welcome recent arrival is the British produced "corn-fed" chicken, reared on a mixture of maize grains. Although it is sold pre-packed, it has special flavour and succulence.

If you can, you should avoid frozen chickens: apart from their lack of flavour, mishandling of them in the home is a common cause of salmonella poisoning. In any case, chilled whole chickens and portions are now widely available in supermarkets.

Cheap, older, boiling chickens may look a bit scrawny but taste wonderful when simmered with herbs and vegetables. Butchers sometimes stock such birds; markets, are a good source.

It is always a good sign if a whole chicken or portions bear the British Chicken Quality Mark (the outline of a chicken with a Union Jack on its thigh), which guarantees production to high standards.

Storage Cover fresh birds to prevent drying, keep in the fridge and cook within three days. Remove giblets beforehand and use them immediately for stock. If you have no fridge, use chicken on the day of purchase. Cooked

Look for the British Chicken Quality Mark (left) when you buy either a whole bird or quarters. It is your guarantee of high standards of production

RULE OF THUMB

Do not be dissuaded by the current exhortations to eat more fresh vegetables, pulses and cereals, from eating meat, poultry and offal sometimes if you enjoy them. Prime cuts of meat are expensive, but from both a health and an economy point of view, a small portion of top-quality meat, .served with two or more fresh vegetables, will be preferable to many ready-made convenience dishes.

Liver, and to a lesser extent kidneys, are highly nutritious, being good sources of vitamin A, folic acid, iron, vitamin B_2, and other B vitamins. It is suggested that meat eaters have liver once a week.

chicken kept in a fridge or cold larder should be eaten within three days.

Nutrition Chickens (roast, meat and skin) contain 215 kcal per 100g (without skin, 142 kcal). This figure is for white meat; dark meat is about 13 kcal more per 100g. White meat, roasted, supplies per 100g, 26.5g protein, 4g fat, compared with 22.6g fat for meat with skin.

Duck Sadly, nearly 70 per cent of home-produced ducks are destined for freezing, to be used in many a gluey restaurant *duck à l'orange*. Only at Christmas and Easter are fresh ducks commonly available.

Britain is famous for breeding stock, and the "superduck" has been bred to produce 275 eggs in a year, as against the more usual 160, and is much appreciated in the Far East. British ducks now have less fat, more lean meat and a smaller carcase than formerly, but you should still estimate about 1½lb per person when buying a small one (up to 4lb) and just over 1lb per person for a larger one (4½-5lb). Fresh, pre-packed duck quarters, comprising either breast and wing or leg, can now be found in some supermarkets, as can partly-boned duck breasts.

When choosing a fresh bird, look for pliable feet and plump breast. It should be possible to bend back the bottom half of the beak.

Storage A freshly-plucked duck will have been hung, drawn and trussed by the butcher, and will keep in a fridge or cold larder for a day or so.

Nutrition Duck contains 189 kcal per 100g (roast, meat without skin); supplies 25.3g protein, 9.7g fat (29g with the skin, which some people think is the best part!).

Turkey Turkeys arrive ready to cook in numerous forms. *Deep frozen:* vacuum-packed, then frozen; white in appearance. *Oven-ready basted:* may be fresh or frozen; before freezing or packing, a basting agent is introduced (butter-based solution, vegetable oil, milk and honey, or broth solution). *Oven-ready chilled:* stocked in the chill cabinet of supermarkets, grocers and butchers' shops; pinkish in colour. *Oven-ready fresh-frozen:* prepared as chilled birds, then deep frozen using blasts of very cold air. *Oven-ready farm fresh or fresh frozen:* produced on farm premises; chilled or air-frozen.

Other concoctions of the turkey trade include turkey chunks, fillets, escalopes, sausages, burgers, and gammon-style steaks trimmed with pork fat.

It is extremely important that frozen birds are not returned, partly-thawed, to the freezer. Only after thorough cooking may this be done.

It is still possible, if the purchase of convenience is not an over-riding need, to buy turkeys free from added water (for which you pay with most of the above) or chemicals. Traditional farm fresh turkey is turkey as it used to be. These birds are less intensively raised, and are kept in open-sided barns on straw and given proper time to mature. They are hand-plucked and sent otherwise intact to the butchers ready to hang for about a week. The British Turkey Quality Mark is one guarantee of a good turkey; another is the Gold Quality Emblem, the mark of the Traditional Farmfresh Turkey Association. *Storage* Keep fresh turkey well wrapped, not next to cooked food to avoid cross-contamination by bacteria.

Nutrition Turkey (roast, without skin) supplies 140 kcal per 100g; 28.8g protein, 2.7g fat.

Game

Game has for centuries played a significant part in the British diet, even when poaching was punishable by death. Although urbanisation and difficulties of distribution have contributed to its decline, promotion of game as part of a healthy diet should mean greater availability. Licensed butchers and poulterers are the only outlets where the sale of game is permitted.

Game may only be killed and prepared (even for freezing) outside specific seasons, known as Statutory Close Seasons, to ensure that the species are protected. Anything classified as vermin, eg, pigeons, can be killed at any time. Rabbits, and quail when farmed especially for the table, are also exempt, and therefore available in shops all year round.

The closed seasons for the most commonly available game are:

Grouse: 11th December to 11th August.
Partridge: 2nd February to 31st August.
Pheasant: 2nd February to 30th September.
Woodcock: 1st February to 30th September (Scotland, 31st August).

The closed season for wild geese and some varieties of wild duck is from 21st February to 31st August; others from 1st February to 21st August. Deer regulations vary according to area, species, gender and degree of maturity.

The best person to ask about the quality of game is the butcher, since few people eat it regularly enough to gain experience in selection. It is important that game is hung so that microbes can break down the tissue and tenderise the flesh. Animals are usually hung by the feet; birds by either the neck or feet. The length of time needed for hanging depends on the type of game and on ambient warmth. Venison needs the longest (10-12 days), wild duck far less (1-2 days), and wild rabbit a day.

Young game birds can be roasted, but all game birds are eminently suitable for braising or casseroling, to prevent them from drying out.

It is strongly recommended that venison (and some other game) is marinated for up to two days before cooking.

A rough guide to estimating quantities is: small birds (snipe, wood pigeon, partridge, teal, woodcock), 2-3 per person; farm quail, 1-2 per person; grouse, half-1 per person; mallard duck, approx half per person. A hen pheasant should serve three, a cock pheasant four, a wild goose about six, a rabbit three to four, and a hare six to eight.

Nutrition The energy/kilocalorie content of some game is: roast pigeon 230 kcal per 100g; roast pheasant 213 kcal per 100g; stewed rabbit 179 kcal per 100g; roast venison 198 kcal per 100g. Venison is highest in protein (359 per 100g), together with roast pheasant (32.2g), the others being all over 20g per 100g.

Offal

Offal is an old English word meaning that which is cut from animals in preparing meat, parts which fall and are thrown away. For Shakespeare, it meant worthless, but today the word is applied to parts of animals which make a valuable contribution to the diet: liver, kidney, heart, sweetbreads, tripe, feet, head, brain, tongue, oxtail.

Although offal is relatively inexpensive, the unfamiliar shapes and textures can be off-putting for those who have never seen or tasted it prepared, or who grew up in a period of relative affluence when such meats bore the

AVAILABILITY OF FRESH GAME THROUGHOUT THE YEAR												
	J	F	M	A	M	J	J	A	S	O	N	D
Grouse								•	•	•	•	•
Guinea fowl	•	•	•	•	•	•	•	•	•	•	•	•
Hare	•	•	•					•	•	•	•	•
Partridge	•								•	•	•	•
Pheasant	•									•	•	•
Pigeon	•	•	•	•	•	•	•	•	•	•	•	•
Quail						•	•	•	•	•	•	•
Rabbit	•	•	•	•	•	•	•	•	•	•	•	•
Snipe	•							•	•	•	•	•
Venison	•	•	•	•	•	•	•	•	•	•	•	•
Wild duck	•	•							•	•	•	•
Wild goose	•										•	•
Woodcock	•									•	•	•

Fresh game is available only at certain times of the year, since it cannot be killed outside the Statutory Close Seasons. Our calendar shows when you might find differing types of game at the butchers.

stigma of poverty. Butchers have responded to lack of demand by stocking less in some parts of the country (a lot of offal goes directly to petfood manufacturers), or not bothering to display it, but most will obtain it on request. Supermarkets do stock liver, kidneys and tripe, but you will have to rely mainly on the butcher for more unusual types.

Liver The most delicate and tender is calf's liver, which is also the most expensive because we do not rear many calves for meat in Britain. As liver is rich, however, 3oz per person is usually ample. Quickly fried in a little butter (it's best when still pink inside) with fresh sage, calf's liver is light, easily digested and delicious.

The flavour of lamb's liver is somewhat stronger, and, like calf's liver, it can be fried, grilled or braised. Fried onions and bacon are traditional accompaniments, but these make for a meal high in fat.

Pig's liver has the most pronounced flavour of all, so is better used in pâtés, terrines and stuffing, though it can be quite palatable grilled if it is first soaked in milk for half an hour, making it milder and more tender.

Fresh chicken livers make an economical meal in themselves, and are especially good in a risotto (8oz should serve three). Frozen or fresh ones are quickly and easily made into chicken liver pâté – an excellent sandwich filling.

Liver is usually sold ready-sliced. It should be absolutely fresh and should not smell unpleasant. All offal is highly perishable, and should be kept in the fridge for two days at most.

Nutrition Liver is the most valuable of offal foods, particularly for vitamin B_{12}, B_6, folic acid and retinol (vitamin A). For this reason, meat-eaters are recommended to have liver once a week. Lamb's liver, fried, contains 232 kcal per 100g; supplies 0.49mg vitamin B_6, $81\mu g$ vitamin B_{12}, $240\mu g$ total folic acid; $20,600\mu g$ retinol, $0.50\mu g$ vitamin D, 10mg vitamin C, 0.46mg vitamin E, 22.9g protein, 14g fat.

Kidneys Lamb's kidneys are the most suitable in texture and flavour for a main course. They can be grilled or, for example, cooked in a wine sauce. Pig's and ox kidneys, first soaked in milk, give flavour to braised vegetable and casserole dishes, and in steak-and-kidney pie. When buying kidneys, look for a good colour and freshness. You will need around two per person for lamb's kidneys, one per person for calf's and pig's kidneys, and three or four ounces per person of ox kidney. To prepare, wash well, cut in half lengthways on the rounded side and remove the "core" with kitchen scissors or a sharp knife.

Nutrition Lamb's kidneys, fried, supply 155 kcal per 100g; 24.6g protein, 6.3g fat, 0.3mg vitamin B_6, $81\mu g$ vitamin B_{12}, $79\mu g$ total folic acid, $160\mu g$ retinol (vitamin A), 9.6mg nicotinic acid, 9mg vitamin C, 0.41mg vitamin E.

Tripe The usual form of tripe is honeycomb (others are blanket and thick seam) which is sold already cleaned and par-boiled. It comes from the stomach lining of the animal. A traditional Northern recipe is tripe layered with chopped, boiled onions mixed with breadcrumbs and herbs, topped with bacon and cooked in a moderate oven for an hour. Mushy peas are a favourite accompanying vegetable. Allow 4-6oz tripe per person.

Nutrition Tripe, sautéed, contains 100 kcal per 100g; supplies 14.8g protein, 4.5g fat.

Hearts These come from lambs, oxen, pigs or calves, and all need long, slow cooking. On their own, they can be rather tough and lacking in flavour, but they are suitable to be stuffed and braised. To prepare, wash, trim away the fatty parts and all strings of the arteries, soak in lightly salted water for about an hour to remove all traces of blood, rinse and dry.

Sweetbreads These are the pancreas or thymus gland taken from an ox, calf of lamb, and are considered a delicacy, particularly on the continent, where offal is more widely used than here. You may have to order sweetbreads from the butcher. One pound of sweetbreads will be enough for three or four people; they should appear pale and bright. Lamb's sweetbreads have the most delicate flavour and finest texture and are suitable for frying. Other sweetbreads need slow, moist oven cooking.

To prepare, wash thoroughly in several changes of cold water, then soak for at least 30 minutes. Plunge into cold water again, drain, remove skin or membrane, rinse and dry.

Nutrition Sweetbreads contain 230 kcal per 100g fried; supply 19.4g protein, 14.6g fat, 18mg vitamin C, $4\mu g$ vitamin B12, $14\mu g$ total folic acid.

Brains The best are calf's, which are prepared in a similar way to sweetbreads. Sold by the set, which will serve one or two people, they should appear bright and pinky-grey, with a fresh smell. Brains are perhaps an acquired taste, but if you have ever tried them Italian style in olive oil as part of a *fritto misto*, you will probably want to repeat the experiment.

Nutrition Calf's brains, boiled, contain 152 kcal per 100g; supply 12.7g protein, 11.2g fat, 17mg vitamin C, 2.3mg vitamin E, 0.12mg vitamin B6, $7\mu g$ vitamin B12.

Tongue There are two kinds available: ox and lamb. Both are fiddly and time-consuming to prepare and are usually sold ready-cooked and sliced to order.

Oxtail Usually sold cut up into segments, though a whole tail will make a satisfying stew for four people, or a hearty winter soup. The tail is not very meaty, but gives extremely good flavour.

Nutrition Oxtail, stewed, contains 243 kcal per 100g; supplies 30.5g protein, 13.4g fat, 0.14mg vitamin B6, $2\mu g$ vitamin B12, $9\mu g$ total folic acid.

Feet Calf's feet are used to make wonderfully thick, gelatinous stock, ideal for adding to pies or to incorporate in gravy. To prepare, wash well, cover with water in a saucepan, bring to the boil and remove the scum. Lower to a simmer until tender. Pig's trotters can be used to add flavour to stews and casseroles.

Fish

We are about to witness the renaissance of fresh fish in our national diet. The past 10 years have, it is true, seen a huge decline in demand, not solely because shoppers suddenly decided fish was no longer to their taste. Frozen fish fingers have proved to be a commercial – if not gastronomic – triumph. Outside factors, such as the Icelandic cod war, the rocketing price of oil which affected transport, and general inflation meant that fish, formerly a cheap and attractive basis for a meal, became expensive, often of poor quality, and lacking in variety. Many people, especially among the younger generation, know little of the characteristics of different fish, or how to cook them. Fortunately, the emphasis on lighter food has led restaurant chefs to experiment with fish, to rediscover its

Fish, for a long time out of favour, seems set for a come-back as we grow more adventurous, more willing to try the many varieties to be found at the fishmongers. Truly fresh fish, simply and lightly cooked, has an incomparable flavour and is highly nutritious.

1. Crab
2. Lobster
3. Scallops
4. Sardines
5. Dover sole
6. Kipper
7. Salmon
8. Red mullet
9. Brown trout
10. Prawns
11. Turbot
12. Squid
13. King prawns
14. Herring
15. Mussels
16. Plaice
17. Mackerel
18. Whitebait

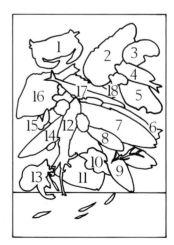

subtlety and versatility, thus helping to revive the public's interest. The Sea Fish Authority, now out of the doldrums, has launched a major promotion campaign and is establishing a Quality Mark for fish retailers.

Although many supermarkets have begun to sell fresh fish, the best person to instil enthusiasm, to give cooking tips and prepare fish to your requirements, is the fishmonger. A good fishmonger will display gleaming, bright-eyed fish on cold slabs, and will allow customers to inspect them thoroughly. The fresher the fish, of course, the better its flavour. During transportation, fish should be kept at a controlled temperature to prevent rapid deterioration. Fish frozen immediately after the catch is preferable to stale, so-called "fresh" fish.

When you unwrap fish at home, it should smell of the sea, not of rotten seaweed. Rinse it immediately, cover it with clingfilm or foil to stop it absorbing other food flavours, and keep it in the fridge. The golden rule with all fresh fish is to consume it as soon as possible, and ideally on the day of purchase.

Nutrition Fish is ideal for anyone who needs to reduce fat intake. In the healthy diet, indeed, fish is invaluable for many reasons. It is satisfying, but not too filling. It provides a wide choice of flavours and textures, while supplying a high level of polyunsaturated fats, protein, vitamins and minerals. Here are some of the nutrients supplied by commonly eaten fish, per 100g. *Cod* (baked with butter), provides 96 kcal, supplies 21.4g protein, 1.2g fat, 0.59mg vitamin E, 0.38mg vitamin B_6, 12μg total folic acid. *Plaice*, fried in breadcrumbs, provides 228 kcal, supplies 18g protein, 13.7g fat, 8.6g carbohydrate, 67mg calcium, 2.9mg nicotinic acid, 0.36mg vitamin B_6, 1mg vitamin B_{12}, 17μg total folic acid. *Herring*, grilled, provides 199 kcal, supplies 20.4g protein, 13g fat, 33mg calcium, 0.18mg riboflavin, 4mg nicotinic acid, 0.30mg vitamin E, 0.57mg vitamin B_6, 11μg vitamin B_{12}, 10μg total folic acid.

Preparing fish

Wash sea fish under running water. Soak freshwater fish in several changes of cold water until there is no trace of mud.

Scaling Some fish, such as herrings, need to be scaled. Lay them on the work top; take a firm hold of the tail and, using the blunt edge of a knife blade, scrape off the scales, working towards the head. Rinse frequently under cold running water. Turn fish over and work on other side. If you use a wooden board, cover it with several layers of newspaper so it does not absorb a fishy smell.

Cleaning In round fish such as herring, mackerel, trout and cod, the entrails are found in the belly. Using a fine-bladed, sharp knife, slit the fish open along its underside from behind the gills almost to the tail. Take a firm grip on the fish and scrape out the entrails. Open fish out and rinse under cold water. If there is a seam of black skin or blood along the spine, use a little salt to rub it away.

If fish is to be served whole, you can merely cut away gills and fins. The dorsal fin may be removed by making deep cuts on either side and pulling hard to bring the root bone away as well. You may, however, prefer to cut off the head and tail. If it is a large fish with a strong backbone, cut down as far as the bone on either side of the head, bend head backwards to snap bone, then use a knife to free it.

In flat fish such as sole and plaice, the entrails are in a cavity behind the head. Make a semicircular slit just below the gills on the darkskinned side and scrape or squeeze out entrails.

Skinning Generally, only flat fish have the skin removed before cooking. Cut off fins, lay fish on a work top, dark side up and slit skin across, just above the tail. Loosen the skin with your thumb, then grasp the tail and peel skin quickly towards the head (dip your fingers in salt for a better grip). Cut it away. The white skin may be left on, or removed in similar fashion.

To skin a fish fillet, lay it skin-side down, use the point of a sharp knife to loosen skin at tail end. Hold the loosened flap of skin down with salted fingers and "saw" the flesh free.

To skin a round fish before cooking, use a sharp knife to cut off a thin strip of skin along the backbone. Loosen the skin on one side, below and beneath the head and gently pull it away. Cut free. Turn over and repeat for other side.

Filleting To fillet a large round fish, first clean, then make a semi-circular cut around the head. Cut along and through the backbone. The fish will yield two fillets.

Working towards the tail now, carefully ease the flesh from the bone, using a short knife which sits comfortably in your hand, and employing slicing strokes. Use knife to free fillet at tail end. Prise second fillet off the backbone and cut away tail. These fillets can be divided up according to their size.

Smaller round fish such as trout may be cooked on or off the bone. To bone a small whole fish, clean it, remove its head and tail and fins, slit along the belly and open the fish out skin side up. Press with your thumb along the back to loosen the backbone. Turn the fish over

SCALING FISH

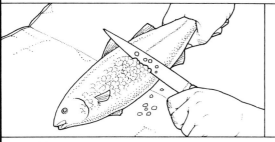 

Lay fish on work top, take firm hold of tail, and use blunt edge of knife to scrape off the scales.

Rinse frequently under cold running water over a colander to prevent scales from blocking the sink.

CLEANING ROUND FISH

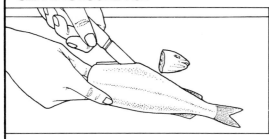 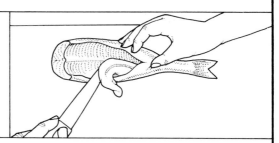

Use a fine-bladed knife to slit the fish open on underside from behind the gills almost to the tail.

Take a firm grip and scrape out the entrails. Open fish out and rinse well under cold running water.

FILLETING ROUND FISH

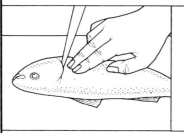 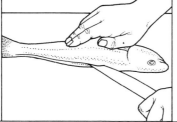 

Clean the fish; make a semi-circular slit around the head.

Cut along backbone. Use knife to free fillet.

Turn over and gently prise fillet off bone. Cut away tail.

FILLETING FLAT FISH

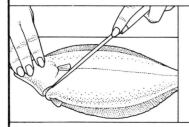 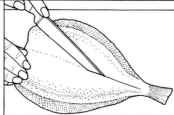 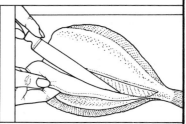

Cut head off, following shape with the point of knife.

Cut through flesh along back-bone, working from tail end.

Hold knife at angle and use slanting strokes to free fillet.

and ease the bone away with the point of a knife, working towards the tail, and at the same time removing as many small bones as possible.

A flat fish yields four fillets. Cut head off, following the shape with your knife. Cut through the flesh, along the backbone from tail. Hold the knife at an angle against the backbone, and use slanting strokes to free first fillet. Use knife to free from tail. Turn fish round and work from tail to head to free second fillet. Turn over and repeat process for third and fourth fillets.

Preparing other seafood

Oysters A plate of fresh raw oysters, preferably eaten within the sound of the sea, is an unforgettable experience. The best are native to our coasts. Others have been brought over from the Pacific and established here: they are

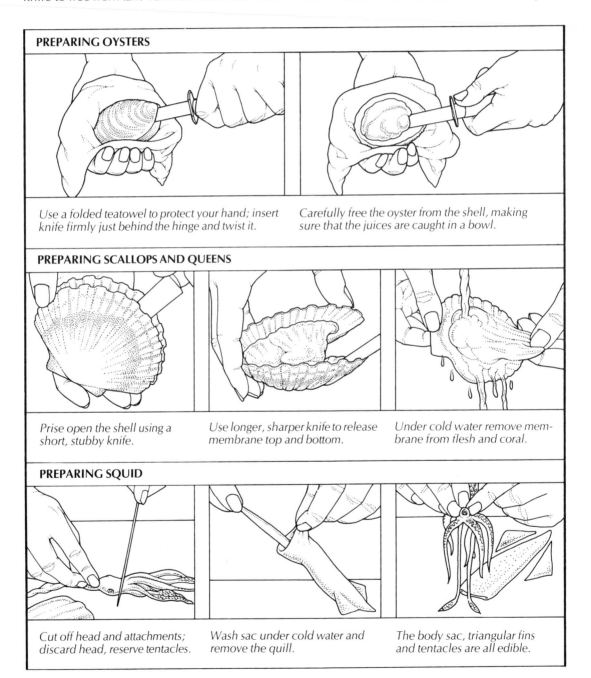

PREPARING OYSTERS

Use a folded teatowel to protect your hand; insert knife firmly just behind the hinge and twist it.

Carefully free the oyster from the shell, making sure that the juices are caught in a bowl.

PREPARING SCALLOPS AND QUEENS

Prise open the shell using a short, stubby knife.

Use longer, sharper knife to release membrane top and bottom.

Under cold water remove membrane from flesh and coral.

PREPARING SQUID

Cut off head and attachments; discard head, reserve tentacles.

Wash sac under cold water and remove the quill.

The body sac, triangular fins and tentacles are all edible.

slightly inferior in flavour.

When buying oysters, make sure they are tightly closed. Scrub the shells thoroughly under running water. To open, use a very sharp knife with which you feel comfortable. Thickly fold a cloth around the hand in which you will hold the oyster. Work over a fine sieve set in a bowl to catch any juice. Insert the knife firmly just beside the hinge; twist slightly to break the hinge muscle but do not cut the oyster itself. Now the shells should be apart, so you can cut the oyster free of the flat half to which it is attached. Squeeze some lemon juice over or add a splash of Tabasco and eat at once.

Scallops and queens Scallops are another expensive delicacy prized by connoisseurs. Queens, a small version from a different family, are just as good and are cooked whole, as are mussels.

Scallops are often sold opened out, so check for firm, slightly translucent, greyish flesh and a bright orange "coral". If the flesh is very white it is a sign that the scallop has been frozen.

To prepare, ease the scallop from the shell with a knife and pull away the black, beard like gill. Delicious steamed or poached, served cold with avocado (see recipe, page 112).

Mussels Buy live mussels and discard any with cracked shells and those which do not close when tapped.

Leave mussels to soak in the sink in several changes of cold salted water for at least an hour. The final rinse water should be clean. Throw away any mussels which float to the surface.

Use a small, stiff brush to scrub the shells, a sharp knife to scrape off barnacles and to pull off the "beards". Mussels are now ready to cook according to the chosen recipe. They can simply be put into a large pan in about ½in of cold water, brought to the boil, covered and steamed for five minutes (discard any that remain closed). But they are perhaps most delicious cooked à la marinière.

Squid Pull away the head, plus its tentacles, from the sac; cut tentacles from head; discard head and innards. Pull out the cellophane-like "quill" from inside the body and thoroughly flush out to leave a clean sac. Rub off the purple membrane which covers the body. Reserve the two fins. Dry on paper towel and cut sac into rings. Discard the inksac if it is attached. Remove "beak" from centre of tentacles. Chop tentacles in half.

Clams Scrub under cold running water to remove sand. To open soft-shelled varieties, simply insert a sharp knife. To open hard-shelled clams, insert the point of the knife next to the hinge and twist to break the muscle. Discard the top shell and use your knife to prise the clam from the shell.

Fish cookery

Fried fish is delicious as an occasional treat, but there are many healthier ways of cooking it (see Recipes for Enlightened Eating, pages 112-14).

In any case, the freshest, most succulent fish deserves better than to be clad in an overcoat of batter or swamped with a sauce, and requires the very lightest, simplest of cooking to enhance its superb natural flavour. Overcooking spells ruin to any fish dish. Flavour is lost, flesh mushed.

Grilling A quick-and-easy method suitable for many types of fish. Set the grill at a moderate heat, and either lightly grease the grill rack or cover it with foil. Brush white fish with a very little oil or melted butter to keep it moist. For oily fish, to be grilled whole, use a sharp knife to make several deep diagonal cuts in the flesh, which will ensure that it cooks through. Grill thin fillets for 3-4 minutes without turning. Thicker pieces and whole fish take 10-15 minutes and should be turned once.

Barbecuing This is particularly suitable for firm-fleshed fish such as cod, haddock, halibut, turbot, monkfish, swordfish and fresh tuna, cooked either in portions or in chunks on a skewer. Oily fish such as sardines and red mullet, and giant prawns in full armour also do well. If you want to cook a whole, large fish such as grey mullet or sea bass, you may think it worth investing in a fish-shaped wire basket tool, so that you can turn it as required and retrieve it still in one piece.

Steaming All kinds of fish may be steamed, but this method, being the gentlest of all, is especially suitable for thin fillets of delicately flavoured white fish, particularly Dover sole. If you don't have a special steamer, place the fish on a lightly greased, heatproof plate, dot it with tiny knobs of butter, season, cover with foil and place over a saucepan of gently simmering water for 10-15 minutes. Alternatively you can use a wok and trivet.

Braising Drier varieties of fish benefit from braising with vegetables in a covered pot on the hob or in the oven, ideally in a fish fumet (stock made with fish trimmings) or wine.

Poaching This is similar to braising, but entails more gentle cooking in a little liquid, usually stock or water, and is suitable for almost any fish from a humble cod fillet to a whole salmon. Allow about 10-15 minutes a pound. If fish is to be served cold, leave it to cool in the cooking

AVAILABILITY OF FRESH FISH THROUGHOUT THE YEAR

	J	F	M	A	M	J	J	A	S	O	N	D
Bass	•		•					•	•	•	•	•
Bream, sea	•	•				•	•	•	•	•	•	•
freshwater		•								•	•	•
Brill	•	•				•	•	•		•	•	•
Carp	•	•	•							•	•	•
Clams	•	•	•	•	•	•	•	•	•	•	•	•
Cockles					•	•	•	•	•	•	•	•
Cod	•	•		•	•	•	•	•	•	•	•	•
Coley	•	•		•	•	•	•	•	•	•	•	•
Conger eel			•	•	•	•	•	•	•	•		
Crab			•	•	•	•	•	•	•	•	•	•
Dab	•		•	•	•	•	•	•		•	•	•
Dover sole	•	•		•	•	•		•		•	•	•
Eels	•		•	•	•	•		•		•	•	•
Flounder		•	•	•	•	•	•	•	•	•	•	•
Greenland halibut	•	•	•	•	•	•	•	•	•	•	•	•
Grey mullet	•	•					•		•	•	•	•
Haddock	•	•			•	•	•	•	•	•	•	•
Hake	•	•	•			•	•	•	•	•	•	•
Halibut	•	•	•			•	•	•	•	•	•	•
Herring					•	•	•	•	•	•	•	•
Huss	•	•	•	•	•	•	•	•	•	•	•	•
John Dory	•	•	•	•	•	•	•	•	•	•	•	•
Lemon sole	•	•	•	•	•	•	•	•	•	•	•	•
Lobster			•	•	•	•	•	•	•	•	•	
Mackerel	•	•	•	•	•	•	•	•	•	•	•	•
Megrim	•	•	•		•	•	•	•	•	•	•	•

*Weather and water conditions will affect both the quality and the
quantities of fish available, and will determine the price you pay. The
quality of wild seafood also varies according to the season*

liquid (but see page 102). Reserve the liquid for use in a sauce or soup. A fish kettle is ideal for poaching large whole fish.

Baking There are many ways of oven-cooking fish, for instance, *en papillote*, with individual portions parcelled in greaseproof paper or foil, with a little chopped parsley, lemon, salt and pepper and a small knob of butter. They can be placed in stock or milk in a covered dish. A clay fish brick is ideal for baking smallish, whole fish at their freshest. As a guide to cooking times, small fillets placed in a shallow dish at the centre of a moderate oven (gas mark 4, 180°C, 350°F) will take 10 to 12 minutes; thicker cuts will take 20 minutes; and small whole fish up to 30 minutes. A larger fish such as mackerel, stuffed, may take up to an hour.

Frying For deep or shallow frying, coat the fish with batter or breadcrumbs to preserve moisture; use this method only occasionally.

Food irradiation

While much interest has been focused on food additives, little attention has been paid to a process which has far more serious implications to our food supplies: irradiation.

	J	F	M	A	M	J	J	A	S	O	N	D
Monkfish	•	•	•	•	•	•	•	•	•	•	•	•
Mussels	•	•	•						•	•	•	•
Oysters, native	•	•	•	•					•	•	•	•
Portuguese	•	•	•	•	•	•	•	•		•	•	•
Pike	•	•	•				•		•	•	•	•
Plaice	•	•			•	•	•	•	•	•	•	•
Pollack				•	•	•	•	•	•			
Prawns	•	•	•	•	•	•	•	•	•	•	•	
Redfish		•		•	•	•	•	•	•	•	•	•
Red mullet				•	•	•	•	•	•			
Rock salmon	•	•	•	•	•				•		•	
Salmon		•	•	•	•	•	•	•	•			
Scad					•							
Scallops	•	•	•							•	•	•
Shrimps		•	•	•	•	•	•	•	•			
Skate	•	•			•		•		•	•	•	•
Smelts	•										•	•
Sprats	•	•	•							•	•	•
Squid					•	•	•	•	•			
Trout, rainbow	•	•	•	•	•	•	•	•	•	•	•	•
sea				•	•	•	•	•				
Turbot	•	•		•	•	•	•	•		•		•
Whelks		•	•	•	•	•	•	•				
Whitebait				•	•	•						
Whiting	•	•						•	•	•	•	•
Winkles	•		•	•						•	•	•
Witch	•	•			•	•	•	•	•	•	•	•

Behind the scenes, some members of the food industry have been quietly assessing its value and are reaching the conclusion that the manipulation of foodstuffs by delaying deterioration could be of definite benefit to the mass market, on the assumption that, if food is safe and looks all right, the public will buy it. If fruit and vegetables, meat and fish can be prevented from showing their age, it will be a boon to the large-scale producers frustrated by the short shelf life of, say, strawberries or chickens. The USA and many European countries have given the go-ahead to this revolutionary technique, so why not Britain?

The name could obviously be a problem. Even before the Chernobyl disaster, the word "radiation" had sinister overtones for many people. And if the public worried about low-dose X-ray used in medical treatment, how could the process be made to seem acceptable when applied to food?

A lavishly-funded promotion campaign, offering explanations and reassurance, would have to follow any lifting of the ban on food irradiation in this country (applied except in cases where hospital patients needed a sterile diet). But first Government, civil servants and scientists must be persuaded of its safety. Once it had the sanction of a MAFF/DHSS report, ran the thinking, there would be little to prevent it being incorporated in the Food Act Regulations and embraced as a major advance. The public would be presented with a *fait accompli*.

In 1985, certain rumblings in the press suggested that, even though food irradiation was illegal in Britain, some of us were likely to have eaten irradiated food. Why were strawberries staying fresher for longer? The process was allowed in the Netherlands and, since no food inspector had any means to test for it, there was nothing to stop the entry of irradiated food via the ports. Still, this was only surmise.

Journalists were alerted that the Government would shortly, without public debate, give approval for irradiation, and a way was found to bring the subject into the open. In March 1986, a daily newspaper revealed that Young's Seafoods, owned by the mammoth Imperial Foods Group, had decided that a consignment of Malaysian prawns did not reach their own stringent safety standards. Young's therefore sent their prawns to the Netherlands, where any bacterial spoilage could be neutralised by irradiation. The cargo was then re-imported illegally and sold here, principally to caterers.

In April 1986, the Government Advisory Committee on Irradiated and Novel Foods produced a report on "the Safety and Wholesomeness of Irradiated Foods". A distinguished panel of scientists, chaired by Sir Arnold Burgen, Master of Darwin College, Cambridge, reached the conclusion that, taken overall, there were no serious objections to allowing the use of food irradiation here. The panel was advised on the practical aspects of industrial food irradiation by Frank Ley, Marketing Director of Isotron, which is the leading British Company with irradiation facilities.

The Committee admitted that irradiation could lead to nutritional depletion, but no more than could other processes such as pasteurisation, dehydration, freezing and cooking. The Report, in regarding irradiation as a process, implicitly assumed that irradiated food was not fresh food as it is commonly understood. However, the Panel on Novel Foods, investigating nutritional aspects and chaired by Professor Arnold Bender, disagreed with this view (Appendix E). "Since irradiation does not usually replace the subsequent cooking procedures, any losses that occur with irradiation must be regarded as additional to, rather than instead of, losses that would subsequently take place when the product is cooked."

Perhaps understandably, there was no mention of its effect on flavour, even though some members of the food industry, who were privileged to attend tastings of irradiated foods at the Leatherhead Food Research Association, had observed a metallic odour in ham and a fishy smell in raw chicken which, it was blithely assumed, would disappear with cooking. Anyway, one member felt confident that consumers were less likely to reject food on grounds of flavour than they were on colour and general appearance.

At the time of writing, a consultation period is in progress. Unless any serious objection is sustained as to its effects on health or its commercial viability, irradiation will eventually be legalised under the Food Act, probably with the proviso that irradiated food should be labelled as such. Whatever graphic device is dreamed up for the irradiation symbol, it will be of little help to the bewildered consumer.

What is food irradiation?

This is basically a method by which food can be made to last longer, using the energy from ionising radiation. It can retard sprouting (eg in potatoes) or ripening (eg in strawberries and mangoes), and reduces the level of microbial loading. Some bacteria which cause food poisoning may be destroyed. Ionising radiation alters the chemical structure of material, so is damaging to living organisms, but it can sometimes be useful to eliminate health hazards in food.

The two radioactive materials which produce low enough energies for safe food irradiation are Cobalt 60 (a radioactive isotope of cobalt which gives off gamma rays) and Caesium 137, both by-products of nuclear reactor technology.

It is also possible to irradiate food using beams of electrons, but this is more expensive, and electrons do not penetrate materials as efficiently as do gamma rays.

Careful control of the radiation dose is crucial in maintaining the characteristic textures, flavours and colours of food, and in ensuring the safety of the process. The higher the dose of radiation, the more dramatically food will change – for better or worse. A low dose is used to delay the ripening process; a higher dose to destroy parasites in meat. The food itself does not come in direct contact with the radioactive source, so it cannot become radioactive, at least at the doses advocated.

Although the irradiation process was patented as long ago as 1930, its development was spearheaded by Eisenhower's "Atoms for Peace" policy, and from the Fifties to the Seventies research was carried out throughout the USA into its safety and feasibility. Several countries have been employing irradiation for certain foods since 1963. In spite of the fact that international standards have been established and recently revised, many people have reservations about the limitations of the safety tests so far conducted, as well as being loath to see yet another development of, and justification for, nuclear technology.

Advocates of the use of food irradiation will point to the following advantages.

A low dose of radiation (usually below 0.1 M Rad) will delay sprouting in vegetables such as potatoes and onions, so they will last long. It will delay the ripening process in fruits so that they can be transported long distances without deterioration. It will kill insects which infest grains such as wheat and rice, spices and some fruits, thus observing the need for gas storage or fumigation treatments.

A medium dose of radiation (between 1 kGy and 10 kGy or 1.0-M Rad) will reduce micro-organisms such as yeasts, moulds and bacteria which cause food spoilage, so prolonging the life of foods and decreasing the risk of poisoning by salmonella in chicken and fish.

A high dose of radiation (above 10 KGy or 1.0-M Rad) will completely sterilise food by eliminating all bacteria and viruses so, for example, meat products could be kept indefinitely.

Food irradiation will particularly benefit certain sectors of the food industry.

BAKERS The irradiation of wheat improves the baking and cooking quality of flour, and ''improves'' the elasticity and volume of dough in bread-making.

BREWERS, WINE AND SPIRIT MAKERS Irradiated barley may increase the yield during malting by 7 per cent. Irradiation can be used to ''age'' spirits and to make grapes produce more juice in processing.

PACKET VEGETABLE MANUFACTURERS Dehydrated vegetables need less time to reconstitute and cook if they have first been irradiated. Carrots are claimed to ''improve in flavour'' after irradiation.

The general arguments put forward for irradiation point out that if consumers want a reduction in the use of chemicals in food processing, irradiation provides an alternative. Most frequently, manufacturers cite the growing incidence of salmonella, particularly in poultry, which could be checked by irradiation. Many point to the safety record of irradiation, and to its ''wholesomeness'', reminding us that it is in common use for specific food products in Belgium, Canada, Denmark, Israel, Italy, Japan, and Netherlands, South Africa, Spain, the USA and USSR. The process has been in selective use

for 25 years with no apparent serious side effects. Some even go so far as to say that, in many parts of the world where vast quantities of food (30 to 40 per cent) are lost through spoilage, irradiation could help to solve the problem of hunger.

The conclusions of the Committee on Irradiated and Novel Foods, while not actively promoting irradiation, raised no objections to its use. They recognised that it would cause a reduction in, for instance, vitamin contents, but dismissed this as insignificant in the diet as a whole.

An important clause ended the Committee's conclusions: ''Since food irradiation is a novel process, there is a need for monitoring the extent of its use. Industry should assess the effects of irradiation on the nutrient content of the foods they propose to irradiate, including carrying out simple analyses that are reliable.''

Once again it was assumed that the food industry would be self-regulatory, and this assumption has provoked strong dissension. It has been pointed out that the watchdogs of the food industry, the Trading Standards Officers, have no training or equipment to carry out the monitoring of irradiated food.

Unscrupulous food manufacturers could benefit by sterilising previously contaminated and useless food by irradiation, then releasing it for public consumption as ''safe to eat''. This practice has been condemned by a joint expert committee of WHO/FAOm, but not all committees share this view.

The London Food Commission's *Food Irradiation in Britain* (£2.50 from London Food Commission Promotions Ltd, PO Box 291, London N5 1DU) comes down firmly against the process for a variety of reasons, many of which are shared by other authorities.

Their main concerns are not primarily to do with technological safety, for with efficiently funded and trained inspectors, the process could be as safe as others now in use. The first question raised by the writers of the report is whether or not, given all the sophisticated techniques for the transportation, preservation, distribution and storage of food, we *need* irradiation. There are potent reasons for saying no.

If our first priority as consumers is cheaper fresh food, so that all may benefit from a healthy diet, we should be aware that the high capital cost for irradiation facilities is unlikely to be offset by the economic advantages of prolonged shelf life. Fresh food will probably cost *more* not less. Furthermore, irradiation depletes nutrients, a factor which runs counter to the advice that they should be obtained from "a wide variety of fresh foods". The LFC Report states: "The full nutritional impact of irradiation on the diet has not yet been fully assessed. Further studies in this area are needed before authorising its use in the UK."

It is true that cases of salmonella poisoning are on the increase, but irradiation would not automatically eliminate the problem. Food can easily be recontaminated after irradiation, and few people would relish the thought of yet another excuse for manufacturers to make use of substandard food, whatever the apparent safety. Irradiation will kill some micro-organisms, but not others, for example those causing botulism. It is also conceivable that some organisms could develop immunity to radiation, and not enough is known about what happens to the genetic structure of pathoegenic organisms which are damaged but not completely destroyed. Scientists are by no means universally confident of the health safety of irradiated food.

We must not forget that irradiated fresh food would not only be bought to take home; it would also be used in convenience items so food could well be irradiated twice in the name of safety. Nor would this obviate the need for food additives; some might still be used, for example, to prevent discoloration. Think of the additional effect on the generally poor texture and flavour of most convenience foods.

The arguments against the irradiation of food are not primarily centred on its hazard to health, for it is highly unlikely that anyone will become undernourished, ill or even die from consuming it, even though there are still some questions scientists would like answered. There are two main causes for concern. At the moment there is no way for the consumer or the public health inspectors to find out if food has been treated or not, and this can only add to public suspicion of our increasingly manipulated food supply. Since the Chernobyl disaster, even those formerly in favour of the use of nuclear energy are changing their minds. Do we need yet more expensive radiation technology with the evident risks to those working with it, as well as to the population as a whole? It is difficult to be convinced that the high cost and possible dangers of a further development in our nuclear industry, which will give questionable benefit to some food manufacturers, will in any way be offset by a major contribution to our diet, in terms of health, wider availability or lower prices.

PART THREE

MANUFACTURED FOOD

The loving care of the skilled gardener or cook can never be reproduced by the processes of mass manufacture and distribution, despite advertisers' claims of "garden freshness" and "country style". But at least the mounting public pressure on the food industry to offer more natural products, to use fewer additives and better ingredients, and to provide more information on labels, has led certain sectors to concentrate their efforts on making manufactured food more appealing. The thrust has come mainly from the large supermarket chains, who are able to respond quickly to consumer demands, and who can dictate standards to the manufacturers who rely on their custom. (Sainsbury and Tesco together control nearly a third of the packaged-groceries market in this country.)

This is good news for car-owners and people who live near large supermarkets, where the weekly shopping can be conveniently accomplished, but it is not so encouraging for those on low incomes, or with poor mobility, who must rely on whatever is available locally.

The smaller retailers are having a hard time of it. They generally pay higher wholesale prices than supermarkets for identical products, since they cannot buy nearly as much stock as the chains do. Because they have a relatively low turnover, they offer fewer fresh foods, and frequently stock up on inferior goods with a long shelf-life. Rents and rates are high, and almost inevitably the customer pays more.

Still, the small shopkeeper also has to depend on what the customers buy – or do not buy. As long as we are vociferous in our demands, all sections of the food trade and industry can be expected to respond sooner or later.

"Healthy" potato crisps Increasingly, goods are being marketed as containing no – or only essential – additives, reduced fat, low sugar, no salt, added fibre. Real and important changes are being made by some manufacturers, while others merely jump on the fast-rolling bandwagon.

Take the Great Potato Crisps Debate. Suddenly this much-maligned snack has pretensions to a "health" food and has claimed a whole new set of credentials. Crisps, the manufacturers say, on the basis of new analytical data, and with the encouragement of a specially retained expert on nutrition, have more fibre, weight for weight, than wholemeal bread. Yes, say the detractors, but not portion for portion. Crisps supply twice the vitamin C of an apple, and three times the energy. But then, apples aren't notable for their vitamin C content. And, for energy, if you will, read kilocalories – many of them, in crisps, deriving from fat. All right, allow the exponents, crisps do have a high fat content, and they do contain salt, but the fat is polyunsaturated vegetable oil, while the salt content is less, weight for weight, than in some popular breakfast cereals. One packet of crisps, comes the reply, contains 90 times the fat of a baked potato, 50 times the salt of an apple. Anyway, weight-for-weight evaluations are misleading, and it is illogical to compare a snack food with a breakfast food, since the one is extraneous to and the other a part of the daily diet.

The multi-million pound crisps industry, having satisfied itself as to its product's credibility, breathes a sigh of relief and launches a "healthy snacking" campaign, assured of a healthy boost to sales.

Jam today

The enlightened eater, while not underestimating the progress which has been made towards better fare, must continue to be alert to marketing ploys, and should be aware that some compromises are deemed necessary in the mass-production of food.

Not all of it is junk. Some is actually quite good; some is appalling. Better labelling now enables us to determine certain nutritional qualities before we buy. But gastronomically we can still make expensive mistakes.

Manufacturers, anxious to ensure that we continue to buy their products, and drawing on their experience of successful sales, have isolated those factors which provide the basis of profitability. These are consistency, availability, cheapness, long shelf-life, and appeal to the lowest common denominator of taste, all of which militate against the production of the very best quality food, which can be unpredictable, scarce, expensive, and distinctive in flavour.

Consider the implications of the specifications in commercial food production. First, **consistency** and the assumption that we expect a food to taste the same every time we buy it. Jam provides the perfect example of this thinking at work. In order to fulfil the first criterion, the manufacturer needs a source of large-volume supply which will be regular throughout the year; he also needs a cooking formula which is entirely predictable and will always produce the same colour, texture and flavour. He will therefore favour the bulk supplier of cheap, imported frozen fruit over the smaller, less predictable supplier of more expensive, home-grown, better-flavoured and seasonal fruit, or he will stock his own orchards with fruit varieties whose main characteristic is abundant yield, with flavour of secondary importance. Consistency is the antithesis of distinction.

Next, **availability**. If it is to have brand impact, a jam must be seen and identified in as many outlets as possible, from the corner shop to the supermarket. So standards may be sacrificed to volume production.

Most households buy jam, and in the weekly shop, **cheapness** may be the deciding factor. The manufacturer who can sell for 10p less than his competitor, therefore has an instant advantage. It would not be possible, however, to keep the price down if the retailer had constantly to replace his stocks because of deterioration. Hence the perceived need for jam that lasts a long time and does not fade. So in go the preservatives to a level permitted by food regulations, in goes artificial colour (cheaper than from natural sources). And the achievement: long **shelf-life**. If, by this stage, the natural flavour has diminished, more can be added – artificial or otherwise.

As long as the jam looks as expected – bright red for strawberry, bright orange for apricot – and tastes as sweet as anticipated (lots of sweetener), and has a bold, recognisable label with a picture recalling fresh-picked fruit, the undiscerning consumer will be happy – or so runs the manufacturers' wisdom.

The result has been mass-produced jam, a relatively cheap, anonymous confection which all the family will accept. And, since few people these days make their own jam, comparisons with the beautiful, fruity, natural version are not easy.

It is the same story with many foods, but the demands of the health lobby are beginning to bring about the expected as well as incidental improvements in standards. In the case of jam, they called for less sugar, no additives, and manufacturers took heed. Reduced sugar meant reduced potential for good preservation and setting qualities. Without added preservatives, flavours or colours, makers had to use better fruit, to accept the natural colour of jam, to rely more on pectin (familiar to home jam-makers) for setting, and to advise consumers to keep the jar in the fridge once opened. This type of jam is slightly more expensive than the type we have grown used to, but a look at the label will confirm its qualities. And you can cut down on quantity to be able to afford a better product.

Any jam, even "sugar reduced", will of course be high in sugar. But since it is something which four out of five households buy (in 1984, the retail sales of jam and marmalade produced over £100 million), it is worth bearing in mind the sugar content laid down by the 1981 EEC Preserves Directive:

Standard jam: for most fruit this must contain 35g of fruit per 100g jam and have a total sugar level of at least 60 per cent.
Extra jam: must contain at least 45g of fruit per 100g jam, and have a total sugar level of at least 60 per cent.
Reduced sugar jam: must contain at least 35g of fruit per 100g jam, and have a total sugar level of at least 30 per cent and at most 55 per cent.

If you appreciate a fruity jam or marmalade, cut down on quantity, pay a little more and go for the "Extra". But, to cut down on sweet things, Reduced Sugar is the obvious choice.

What's on the label

In gloomier, paranoid moments, one could imagine a food industry operating a sort of free-for-all, with the "big boys" going to any lengths to deceive us, to cheat us, and worse ("How the Food Trade Poisons Us", ran a headline in New Society on January 17, 1986). Heightened awareness of food has brought increased anxiety, and we are now demanding illumination of the whole subject, wanting the truth, with everything in black and white, with labels saying "good" or "bad", so that we can quickly get on with the business of living, and have no more headaches over eating.

Well, some abuses are perpetrated by the food industry, as by other industries, and inspectors are too few to keep a constant check on culprits. However, these abuses almost always involve short-cuts on quality, rather than infringement of government regulations concerning proportions of chemical additives. After all, it needs only one contamination scare to bankrupt a manufacturer.

In general, manufactured foods present far less risk to life and health than does the family car. The major, and increasingly common, hazard of food poisoning arises from poor hygiene during preparation, often in the home. But the fact that standards of hygiene should concern us more than the contents of branded foods, does not mean we can be complacent about reading the labels. We must all make up our own minds about the acceptability of certain additives, and we should have a basic knowledge of nutrition. We must study the ingredients of the foods we buy, for with the sophistication of today's products, it is not enough to trust to the tastebuds. The clever food technologist using artificial ingredients can confuse the most discerning palate.

Since the mid-Forties, food regulations have been expanded to protect consumers against unscrupulous practice. Compositional standards were set for such foods as ketchup, margarine and fishcakes. Regulations were brought in to govern food safety, and to determine nutritional quality. Over the years the rules have been refined and augmented. A company manufacturing, for example, butter or margarine, is subject to controls as to what it may add and in what quantities. There are restrictions on the amount of water which may be added to some dairy produce; regulations as to the minimum meat content in, say, sausages; regulations regarding the sugar content of jam. Safety clauses stipulate the maximum levels of potentially dangerous substances.

For 40 years it has been regarded as a duty of government constantly to review food regulations, but the Ministry of Agriculture, Fisheries and Food, responsible for drawing them up, has come to realise that labelling alone cannot ensure standards, nor can the Ministry keep pace and lay down compositional requirements for all the proliferation of convenience foods, which involve new ingredients and new techniques. It therefore concentrates on setting standards for those staple foods (bread, meat products etc), which are "nutritionally significant in the national diet". The manufacturer has become more directly responsible to the public for providing information on, for instance, the increased water content of some foods as a result of new processing techniques, or on the extent to which substitutes have been used instead of more expensive ingredients. Recognising that "substandard versions of commonly known and well recognised foods" could become common, the Ministry's 1979 report on food labelling says, "accurate and positive labelling is especially important if the consumer is to be fully informed". The implications of this message are that we will become increasingly reliant on what manufacturers choose to communicate on the label, and that we, the consumers, must ourselves be the watchdogs of the food industry.

Food labelling descriptions are covered by Ministry of Agriculture, Fisheries and Food regulations, which form part of the Food Act (1984) and which are periodically updated or altered. Here is the straightforward information you can expect to find on the label of pre-packaged foods.

- Name by which product is usually known.
- Ingredients listed in descending weight order (as additives usually form the smallest component, they are listed last, either by E number or chemical name).
- Name and address of manufacturer/distributor.
- Date (on certain goods) giving minimum time the product is expected to last.

Labelling regulations

A new set of regulations has been drafted to supplement existing ones, to take account of current nutritional concern about the quality of our national diet. Fat labelling, for example, will become a legal necessity in 1988, with further nutritional labelling a voluntary option. The basic requirements for labelling fats in food stipulate that the proportion of saturated fat should be shown. Manufacturers may choose to provide further nutritional information, which must be listed in the order of fat, protein, carbohydrate and energy. Additional intelligence may follow, on energy content (kcals and kJ), breakdowns of sugars and fibre under carbohydrates; polyunsaturates and mono-unsaturates under fat, plus details of sodium, vitamins and minerals. The draft regulations clearly lay down "a limit on the amount of information to be given within the guidelines format".

Many nutritionists, while welcoming more information on labels, are concerned that this information is incomplete and often given in a form which the consumer cannot readily assimilate. Some would go so far as to say that, far from clarifying nutritional issues, the new labelling has contributed to confusion.

The main objection is that the regulations, which were given impetus by the COMA report, make it necessary only to give certain information about fat. Data about sugar, salt and fibre are as yet optional even though intake of these should be monitored. And even such information as must be given about fat, tells only part of the story. For, while it is important to know the saturated fat content and total fat content of foods, both of which must be declared, it is as important for the aware consumer to know the proportion of polyunsaturated fat, which need not be stated.

Any additional information which manufacturers may elect to provide can be given only according to certain formulae. The sugar, fibre and starch contents of foods are grouped under the umbrella term "carbohydrates", which is no use to anybody wishing to reduce sugar intake and increase fibre intake. You may be told that your bar of milk chocolate has 59.4g carbohydrate per 100g, or that a brown roll contains 57.2g carbohydrate. But how are you to know that the brown roll contains just 2.1g sugars and about 5.9g dietary fibre, or that the chocolate bar contains 56.6g sugars and no dietary fibre?

Nor are manufacturers required to list the amounts of added salt or sugar.

Many savoury manufactured foods contain "hidden" sugars, a practice which subtly maintains the habit of eating too many sweet things. Corned beef and tendersweet bacon commonly have added sugar, as do soups, convenience foods such as made-up macaroni cheese and spaghetti bolognese, and most tinned vegetables, particularly peas, red kidney beans and tomatoes. Other products which

A dash of 1-(p-hydroxyphenyl)-3-butanone, a soupçon of 2,5-dimethyl-N-(2-pyrazinyl)pyrrole, a drop of ethyl vanillin et voila!

reinforce the craving for sweetness by including sugar, are gravy browning, chutneys and relishes, ketchup, baked beans, breakfast cereals, meat extract.

When you start to cut down on sugar, you do become more sensitive to its presence in savoury foods, and it is becoming increasingly possible to find sugar-free alternatives.

Once again, read the labels. And don't forget that sugar may appear as caramel, sucrose, dextrose, glucose syrup and glucose powder.

Write to the manufacturer (name and address on label), or, with own-brand products, to the supermarket, to obtain missing information on sugar, salt and fibre contents of those foods which you buy on a regular basis.

Flavour labelling

Some labels may be ambiguous, some positively misleading. The description of flavours, in particular, can be perplexing, and manufacturers use different labelling criteria, but, in practice, there do seem to be certain conventions.

If you wish to buy a raspberry dessert, you may find three versions with slightly different tags. "Raspberry dessert" should be what it says: a dessert made from raspberries, with no additional flavour. "Raspberry flavoured dessert" will contain both raspberries and additional flavouring. "Raspberry flavour dessert" will contain no fruit, only flavouring.

This can only be a rough guide, and there are exceptions, so you need to read the small print. And there may still be few clues as to what "flavouring" implies. According to regulations, the picture of a fruit or vegetable can be used only if the flavour is derived wholly or partly from it. What is not specified is the origin of all the flavours used, and natural and artificial ones are frequently used in combination. Synthetic flavours, being cheaper, are the most widely used. Here is a recipe for synthetic raspberry flavour which can contain, in varying porportions, vanillin, ethyl vanillin, alpha-ionone, maltol, 1-(p-hydroxyphenyl)-3-butanone, dimethyl sulphide, and 2,5-dimethyl-N-(2-pyrazinyl)pyrrole.

Many labels now proclaim, "no artificial colouring, flavouring or preservatives", but "artificial" refers to the manufacturer's rather than the public's understanding of the word. A substance which is "not artificial" can be similar to a substance occurring naturally, an extract of a natural substance, or even a synthetic copy of a natural substance. Most flavours used are "nature identical", one example of this being ethyl vanillin, which is not classified as artificial, and is used as a substitute for the more expensive and erratically obtainable vanilla pod. "Nature identical" flavours are not quite that. One naturally occurring flavour can contain 3000 chemical components and, as it would be impractical to assemble these in the laboratory, food chemists use far fewer, to produce a crude version of the original.

Manufactured flavours are used increasingly as substitutes for real, more expensive ingredients and processes. Frozen pizza may contain tomato and cheese flavours to enliven a thin and poor-quality topping, or even to make possible the use of artificial cheese. Smoked flavours can be a cheap shortcut for bacon or fish. Soya protein products and reconstituted meat wastes are particularly dependent on added flavours.

Fruit juice and squash
If you have ever wondered at the variation in the fruit taste of drinks, here is the reason for it. "Fruit juice" and "concentrated fruit juice" do contain the juice, and not other parts, of fruit. However, flavour may have been added to boost insipid taste, and this need not be declared on the label. If sulphited fruit has been used for reasons of preservation, the juice is permitted to contain up to 10mg per litre of residual sulphites, and again, this is not necessarily declared on the label.

"Fruit drink" makes use of whole fruit and skins to extract maximum liquid. Benzoic acid (E210), to which asthma sufferers may be sensitive, is usually added as a preservative.

"Squashes", "cordials", "crushes" and carbonated (fizzy) drinks may possibly contain some fruit, but usually rely on flavouring essences mixed with water, sugar, preservatives (sodium benzoate and/or sulphites), and artificial colours.

Colours are another area of confusion. E160(b), annatto, is a natural yellow colour obtained from the seed covering of the annatto tree, and is commonly found in food products, where it is used to heighten natural colour. The result is still artificially intensified colour, from whatever source.

Meat products
Water is a major natural component of many vegetables, but meat, also, contains a fair proportion. Raw chicken contains 67g per 100g, but frozen chicken considerably more, for which the customer pays dearly, and this additional water does not have to be declared on the label. Poor-quality frozen fish has added

The mass-produced hamburger or beefburger may be a very poor relation indeed of the traditional American-style hamburger made from top-quality lean mince

water, and many made-up dishes rely on watery liquids distantly flavoured by tomato concentrate. Water can represent profit for the manufacturer; expense and loss of flavour for the consumer. (See table of additives, page 89: water-retaining properties of polyphosphates.)

Once meat is made up into a meat product, there is much more scope for disguising the ingredients. Any part of the flesh – including fat, skin, rind, gristle and sinews – can be used and is classified as meat. Permitted offal includes the diaphragm, muscle and fatty tissue from the head, the heart, kidney, liver, pancreas, thymus, tongue and tail meat. The superior grade is described as "lean meat" – that is, meat where the connective tissue and fat have been trimmed away (although 10 per cent fat is still permitted). There are stipulations as to the proportion of "meat" to "lean meat" in certain products. Take, for example, the variations on the theme of hamburger, which in true American style should be made from top-quality lean mince.

Burger Must contain at least 80 per cent "meat" (according to the definition given above), of which 65 per cent (that is, 52 per cent of the total) must be "lean".

Beefburger "Meat" content must be at least 80 per cent beef in origin, otherwise as above. (A "turkeyburger" must be at least 80 per cent turkey in origin.)

Hamburger Must be made from either beef or pork, or both, and must contain at least 80 per cent "meat".

Economy burger Need be only 60 per cent "meat", and 65 per cent of this (ie, 39 per cent of the total) must be "lean meat".

Ham This has undergone a depressing metamorphosis over the years. Most of what is offered for sale today is scarcely deserving of the name ham.

Much of the ham we eat, both at home or in pub and canteen sandwiches, is put together from bits and pieces of different pigs, thrown into a machine, and perhaps made extra-moist by the addition of water-absorbing polyphosphates. The meat scraps are pummelled, stuck together and moulded to give the familiar pink, slimy meat.

At least, however, the Bacon and Meat Manufacturers Association have decided on a code of practice which will mean better labelling. Ham which is reconstituted has now to be labelled "formed from" or "made up from" cuts of the leg (if this is the case); or "sectioned" if it is made from meat from different pigs. If the ham includes inferior bits of meat, either mince or slurry (liquefied scraps), added in for bulk, the label will state "re-formed". Only products worthy of the name will be labelled "ham" or "traditional ham".

Sausages Before you reach for the packet of mass-produced bangers – and there are few households which don't have one in the fridge – pause to consider if you really fancy them.

According to the Meat Product Regulations, a sausage must contain not less than 50 per cent meat. A sausage labelled "pork" must contain not less than 65 per cent meat, of which 80 per cent must be pork. Sausage meat is defined as "Flesh, including fat, skin, rind, gristle and sinew in amounts naturally associated with such flesh . . ."

A pork sausage can easily contain 45 per cent saturated fat. Sausages can be further filled out by making use of the waste left on animal carcases after trimming. By heating and pressurising the bones, the meat is made to flow out in a slurry known as Mechanically Recovered Meat (MRM), which a food analyst would be hard-put to distinguish from "proper" meat. Another aid to the cheap and nasty sausage is dehydrated granules of rind, not above 10 per cent of the "meat" in a pork sausage. Gristle, too, is a likely ingredient, as technologists have found a way of chopping it into a glutinous material which combines with "meat".

Meat and fish spreads For those who have wondered why branded meat spreads, pâtés, pies, pasties and sausages often taste like the

A cheap-and-nasty, commercially produced sausage will be high in saturated fat and may contain dehydrated rind granules as well as mechanically recovered meat

ghost of what the butcher used to sell, here are some further clues.

A meat or fish "spread" need be only 70 per cent fish or meat – and only 65 per cent of this has to be what is generally meant by meat and fish. Only half of the minimum meat content of pâté, need be "lean meat"; the rest may be offal. The award for the lowest total meat content of all goes to the sausage roll, with a minimum 12.5 per cent meat.

The important issue is not what is permitted in such products, but the fact that some manufacturers have been able to get away with selling products no one would dream of making in such a fashion at home.

The demands for healthier food will not necessarily mean better meat products. Low fat is not in itself any guarantee of high quality. Those butchers who make their own sausages and pies from prime ingredients should be rewarded with long queues of customers.

To some extent, we must blame ourselves for declining standards. Because we have persisted in buying them, we must bear responsibility for what has happened to convenience foods which used to contain decent ingredients and to provide a tolerable alternative to home cooking, but which then degenerated into tasteless parodies of the original.

Little has changed on the label, but much has changed in composition, as may be seen from this case history, compiled by David Walker of Shropshire County Council.

1962 A local authority analyses samples of fishfingers. Average fish content 78 per cent.

We should give encouragement to those good family butchers who make their own sausages and pies from prime ingredients

1968 Analysis of 20 different fishfingers shows an average fish content of 65 per cent.
1969 Analysis reveals an average fish content of 62 per cent.
1971 Six brands analysed. Average fish content ranges from 49 to 71 per cent.
1976 Analysis of fishfingers from three leading manufacturers shows an average fish content of 58 per cent. One brand has about 35 per cent.
1978 Twelve local authorities analyse 121 packs. Average fish content 58 per cent.
1983 A further survey reveals an average fish content of 56.5 per cent; 13 per cent of the sample has a fish content of under 50 per cent.

Shelf life

As well as listing ingredients, food labels frequently give an idea of how long a product will "retain its specific properties if properly stored". The label does not indicate the date beyond which the product might be a health hazard; it is assumed that appearance, mould growth and smell will betray food unfit for consumption. There are two time limit indications: "best before" or "best before end", and "sell by". According to the food regulations, only "best before" dates are required for longer-lasting products. Foods which keep for up to three months give a "best before" date, stating the day and month of expiry; products which keep for more than three months give the day, month and year. The label should also indicate if special storage conditions are needed, such as darkness, or a cool atmosphere.

Any short-life item, to be eaten within six weeks of packing, should be labelled with a "sell by . . ." date, with an indication of how long the food, once bought, can be expected to last in order to retain its "specific properties".

Many foods may be sold without date marking. These include products with a shelf life of at least 18 months; baked products and bread (expected to be eaten within 24 hours); vinegar and salt; sugar and sugary products; deep-frozen and quick-frozen foods; ice cream; cheese intended to ripen fully in its packaging. This does not mean the products are expected to last for ever and cannot go stale, and the best bet is to buy them from a shop with a rapid turnover.

However closely you scrutinise food labels, the first impression created by bold visual images and large type is likely to stay with you, and to influence your decision to buy or not to buy. Attractive representations of fruit and vegetables displayed on such goods as yoghurt, vegetarian ready-meals, or even dehydrated mixes, are designed to say "healthy", irrespective of the added colours, flavourings, emulsifiers and preservatives. You do well to question anything which boasts of being country style, farm fresh, hand-picked, prime, premium, extra, essential, low salt, low fat, dairy, homemade, improved, enriched, pure, natural, traditional, organic. Although the Food and Drugs Act makes it an offence to mislead the public about food qualities, the products are too numerous to control, and not all manufacturers can be trusted to be self-regulatory. If you have reason to doubt the claims on a label, you should contact your town hall for the local Trading Standards Officer or Consumer Protection Department.

The Food Standards Committee 1980 Report, published by the Ministry of Agriculture, Fisheries and Food, gives guidelines as to the ways in which many of the above descriptions should be used.

Staple foods and their contents
Bread

Nearly two-thirds of our bread comes from two large companies, Allied Bakeries (a subsidiary of Associated British Foods) whose brands include Sunblest, VitBe, Allinson; and British Bakeries (subsidiary of Rank Hovis McDougall), who market Mother's Pride, Hovis and Windmill. If other bakers use Hovis flour, they can call their bread Hovis. These two companies also supply own-label bread, mostly sliced and wrapped, to the supermarkets. Because of bulk supply, supermarkets can obtain this bread at a great discount – so fresh, crusty, individually-baked bread has to come at a premium, albeit a worthwhile one.

Mass-produced bread relies on the Chorleywood and the Activated Dough Development (ADD) systems of manufacture which speed up the process to achieve fast bulk production and uniformity of result. Chorleywood uses vigorous, intensified mixing to raise the dough, thus reducing by several hours the time needed for fermentation. The main feature of ADD is the blending of ingredients with an amino acid, cysteine, and ascorbic acid which act as "improvers". Could these processes be the reason why it is almost impossible to buy an English-baked "French stick" with the crustiness, aroma and texture of its Continental counterpart? The answer, perhaps unexpectedly, is that human intervention, rather than techniques of manufacture, is usually to blame. There is no reason why "real bread" should not be made with the Chorleywood and ADD systems, provided that the dough is handled

Only the inner part of the wheat grain is used for making white bread, while wholemeal bread is made from wholemeal flour which uses the entire grain, or from white flour with bran and wheatgerm added

properly after mixing and fermentation. At this stage, large gas bubbles must be retained in the dough, and this requires extremely delicate handling and a lengthy, cool rising period. The additional human care (which is labour intensive) and necessary time are usually sacrificed by manufacturers in favour of speedy distribution. The delicious flavour of fresh bread depends not on any particular flour, as is sometimes thought, but principally in the crust formed by careful and expert baking.

Although bread comes in many shapes and sizes, it conforms to three main types which are made from three different sorts of flour.

White bread is a mixture of milled wheat flour, manufactured from the whitish inner part of the wheat grain, yeast and water. It relies more than other breads on additives, not all of which have to be declared, as they form part of the technological processes. Apart from wheat flour, typical ingredients are water, salt, yeast, soya flour, wheat gluten, vegetable fat, preservative (E282), emulsifiers and flour bleaches and improvers (E300, 920, 924, 926, 927). The white flour must by law contain a minimum of 1.65mg iron, 0.24mg thiamin, 1.6mg nicotinic acid, a minimum of 235mg and a maximum of 390mg chalk per 100g.

Brown bread (formerly called wheatmeal) is made from brown flour with some of the bran removed. It must have a minimum of 0.6 per cent fibre, may contain caramel, plus any of the additives allowed in white bread.

Wholemeal bread is made from wholemeal flour (which uses the whole of the wheatgrain), yeast, water and other additions. Some wholemeal bread is made with white flour, with bran

and wheatgerm added, and some is termed "stoneground", when traditional stone grinders, instead of modern steel rollers, have been used in milling the flour. Stoneground has a coarse texture, more like home-made.

Other types of bread include the following.

Granary (or malted loaf) is made from brown flour plus added malted flour and wheat kernels. In malted flour, wheat grains have been moistened, germinated, then roasted.

Wheatgerm Brown or white bread flour plus 10 per cent processed wheatgerm.

Bran enriched Made from white, brown or wholemeal flour with added bran.

Rye bread is made from wheat flour with 20 to 60 per cent rye flour, plus flavouring additives.

Aerated bread This is given a long fermentation period to "blow up" the volume of gas, and has a high gluten content.

High fibre white bread is made from white flour with added fibre from sources other than wheat (eg the skins of peas).

Milk bread is made from white flour plus added milk or milk powder.

Soda bread is made from white flour containing sodium bicarbonate.

Starch-reduced bread must have less than 50 per cent carbohydrate in the dry state.

Wrapped bread usually has a sell-by date, and it will last three days stored in a dry, cool place. Keeping bread in the fridge is the quickest way to firm up the crumb and make it suitable for toasting; it also inhibits moulds, which are a potential health hazard.

It is not advisable to cut off slightly mouldy crusts and eat the inside of the loaf; throw it out.

Unwrapped bread, freshly baked, should last about two days, although French sticks will be rock-hard the next day. Small rolls and French sticks can be revived in a moderate oven, but because bread has low heat conductivity, large loaves are not suitable and will dry out.

Margarine

The search to find a cheap butter substitute resulted in margarine, originally made in the 19th century from suet. Although its contents have changed, margarine is still regarded in law as a product whose texture and composition has to resemble butter. What yet eludes the manufacturers is how to make it taste like butter.

Margarine has recently found new favour,

Loaves come in all shapes and sizes, but the many variations of the theme – granary, rye, soda bread, high fibre, bran enriched, starch reduced – conform to three main types, white, brown and wholemeal

---

RULE OF THUMB
Wholemeal bread can play an important role in healthy diet since it is high in insoluble fibre, which has implications to bowel functioning. Remember when buttering bread, that it is important to strike the right balance between fat and carbohydrate intake. A thin slice of bread with generous butter will supply around 150 kilocalories, of which some 90 (ie, 60 per cent) will come from fat. Cut the bread more thickly and be very sparing with the butter, or with a margarine which is high in polyunsaturates.

chiefly because *some* brands are high in polyunsaturates. By law, 80 per cent of margarine must be fat, with a maximum water content of 16 per cent, as in butter. The remaining ingredients are whey; emulsifiers which help to bind oils and water; salt; flavouring agents – usually butter flavour cis-4 heptanol; colour – usually annatto, E160(b); and vitamins A and D.

Manufacturing process The oils used in margarine are chiefly from groundnuts, coconuts, palm kernels and palm, as well as from fish such as herring, anchovy, pilchard and sardine. At the start, any odours must be removed, and the oils are mixed with a cleaning agent and heated. Impurities, together with the cleanser, drop to the bottom of the container tank, and these residues are removed. Any remaining impurities are removed by a second process where the oils are washed several times with a weak solution of salt, or with water; Fuller's earth is added, the mixture is filtered and finally steam is bubbled through to eliminate any identifying smell.

Once purified and deodorised, the oils may be hydrogenated, depending on whether soft or hard margarine is required. This process hardens the oils by adding hydrogen atoms to their fatty acids. The more hydrogen atoms are added, the harder and more stable the oils become – but at the same time, initially unsaturated fats change into saturated ones. Solid, block margarines are heavily hydrogenated so are high in saturated fats; soft, spreadable margarines are lightly hydrogenated and contain more unsaturated fats. The process of hydrogenation, apart from producing margarines of different consistencies, also enables different oils to be blended, and whichever oils happen to be cheapest may be utilised.

When the oils have been selected, blended

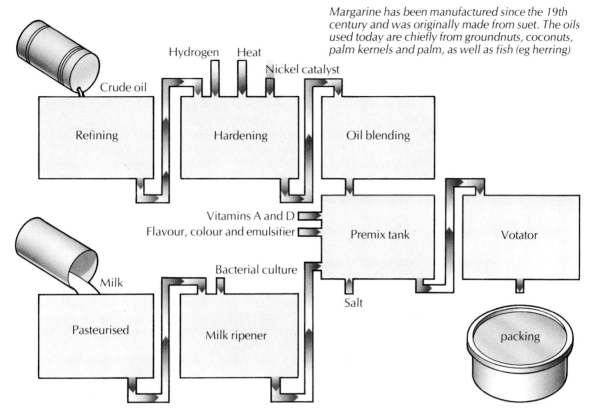

Margarine has been manufactured since the 19th century and was originally made from suet. The oils used today are chiefly from groundnuts, coconuts, palm kernels and palm, as well as fish (eg herring)

and hardened to the desired level, they are emulsified. The purified oil, water, whey or milk powder, colouring (annatto or carotene) and synthetic butter flavour are stirred vigorously in an emulsion kettle until they coalesce to make soft margarine. The emulsifying process acts as a preservative because the water clusters are broken down to such an extent that organisms are unable to grow. This is significant, as pre-

It is increasingly possible to buy reduced-fat milk products. Of those pictured, crème fraîche *is highest in fat (up to 50 per cent). Some yoghurts have as little as 0.5 per cent fat; skimmed milk has 0.1 per cent*

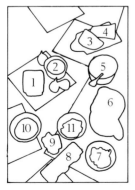

1. *Quark*
2. *Crème fraîche*
3. *Ricotta*
4. *Feta*
5. *Buttermilk*
6. *Skimmed milk*
7. *Curd cheese*
8. *Strawberry flavour low fat soft cheese*
9. *Fromage frais crème*
10. *Yoghurt*
11. *Cottage cheese*

servatives are not allowed in margarine. Low-fat spreads which are not labelled "margarine", do, however, contain preservatives, the mould-inhibiting sorbates, and sometimes anti-oxidants. Such spreads may also have a water content above 10 per cent. St Ivel Gold, marketed as a "dairy spread", is one example, an emulsion of cultured buttermilk with butter-oil and soya bean oil, to which emulsifiers and fortifying agents are added.

Margarine will keep in the fridge for several weeks, but if contaminated by other foods such as jam or cheese, it will quickly go rancid.

Milk products

Milk is a natural oil-and-water emulsion and is graded according to its tendency to cream, which is related to the milk fat content, as well as according to its purity.

Commercial milk production uses two main criteria: safety and keeping qualities. The most efficient heat treatments, sterilisation (heating to 120°C for at least 20 minutes) and ultra-high-temperature treatment (heating to 132.2°C for 1-3 seconds) remove all harmful bacteria, but impair flavour and deplete nutritional content.

Pasteurised milk is heated to a temperature of

about 72°C for 15 seconds. The following grades of milk are all pasteurised.

Silver top contains 3-4 per cent milk fat; cream at top of bottle.

Red top 3-4 per cent milk fat; homogenised (the fat globules are broken down and distributed evenly throughout).

Gold top has 4-5 per cent milk fat; distinct layers of cream at top. From Jersey or Guernsey cows.

Red-and-silver top is semi-skimmed with 1.5 to 1.8 per cent milk fat. Reduced vitamins A and D. Can also be sterilised and ultra-heat-treated.

Blue-and-silver top skimmed milk with 0.1 per cent milk fat. Vitamins A and D lost. Other nutrients similar to those in other milk. Also obtainable sterilised and ultra-heat-treated. Not suitable for babies or young children.

Untreated (unpasteurised) milk has the most genuine flavour, but does present a certain health risk, particularly if consumed in quantity, the major hazard being salmonella infection. 1985 legislation allows untreated milk to be sold in sealed containers, but it must be labelled as raw, unpasteurised milk. Caterers may not use it, nor may anyone serving the public (restaurants, schools etc), for fear of the risk of a mass outbreak of infection. The Soil Association has come out strongly against this legislation, maintaining that the ban has been imposed against the wishes of consumers, farmers' unions, nutritionists and doctors, "on the basis of flimsy and contradictory scientific evidence". The demand for untreated milk and cheese is growing, standards of hygiene on British farms are generally very high, and untreated milk is higher in vitamins, some proteins and anti-microbial agents than pasteurised milk.

Sterilised milk has a fat content as for silver/red top. Heat treated and homogenised. Reduced vitamin content. Long-keeping milk has "cooked" flavour.

Long life milk (ultra-heat-treated or UHT) has undergone heating to 132.2°C for four seconds; is homogenised and contains 3-4 per cent milk fat.

Evaporated milk is made from pasteurised milk, whole or skimmed; often has added vitamin D.

Condensed milk contains 44 per cent added sugar; suffers loss of vitamin C and B complex.

Storage Pasteurised milk keeps fresh for up to five days in the fridge. Sterilised and UHT milk will keep for several months unopened. Once open, use as pasteurised.

Yoghurt This milk product is the result of specific bacteria which curdle milk and give it a thick consistency. These bacteria produce lactic acid which helps to prevent the growth of harmful micro-organisms. Yoghurt can contain live bacteria, though commercial pasteurised brands have been subjected to heat treatment after fermentation, and the culture is therefore dead. Low-fat and fat-free yoghurts are made from skimmed milk; others from whole-milk which is boiled to destroy harmful bacteria. Fruit yoghurts contain added sugar.

Curiously, yoghurts are not covered by food regulations, though the Dairy Trade Federation has a code of practice which recommends that very-low-fat yoghurt should contain less than 0.5 per cent fat; low-fat yoghurt should contain *not* less than 0.5 per cent fat; other yoghurts should contain not more than 2 per cent fat. The minimum milk protein in all cases should be 3 per cent, and plain yoghurts should have no added colours, preservatives, stabilisers or thickeners.

Fruit yoghurt, other than fruit flavour or flavoured, should contain not less than 5 per cent whole fruit or fruit pieces (think what you would use if you were adding your own!). Emulsifiers (soya lecithin or glycerol monostearate) are sometimes used in fruit yoghurt, and the use of stabilisers is widespread. Alginates, agar, locust bean gum, guar gum, gum arabic, tragacanth, xanthan gum, pectin, cereal starch, carrageenan, gelatine, hydroxymethyl-cellulose, sodium-carboxymethyl-cellulose and microcrystalline cellulose may all be used in regulated proportions. Food dyes may also be found, as no regulations except "good manufacturing practice" govern their use. Fruit yoghurts may also contain preservatives, including sulphur dioxide, benzoic acid and other benzoates.

On the whole, the more solid the yoghurt, the higher the fat content. But, although a creamy yoghurt might have around 3.5 per cent fat, and sheep's and goats' milk varieties average 8-10 per cent fat, this is still only about half that of single cream.

Soured cream is single cream thickened to the consistency of double with lactic-acid-producing bacteria. Sometimes rennet is added. The fat content is 18-20 per cent.

Crème fraîche is a French version of double cream, found in some delicatessens. It has been allowed to ferment for just long enough to develop lactic acid. The result is thick and refreshing, less sickly than double cream. But it does contain about 30-50 per cent fat.

Clotted cream has a minimum fat content of 55 per cent.

Double cream has a minimum fat content of 48

per cent.

Whipping cream has a minimum fat content of 35 per cent.

Single, sterilised and UHT cream minimum fat content 18 per cent.

Half cream minimum fat content 12 per cent.

Aerosol cream, used by confectioners and caterers, can contain certain additives which are not permitted in retailed fresh cream. They include up to 13 per cent sugar, stabilisers, emulsifiers. Cream in aerosol cans may also contain nitrous oxide as a propellant.

Butter This can be made either from fresh cream (sweet butter) or from cream into which lactic-acid-making bacteria have been introduced for a few hours before churning. The content of butter is chiefly saturated fat, but the process of separating the emulsion concentrates the fat-soluble vitamins. Salt is often added in regulated amounts (around 2 per cent) to act as a preservative and to bring out flavour. Food regulations do not permit the use of emulsifiers, but do allow natural colour (carotene, annatto, turmeric), salt and lactic acid culture. Colour varies depending on the time of year.

Cheese In cheese production, the milk solids (curds) are separated from the whey (the watery substance containing most of the lactose and water-soluble vitamins) through the action of lactic acid or rennet, an enzyme taken from the stomach lining of calves and lambs. Once separated, the solids are treated in a succession of processes which differ according to the type of cheese made. The final stages may involve maturing, curing, ripening and ageing. Most cheese is made from whole milk, but skimmed milk is used for others. Commercially manufactured cheese is made from pasteurised milk. Non-pasteurised milk undoubtedly gives a better flavour (to taste the difference, visit local cheese-makers in Britain. Some hand-made cheeses are imported from France, and can be found along with English ones, in specialist shops and enterprising grocers).

NUTRITION Generally, the harder and drier the variety, the greater the fat and protein content, the average composition being one-third each of water, protein and fat. Cream cheeses contain considerable fat, but more moisture and less protein than harder cheeses. A low-fat French version of cream cheese, *fromage frais,* has recently appeared in supermarkets. It is made from fermented, skimmed milk, and may have either 1 per cent or, if cream is added, 8 per cent fat content.

Packaged soft cheeses have by law to be labelled in a certain way. Their fat contents are as follows.

Full fat soft cheese: not less than 20 per cent.

Medium fat soft cheese: less than 20 per cent but not less than 10 per cent.

Low fat cheese; less than 10 per cent but not less than 2 per cent.

Skimmed milk soft cheese: less than 2 per cent fat.

A kind of soft "cheese" featured in vegetarian and Chinese cookery is made from soya milk and is known as tofu or soya bean curd. It is a good source of protein, but is bland and needs to be marinated or mixed with strong flavours (see recipes, page 118). The fat content is low at 4.2g per 100g (steamed), which makes it useful for dressings and fillings.

Processed cheeses and cheese spreads are an example of sheer convenience foods which have little to do with the beauty of cheese. They are made by grinding together different cheeses, heating them to 60°C to produce a characterless mass which is then cooled and packaged. Cheese spreads, made in a similar manner, are higher in moisture, and rely on artificial stabilisers. One cheese spread we looked at contained emulsifying salts, pentasodium triphosphate E450(b), sodium polyphosphates E450(c), sodium dihydrogen orthosphosphate E339(a), colours (unspecified).

The energy content of some cheeses per 100g is as follows: Camembert 300 kcal; Cheddar 400 kcal; Danish Blue 355 kcal; Edam 300 kcal; Stilton 460 kcal; Gouda 390 kcal; Gruyère 465 kcal; cottage cheese 100 kcal; cream cheese 430 kcal; processed cheese 311 kcal. Except for cream cheese, cheeses are a prime source of protein, calcium, vitamin A and riboflavin (vitamin B_2).

Eggs With all the furore over battery hens cooped up indoors to over-produce flavourless eggs, many people are prepared to pay the higher price for eggs labelled "free range". These words conjure up visions of the farmyard, of hens scratching around in open-air runs for natural feed and if the odd feather or scrap of farmyard dirt clings to a shell, it only serves to reinforce this image. Until 1985, when the EEC stepped in to clarify terms applied to eggs, producers dreamed up all manner of emotive variations on the farm-fresh theme. Labelling regulations are still inadequate, but here are a few clues as to what the descriptions really mean. If the box is labelled "farm eggs", you are entitled to ask by which method the eggs have been produced.

Battery eggs do not have to be labelled as such,

Free-range eggs come from the happiest hens. Perchery or barn eggs are from hens kept 25 to a square metre

and "country fresh" or "farm fresh" may mean the same thing.

Free-range eggs are from hens which have all-day access to open-air runs, with only one hen per 10 square metres of ground.

Semi-intensive eggs also come from hens with all-day access to open-air runs, but with less space (one hen per 2.5 square metres).

Deep-litter eggs are from hens kept in sheds with no access to the open air. Each square metre should accommodate no more than seven hens.

Perchery or barn eggs are from hens kept indoors: 25 hens are allowed per square metre, and each bird must have at least 15cm of perching space.

Additives

Food additives were given numbers by the EEC (hence, E) so that member countries would benefit from a standard ingredient listing. The EEC decides which additives can safely be used, though member countries disagreeing with certain decisions are sometimes allowed numbers unique to themselves. The permitted list is subject to constant review and revision, which accounts for some variations in labelling. The original idea was to facilitate trade, rather than to enlighten the shopper.

Our own Food Act serves as a basic safety-net for all food processes and additives, as all food is required by law to be fit for human consumption and not injurious to health. Government committees carry out periodic reviews of certain additives, and in some cases research laboratories conduct toxicological testing to provide additional evidence for the committees. Additive and food manufacturers also carry out their own testing, but custom and practice has widely been the major criterion for use. Currently, the use of, necessity for, and possible harmful effects of, food additives are the subjects of close investigation.

The E factor

The form of labelling is laid down by the EEC. Ten per cent of food additives in use have each to be specifically identified by either E number or chemical name. You'll notice that some additives have a number but no E: this means they have either been considered and rejected by the EEC Committees but allowed for UK use only, or they are presently or imminently being considered for inclusion in the E category. The remaining 90 per cent includes the largest group, flavourings, which are currently under consideration for E numbers, and processing aids, enzymes, modified starches, solvents and carriers, additives which have no technological function in the finished product, but which nevertheless play a part in some stages of manufacture. Theoretically, they should have completely disappeared by the time the food is ready for consumption.

E100-E180 Food colour agents

The most important groups of additives in terms of the consumer's awareness are colours and preservatives. Food colouring agents are used to heighten the colour of foods which have faded or become murky during processing, and give them the colours which we have been conditioned to expect. They are also used particularly to attract children in sweets, jellies and manufactured drinks. A further function is that of colouring pills in the drugs industry in order to differentiate between medicaments. Colour ensures a standardisation of appearance in such products as jams and cheese, where this might not naturally occur, again something we have been conditioned to expect.

This group covers artificial colours (manufactured chemicals that do not occur naturally/in nature) as well as "natural" colours (extracts or manufactured copies of chemical substances from trees, plants, vegetables or fruit).
★ Indicates an azo dye, synthetically made. Other azo dyes are Yellow 2G (107), Black PN

(E151), Brown FK (154), Chocolate Brown HT (155), Pigment Rubine (E180).

● Indicates a "coal tar dye" synthetically made, not occurring in nature. Another coal tar dye is Brilliant Blue FCF (133).

E101 Produced from yeast (also synthetically). Occurs naturally in liver, kidneys, green vegetables, eggs, milk. (Yellow)

★ *E102* Tartrazine. (Yellow) This particular colour appears in most products (packet convenience foods, cheese rind, smoked haddock and cod, chewing gum, sweets, lime, lemon and orange dilutable drinks, seafood dressing, mint sauce and jelly, packet desserts, tinned fruit pie filling, tinned processed peas, salad cream, pre-packed cakes, marzipan, piccalilli, brown sauce, maple flavour syrup, fizzy drinks, casing for medicinal capsules).

● *E104* Quinoline Yellow.

★ *E110* Sunset Yellow (Orange)

★ *E122* Carmoisine. (Red)

★ *E123* Amaranth. (Red)

● *E127* Erythrosine. (Red)

★ *128* Red 2G. (Orange)

● *E131* Patent Blue V.

● *E132* Indigo Carmine.

E141 Copper complexes of chlorophyll and chlorophyllins. (Green)

E142 Green S

E150 Caramel, also synthetic. Used more than any other colour. (Brown) Produced by the action of heat or chemicals on carbohydrates.

E160 (a) Alpha-, beta- and gamma-carotene. (Yellow) Extracts of natural plant pigments found in carrots, green vegetables, apricots, rosehips, oranges.

E160 (b) Annatto, bixin, norbixin. (Peach) Vegetable dye from the seed coats of the tropical annatto tree.

E160 (d) Lycopene, from tomatoes. (Red)

E162 Extract of beetroot. (Red)

*E163*Anthocyanins. Plant pigments. (Purple) Plant and fruit extracts such as apple juice, strawberry, parsley, lemon, which give both colour and flavour, are not classified as additives. The following colours are being considered by the EEC for an E number in 1986: 101 (a), 107, 128, 133, 154, 155.

E200-E321 Preservatives and anti-oxidants

Preservatives delay the deterioration of food through the action of micro-organisms (fungi, mould, bacteria and yeast). Anti-oxidants delay the production of chemicals which cause rancidity (unpleasant taste and smell) in fats and oils. Poisoning from bad food can cause anything from a slight stomach upset to death.

Harmful micro-organisms can be destroyed in a number of ways such as:

1 Heating: sterilisation, cooking and pasteurisation. Cooling: chilling, refrigerating, freezing, quick-freezing.

2 Drying: concentration, desiccation, use of solvents.

3 Reducing water content by raising osmotic pressure: sugaring and salting.

4 Raising the acidity level to reach a pH of 4.5. Below this, pathogens causing food poisoning do not survive. This can be achieved by adding acids, or by fermentation (lactic acid is produced by lactic fermentation).

5 Controlled industrial fermentation to limit the development of undesirable micro-organisms in wine, beer and vinegar.

6 Regular cleaning and disinfection of equipment used in manufacture and food storage.

7 Use of permitted chemical preservatives.

8 Irradiation, as yet given only special medical dispensation in this country, but under consideration for wider use.

9 Pickling: use of acid and salt which dehydrate the cell-wall, killing bacteria.

10 Smoking: fish and meats.

The use of chemical preservatives is by far the cheapest method of keeping food fresher longer, but although this prevents the additional growth of micro-organisms, these may still survive. Once food is contaminated, it remains contaminated. The strictest standards must be maintained in processing and distribution when chemical preservatives are used.

Main preservatives

E200 Sorbic acid Occurs naturally but is generally produced synthetically. Also derived from sorbic acid are: E201, E202, E203.

E210 Benzoic acid and benzoates Occur naturally, mostly prepared synthetically.

E211-E219 Derivatives of benzoic acid used in a range of foods, including fruit pies, soft drinks.

E220-E227 Sulphur dioxide and sulphites Sulphur dioxide is a gas formed when sulphur is burnt. Used as a preservative, anti-oxidant (and has been for generations), improving agent, bleaching agent in dried fruit, vitamin C stabiliser. Also used in preserving alcoholic drinks, fruit juices, dried fruit.

E249-E252 Nitrites and nitrates Preservatives and curing agents. Commonly added to delicatessen meats, sausages, bacon, pork, tinned meats. Nitrites and nitrates are used together. Nitrites act as the preservative, nitrates as a reserve or "back-up" system. When nitrites are added to meat, they react with muscle myoglobin producing a pinkish colour and also add some flavour. Another effect of nitrites is either to reduce the heat resistance of *Clostridium botulinum,* or to inhibit its growth so that less heat processing is needed.

E260 Acetic acid Manufactured chemically under high pressure at a high temperature. Acetic acid is formed by a bacterium acting on the alcohol in beer, in malt vinegar, or in cider or wine in those vinegars. Used in pickles, chutneys, sauces, mint jelly and salad cream.

E270 Lactic acid Naturally occurring, produced by milk-souring organisms; also manufactured by fermentation of a carbohydrate.

E280 Propionic acid Naturally occurring fatty acid; produced by fermentation.

296 Malic acid One form found in apples, pears etc; another produced chemically.

297 Fumaric acid Naturally occurring. Prepared commercially by fermentation.

Main anti-oxidants

Heat, light, water and contact with metals affect food fats and lead to their deterioration. Producing rancidity from contact with the atmosphere, they combine with oxygen and become oxidised (converting to oxygen compounds which may be harmful). Oxidisation may also affect the vitamin content, diminishing the nutritive value of fat. Anti-oxidants, either natural or synthetic, inactivate the initial or intermediate compounds of oxidisation reaction, preventing harmful end products being formed. There are two kinds of anti-oxidants: *primary* ones, and *synergists* which, while not possessing an anti-oxidant quality, reinforce the anti-oxidant capacity of other additives. Frequently two primary anti-oxidants are used together (eg gallate and BHT), reinforced with a *synergist* (eg citric acid). The use of anti-oxidants tends to be cheaper than other methods of preventing food fat deterioration.

E300 L-ascorbic acid (vitamin C), occurs naturally, but also produced synthetically.

E306-E309 Tocopherols (vitamin E), occur naturally, but also produced synthetically. Extracted from soya bean oil, rice germ, cottonseed, maize and green leaves.

E310-E312 Gallates (propyl-, octyl- and dodecyl) The first anti-oxidants to be synthesised (propyl gallate patented 1942). They are unstable in the presence of moisture and can cause unwanted colouring.

Before the use of an additive is allowed, it must be passed by a number of official bodies. It will then be given a number by the EEC (hence, E). The permitted list is under constant review and revision

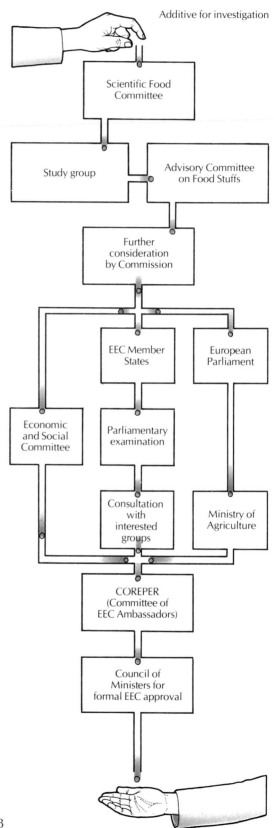

Additive for investigation

Scientific Food Committee

Study group

Advisory Committee on Food Stuffs

Further consideration by Commission

EEC Member States

European Parliament

Economic and Social Committee

Parliamentary examination

Consultation with interested groups

Ministry of Agriculture

COREPER (Committee of EEC Ambassadors)

Council of Ministers for formal EEC approval

E320-E321 BHA (butylated hydroxyanisole) and BHT (butylated hydroxytoluene). Lack the disadvantages of gallates, and are reasonably heat resistant, hence can be found in many baked products (biscuits, pies), packet foods, crisps, margarine, lard, oils, soft drinks.

E322-500 Emulsifiers, stabilisers, etc.

This group improves the consistency or texture of food, modifying or stabilising it. (Some of these additives are multi-functional.) The *modifiers* include emulsifiers, stabilisers, thickening agents, gelling agents, gelling delayers, dispersing agents, leavening agents, foaming and anti-foaming agents and anti-caking agents.

Certain food substances comprise two elements which are mutually antagonistic: eg margarine, an emulsion of water in oil, is both lipophile (having an affinity for fatty substances) and hydrophile (having an affinity for water). These conflicting elements tend to separate. *Stabilisers* reduce collision between the droplets of the emulsions; *emulsifiers,* whose structure is part hydrophilic, part lipophilic, act as a ''binder'' between the two elements.

Main emulsifiers and stabilisers

E322-327 Lecithins Mostly obtained from soya beans, but also from egg yolk. Present in all living cells.

E442-450(c) Phosphates and polyphosphates Used mostly in chickens, delicatessen meat products and sausages in order to improve homogenisation. They also retain water during cooking, produce succulence in chicken, particularly frozen birds, and prevent a stringy texture in ham. Water can be added over and above the amount needed for texture and succulence. Phosphates and polyphosphates are multi-purpose additives to be found in bread, cheese, dried milk products, packet cake mixes, cooked meats and sausages.

E471-472 (e) Mono- and diglycerides, from food fatty acids.

E473-495 Glycerol esters Semi-synthetic derivatives of fatty acids: mono-glycerides and di-glycerides, their esters from acetic acid, lactic acid, citric acid and tartaric acid, sucrose esters. This group includes some purely synthetic compounds such as sodium stearoyl-2-lactylate (E481) and calcium stearoyl-2-lactylate (E482) used in biscuits, bread, cakes and in gravy granules respectively.

Lecithins, the glycerides and sucrose esters are frequently added to margarine, and to fats to prevent spattering in frying. Lecithins and sucrose esters are used in mayonnaise, sauces and emulsified seasonings. Emulsifiers are important in chocolate to reduce stickiness and to create a uniform texture. Powders (eg packet desserts) mix with water more easily if they contain emulsifiers, helped by lecithins, glycerides, sucrose esters. Another principal use of emulsifiers is in baking and pastry-making and in products containing starch, the deterioration of which they inhibit. These products last longer and have a more uniform texture, and are more gluten stable with emulsifiers.

Thickening and gelling agents

Widely used in the preparation of meat products, pastry, confectionery, milk-based desserts, ice creams, to thicken, gell or make products last longer. They have other properties such as preventing the formation of ice crystals in ice cream as it cools; stopping milk curdling when it contains citric or tartaric acid. The following are natural agents:

E400-407 Alginates Extracted from brown seaweeds, agar (Japanese isinglass), carrageenan (Irish moss). Carrageenan is used in all forms of desserts, ice-cream, pastries, biscuits, salad dressing and alcoholic drinks.

E410-416 Gums. These include different gums extracted from the seeds of the carob tree; those of an Indian member of the pea family (guar gum); from an exudation of the trunk and branches of *Astragalus gummifer* (tragacanth); from African acacia trees; from the fermentation of carbohydrate (corn sugar gum); from a plant found in China (karaya gum). Used as stabilisers, thickeners, emulsifiers in many foods, eg Scotch eggs, carton coleslaw, dessert topping.

E440 Pectins When acid fruits ripen, pectin is made in the cell walls. Commercial sources are apple residues from cider making and orange pith. Pectins form solid gels in the presence of water and thicken jams, jellies, desserts.

E460-466 Cellulose and its derivatives. Manufactured from the cellulose walls of plant fibres or wood pulp. These additives delay crystallisation, lighten pastry, act as binders, thickeners, bulking agents. Found in bread, cake, biscuits, sweets, cheese, snacks, low-calorie mayonnaise and sauces. Mostly used in powder desserts and packet topping.

Synthetic sweeteners

E420-422 Sorbitol used extensively, particularly in diabetic foods like jams, also in toothpaste. Mannitol and glycerol E421, E422 are used as sweetening agents. Also used as a humectant (substance which absorbs water vapour from air and prevents food drying out). *Sorbitol* is synthesised chemically from glucose but occurs as a six-carbon sugar found in some fruits and also metabolised in the body. *Mannitol* is usually manufactured from seaweed or manna. *Glycerol* is manufactured from oils and fats; found naturally in plant cells.

E620-635 Flavour enhancers

These heighten or mask the taste or smell of food. They are particularly used where flavour is weakened by heat or drying treatments. None at present has an E number.

620 L-glutamic acid An amino-acid which is part of the nitrogen metabolism of plants and animals. Prepared commercially through the fermentation of a carbohydrate solution.

621 Sodium hydrogen L-glutamate (monosodium glutamate, MSG). Frequently found in packet soups, sausages, meaty flavoured crisps and snack foods.

622, 623, 627, 631, 635 These are all flavour enhancers (non-sequential numbers indicating many dropped by EEC).

Flavouring agents

The word "flavour" embraces the flavouring ingredient itself, and the end result of its action. Flavours, in the context of the food industry, usually refer to the *flavouring ingredients.* No one has classified all the flavours in use in Britain, but estimates of their numbers range from 3000 to 6000, both natural and synthetic. Present legislation excludes flavours from labelling requirements and food regulations relating to additives, even though in 1976 the Food and Contaminants Committee recommended their regulation. The EEC is currently devoting itself to compiling a positive list of these. They can be divided roughly into five categories:

1 Aromatics are obtained from plants, parts of plants and trees, from certain animal products, and are either used raw or lightly processed (dried or roasted) for their distinctive taste or smell (fruits, spices, roots, etc).

2 Natural flavours are extracted from aromatics by processes such as expression, distillation, maceration or infusion (orange oil, concentrated fruit juices). These processes eliminate the non-flavouring parts (eg cellulose, water) to intensify their effects in food. Unfortunately, natural flavours can change considerably with storage, weakening the smell according to their origin, climate where grown and methods of cultivation, causing problems with consistency. They are vulnerable to extremes of heat and cold used in food processing.

3 Synthetic flavours Analytical technology such as gas chromatography and mass spectrography, have enabled scientists to isolate the chemical substances which give aromatics their characteristic taste or smell. Chemists now synthesise aromatic substances in the laboratory to make copies of the original with molecules identical to those found in nature (citral, menthol or eucalyptol) including those which had until recently escaped analysis (amyl, acetate, diacetyl, etc). These copies can be remarkably like the original; they are cheap and consistent. The additive industry is opposed to their synthesised flavours being described as "synthetic" because it implies something not found "in nature". If what they produce has the same chemical constituency as the natural original, they prefer to call it "nature identical". To complicate matters, there can be a synthetic and "nature identical" version of the original natural substance. For example: vanilla, an extract from vanilla beans, can be chemically copied exactly (vanillin or methyl vanillin), but it is also possible to produce a chemical substance (ethyl vanillin) which mimics the effect of the original. Chemists cannot yet reproduce the subtlety and variation of the "impure" natural aromatic. For the mass-producer of food, however, a manufactured flavour has distinct advantages: it is cheap, supply is reliable, it is more stable during processing treatments and capable of greater consistency.

4 Natural plus synthetic flavours used together An artificial "booster" or "extender" can be added to natural flavours to ensure consistency. A better taste is achieved by mixing the two than by using only synthetic flavour.

5 Treated flavours Heat treatment is used to create the Maillard browning effect, which imitates the roasted flavour in cooking through the reaction of sugar and amino acids. For example, a "meat" flavour is produced by heating a mixture of hydrolysates of offal, usually lungs, and corn syrup.

Other substances

There is another category of chemical substances which are used in food manufacture and which have EEC listings, but these are not found on food labels, and are not required to in law. However, some do remain in the product, sometimes in minute traces; others are entirely eliminated.

1 Lubricating agents Chemical substances can be used in preparing packaging materials and machinery receiving such products as confectionery and jellies so they don't stick. Paraffin oil and waxes are used. Small amounts may stay on the product.

2 Dusting agents Talc and starch are used on the surface of confectionery.

3 Bleaching and decolouring agents The bleaching of flour is permitted in the UK (but not in some other European countries). Sulphur dioxide is used to whiten sugar.

4 Acid treatments As well as their preservative, anti-oxidant and acidulant use, acids are used in intermediate processing. For example, in wine making, if the must (unfermented grape-juice) is insufficiently acid, tartaric acid is added. To prevent spoiling of wine, it is treated with calcium phytate or potassium ferrocyanide.

5 Enzymes These have traditionally been used in wine, beer, cheese and bread making, and were produced industrially in the late Forties. There are three main groups: (a) *Pectinolytic enzymes* which break down pectins. Used in the making of preserves and jellies so they do not solidify; also to clarify fruit and vegetable juices, wines and ciders. (b) *Amylolytic enzymes* break down starches. Used in brewing, baking and pastry-making, and to clarify fruit juices. (c) *Proteolytic enzymes* hydrolise the peptide bonds of a protein or peptide and are used in cheese-making, in home brew kits, particularly wine, in clarifying beer, in tenderising meat and modifying gluten in baking. Enzymes are almost completely inactive long before food is packaged or bottled.

Solvents

There is a permitted list of nine solvents in the UK whose function is to "carry" flavours in liquid or powder form throughout the manufactured food to avoid a blotchy concentration. Isopropyl alcohol (a carrier for colours and flavours), for example, edible gums, starches, rusk and salt are used for this purpose.

Food aliens (contaminants)

Apart from the "intentional", listed and controlled additives, there are frequently small traces of substances whose presence is entirely undesirable, such as hormones, antibiotics, pesticide residues and chemicals which have "migrated" from packaging materials. Dr Gangolli, of the British Industrial Biological Research Association (BIBRA), has listed the following:

Production agrochemicals; pesticides; metals; nitrites, nitrates; polycyclic aromatic hydrocarbons, etc.

RULE OF THUMB

Once again the advice must be to read the labels. If you suffer from asthma or eczema, or if you are sensitive to aspirin, you might be well advised to avoid food products coloured with one of the azo dyes, which are also believed by some to be a cause of hyperactivity in children. In particular, tartrazine (E102), found in a whole range of foods and drinks, has given cause for concern.

Storage mycotoxins (aflatoxin, etc); pest infestation; ethylene oxide, etc.

Processing filtering aids; lubricants; mould-releasing agents.

Packaging lacquers; metals; adhesives; plastics chemicals – monomers, solvents, etc.

Some additives which find their way into food are not there by design. Traces of residues may remain from agricultural pesticides or chemical fertilisers, and also from the materials used to enclose or wrap food. The extent of these residues is monitored, and at a certain point decisions have to be made as to what constitutes a significant level.

A recent example of a widely used material exerting an undesirable effect occurred with plastic clingfilm, which was originally developed, not for use on food, but for wrapping apparatus where its anti-static qualities proved valuable. It was later found that clingfilm could be made incorporating the reverse effect, so that its adherent properties could help keep foodstuffs airtight and delay deterioration. In order to make hard plastic soft and malleable, plasticisers – in this case, dioctyl adipate – are used. Adipates are soluble in fat, but not in water, and a high percentage is needed to alter the hardness of plastic.

Analysts discovered that, with warm or fatty foods, the adipates were provided with ideal conditions to "migrate", and some would leave the plastic film and make their way into food. Clingfilm has not been proved dangerous to health, but it is nonetheless a potential food contaminant and can affect flavour. In order to avoid any possibility of migration, never use clingfilm directly on fatty foods (eg, to store a cut avocado, put it face down in a bowl, then cover the top with clingfilm so that it is not touching the avocado), and do not wrap foods which are still warm.

Clingfilm is perfectly acceptable for short-term wrapping of foods which are cool and kept in the fridge (eg, fish), but the longer it stays on, particularly in a warm atmosphere, the greater the likelihood of contamination. It should *not* be used in either conventional or microwave ovens.

Apart from this disadvantage, plastic wrapping has made food preparation and transportation far more hygienic than it used to be.

Additives in wine

Wine is rapidly gaining in popularity here, but those who consume a lot of it might spare a thought for what (apart from many calories) it contains. The EEC allows any or all the following additives to be used either in processing, or for taste and appearance: sulphur (to inhibit spoilage); diammonium phosphate; ammonium sulphate; thiamin hydrochloride (to feed yeasts); potassium bitartrate and metatartaric acid (to precipitate tartaric acid); tannin (to preserve red wine); copper sulphate (to reduce sulphide level); carbon dioxide (to give fizz to sparkling wine).

Processing may involve the use of: potassium ferrocyanide; silicon dioxide; bentonite; kaolin; tannin; acacia gum (for clarification). Charcoal may be used to remove unwanted colour from white wines and cream sherries. Potassium tartrate, potassium bicarbonate or calcium carbonate (chalk) are added to the more acidic Northern European and British wines, in order to reduce sourness from grape juice. And, much to the scorn of Italian wine producers, whose sun-kissed grapes have no need of added sweetness, sugar from cane and beet is the most common wine additive in other areas.

The cheaper the wine, the more likely you are to pay for additives rather than for distinction. Inexpensive table wine will contain the highest proportion, particularly EEC *Tafelwein*, which is usually a mixture of wines from different countries. Slightly more expensive bottles are far more likely to have been strictly controlled in manufacture, as well as being superior in taste. Recently, as wine scandal followed wine scandal, this message has been taken to heart.

The future for additives

More and more manufacturers have begun to change their policy with regard to the use of certain food additives, and to eliminate the undesirable ones. It is always advisable to read the label. The fact remains that quality is not going to be much improved by the loss of one or two categories of additives, and constant consumer pressure is still needed to keep food producers on their toes.

When confronted by the bewildering array of substances added to basic food ingredients, it is tempting to say, "Let's get rid of the lot!" However, few people today have the time or inclination to bake their own daily bread, make their own butter, cheeses, sausages, preserves and jam, to cure their own meats and fish; nor do they have space or the right conditions to store a vast range of fresh ingredients safely.

It would be quite impractical, not to say undesirable, to call for a ban on *all* food additives.

We argue only against shoddy manufacturing practice, the irresponsible use of food additives and the worst excesses of the food industry.

The enlightened approach

Let's be realistic. Which of us has the time or the inclination to quantify the nutrients in every piece of food we eat, every liquid we drink? It would mean acquiring from HMSO a copy of the nutritionists' bible, McCance and Widdowson's *The Composition of Foods*, plus its supplements, and keeping a meticulous tally of the grams of carbohydrate, fat and protein consumed. It would mean measuring everything, calculating what proportion of the carbohydrate was sugar, what starch, what fibre. It would mean drawing precise distinctions between saturated and unsaturated fats and between animal and vegetable proteins (one amino acid here, another there). There would be all the vitamins, minerals and trace elements to keep track of. And how could you ever work out the variables, when nutrient values of foods are subject to fluctuation, and when the needs of each individual are different?

Thank goodness it is not necessary to be quite so exact. Food is one of life's pleasures upon which your state of health depends, not medicine to be taken as prescribed. We need a thorough understanding of the principles of sound nutrition, but we do not need to be fanatical. Refer to our Rules of Thumb, observe the principles of variety, balance and moderation, and you won't go far wrong.

PART FOUR

THE HEALTHY KITCHEN

The "dream kitchen" image is today so potent that many people think little of spending thousands of pounds on its realisation, often paying for it over years. Yet the healthy kitchen does *not* have to be an expensive one. Rather, it is one in which more has been spent on quality or essential tools than on fancy decor or new-fangled gadgets.

If you are to eat more fresh food, to fry less and to grill, bake and steam more, you may need to make a few additions or replacements. When planning a new kitchen, consider the kind and quantities of foods you will be preparing, and the demands of your favourite recipes, before you so much as set foot in a showroom, where it is all too easy to be side-tracked by shiny new irrelevancies. And bear in mind the following.

The efficient kitchen

The kitchen is usually the most intensively-used room in the house. Food is stored, prepared, cooked and often eaten there. Crockery and utensils are washed-up and stored, cleaning materials are kept.

The ideal arrangement for economy of movement, efficiency and safety is generally considered to incorporate a work triangle of sink, cooker and fridge. And because pan handles project, and pans need to be set down beside the cooker, a work surface on either side of it is desirable. There should be no door to get in your way – particularly with children running in and out – as you move within the triangle, often with hot dishes. The triangle will not necessarily be equilateral, and its dimensions must depend on the overall size of your kitchen; but for maximum efficiency, its three sides will total no more than 7m (23ft).

The height of work surfaces and cupboards depends on who uses them most. Sir Terence Conran suggests the following as suitable:

One-level work-top height of 95cm (37½in)

Work area of 71cm (28in) for sitting down to chop and mix

Kitchen cupboards positioned to give reaching heights of between 76cm and 152cm (2ft 6in and 5ft), with a maximum of 195cm (6ft 4in)

Frequently-used cupboards, drawers and shelves should involve as little bending and stretching as possible

Wall cupboards should be a minimum of 40cm (16in) above the worktop

93

Test your kitchen layout by simulating every step needed to organise a cooked meal, from assembling the ingredients to washing-up. In that way you will find out if everything as far as possible is arranged in a logical and comfortable way, which does not involve too much unnecessary movement.

The equipment

The cooker

One of the first decisions you must make is whether you should go for a free-standing or for a split-level model.

For a small kitchen, an upright cooker is often the only possibility, and in cooking terms it will do just as well. It will also be significantly cheaper to buy.

Today, some free-standing models are designed to slot in, to fit more harmoniously with surrounding units and offer a reasonable compromise where space is limited.

Another major choice you have to make is between gas (if it is supplied in your area) and electricity. You may swear by one or the other, and each has its advantages, or you may wish to combine the two. Split-level cookers give you the option of having, say, a gas hob and an electric oven. And a number of cookers have combination hobs.

Gas is a visible, controllable source of heat. Turn the burner up or down and the effect is instant. An electric ring will not respond so immediately – but does give the benefit of residual heat.

The latest innovation is the tungsten halogen hob, which looks like an ordinary ceramic hob until switched on, when the halogen lamps glow brightly. They are supposed to give the instant responses of gas, but when they were tested by *Which?* in March 1985, the disappointing conclusion was: "Overall, at its current price, this type of hob seems worth considering only for its hi-tech looks and not for any great advantage in cooking performance."

Because you are likely to use the hob more than either the oven or the grill, you should make it your first priority.

Most hobs have rings of different sizes to accommodate large and small pans; some have dual-element rings allowing you to use the whole or just the centre, thus saving fuel.

Self-igniting gas burners save you reaching for the matches, but have an annoying tendency to clog and cease working efficiently.

Ceramic hobs are a little easier to clean than others – but at quite a price. Anyway, all cookers are difficult to clean unless splashes are removed immediately.

With an ordinary electric hob you have a choice between solid plates and radiant rings. Solid plates are usually sealed into the hob and are sturdy and easy to clean. They are slow to cool down and, since they don't normally glow, may present a slight risk of burns. But their slow cooling time (up to 30 minutes) does mean you can make use of residual heat. Radiant rings usually glow, and cool down more quickly. A removable tray slides under the hob to catch any spills that fall through the coiled element.

Oven capacity is clearly a prime consideration and a second oven may be a boon. The wire shelves should provide a firm base even when drawn part of the way out, and there should be stops to prevent them from sliding out and depositing their cargo on top of you. An inner glass door is a must, and a self-cleaning lining a real advantage. The latest fan ovens need no preheating; the heat is spread evenly throughout; cooking times and shrinkage are reduced, and there are fewer food splashes (but some people are expert at putting to good use the temperature variations at different levels in a normal oven).

Most ovens today have an auto-timer. This device allows you to pre-set the oven to switch itself on and off. How many people take advantage of this facility is a matter for conjecture, and the workings of it may be hard to fathom. But it could be useful if you do a lot of casserole cooking, or if you like the idea of coming home to a hot meal. A manual timer, which will switch the cooker off but not on, is of more limited use.

A large, accessible grill is of value in the healthy kitchen, and here the traditional free-standing cookers can come into their own, since some built-in and built-under models incorporate a grill in the oven (which means you can't grill and bake at the same time) or provide no grill at all.

Should you go for a low- or high-level grill? The high-level unit is easier to get at, but gives the cooker a less finished look, and needs clearance around it (at least a foot above and 3-4in to right and left) because of the heat it throws out. A low-level grill, enclosed under the hob, has a flap-down door which is handy for resting dishes and pans on, though it can be a nuisance when you want to get at the oven.

Again, you must decide if you want gas or electricity. Gas is more immediate. It is also, at the time of writing, cheaper to use.

Cookers come with various additional features, such as a minute minder, which alerts you by pinging or buzzing after a pre-determined length of time. A plate-warmer is a great plus, and a warming facility within a low-level grill compartment is especially useful. A rotisserie unit is good for kebabs, though, as with the auto-timer, many people have them and never somehow get to grips with them. Some of the big range-type cookers have non-stick griddle surfaces on which you can cook directly. Good for fat-free frying, but can be messy. A fold-down splashback tidies the cooker away when not in use.

Microwave ovens

Many people are still deeply suspicious of and resistant to the idea of microwaves. They may have been discouraged by scare stories of exploding poodles and of chefs cooking their own livers, or they may simply be reluctant to get to grips with this very different way of cooking. The main worry is that invisible rays can leak from the oven and, in an insidious way, be dangerous to health. Yet the real hazards lie in misunderstanding and consequent misuse of microwaves. There have been reports of babies being scalded when mothers have used the microwave to heat infants' feeding bottles. Other injuries have been caused by exploding eggs, by steam and through contact with hot items. "The underlying cause of such injuries," commented Dr Matthew Maley in *The Lancet* in May 1986, "seems to be that oven users do not understand that microwaves heat in a way completely different from conventional heating appliances. This results in actions which would probably not be considered by someone using an ordinary cooker."

There was, reported *Which?* in December 1985, no evidence that ovens which conformed to the appropriate British Standards, and were properly maintained, were in themselves in any way dangerous. Choose a model which carries the BEAB (British Electro-technical Approvals Board) label, denoting that it has been independently tested and found to comply with the Standards, including tests for both electrical safety and microwave leakage.

Even with this reassurance, you may wonder if there is any place for the microwave, with its associations with Fast Food, in the healthy kitchen. So often it is used in a sloppy and

---

RULE OF THUMB

A refrigerator is essential in the modern kitchen and should be capacious enough to store the quantities of fresh produce upon which good diet depends. Don't pack the contents too tightly. Wipe the fridge interior out regularly with a damp cloth and dry with kitchen towel. Invest in a fridge thermometer and ensure that the inside temperature is around 3-4°C (37.4-39°F) and certainly no higher than 5°C (41°F). This will prevent the proliferation of harmful bacteria, although some moulds and spoilage bacteria can multiply, albeit slowly, at low temperature. Never put warm food in the refrigerator.

---

unconsidered way, to defrost and reheat frozen convenience foods.

Yet once they take the trouble to investigate its potential, many people find a microwave oven to be more than merely a time-saver. It cooks fresh vegetables to perfection so that they retain their colour, bite and flavour. It's good for fish and for cooked fruit, for jacket potatoes, and for making sauces. And it's ideal for a large family whose members have to eat at different times, as a meal or snack can be heated in minutes when required.

With trial and error the microwave user will also soon discover its limitations. For some cooking, such as roasting meat and potatoes, crisping and browning, it will perform nowhere near as well as a conventional oven.

Tomorrow's oven — and there are some of these already on the market — will combine microwave and conventional functions.

The refrigerator

A fridge is an absolute must for storing fresh fruit and vegetables, meat, fish and dairy produce, particularly in modern houses, flats and conversions, which generally have central heating and seldom have a larder ventilated to the outside air. Even one- and two-person households, making a switch from frozen to more fresh produce, can find that a small fridge which tucks away under the work surface will not meet all their needs, particularly in summer. If you are not heavily reliant on frozen foods, a combined model with capacious refrigerator section and small freezer box is ideal. Self-defrosting is a plus, as is a section for keeping foods chilled.

(Continued on page 98)

The food processor may have revolutioned the modern kitchen, but a good set of knives remains the cook's first essential, and other traditional tools for chopping, shredding, slicing, mincing and grating will often do the job better and more conveniently than a machine. A mandoline, for instance (right foreground in photograph) is ideal for thinly slicing fruit and vegetables; an hachoir, with its twin handles and curved blade, for chopping parsley; a ricer (behind the chopping boards) for shredding potatoes, etc, to make purées, and a Mouli for soups.

If a refrigerator has an internal frozen food compartment for the short-term storage of commercially frozen foods, star marking will indicate how soon these should be used.

	Temperature	Storing time for frozen foods
*	−6°C (21°F)	up to 1 week
**	−12°C (10°F)	up to 1 month
***	−18°C (0°F)	up to 3 months

Few fridges have the capacity actually to freeze foods efficiently. A specialist freezer (symbolised by three stars preceded by a large white one) is necessary for this.

The main storage compartment of a refrigerator is intended to keep food at low temperature to extend its storage life for a relatively short time. All domestic fridges should have a temperature gauge (manufacturers please note), but you can buy a special fridge thermometer quite cheaply. The inside temperature should be no higher than 5°C (41°F), and 3-4°C (37.4-39.2°F) is better. Many domestic fridges, particularly old ones, are way off the mark and function simply as bacteria-harbouring cupboards.

The main purpose of a refrigerator is to stop the proliferation of harmful bacteria. It does not, however, destroy these. Once a higher temperature is reached, they will immediately resume growing.

Some moulds and spoilage bacteria can, indeed, grow slowly at low temperature, and are encouraged if warm food is put in the fridge, creating condensation, or if food is packed too closely. A poorly-ventilated, damp, cramped fridge is a favourable environment for moulds

The fridge is not always the safe place it seems and may function as a bacteria-harbouring cupboard

and yeasts. Wipe the fridge interior regularly with a damp cloth and kitchen towels.

The freezer

A freezer, like a microwave, can be a real asset in the healthy kitchen, provided it does not encourage a heavy reliance on convenience foods and ready-meals of indifferent quality.

The great advantage of freezing is that it retains more of the natural properties and nutrients of foods than other methods of home preservation. Indeed, food frozen in peak condition may actually be more nutritious than fresh food that is past its best. Green vegetables kept at 15-21°C (60-70°F) may lose 15 per cent of their vitamin C content per day, and other vegetables and soft fruit can suffer similar depletion.

A freezer makes for flexibility. You can take from it a single portion or enough to feed the hungry hordes. It allows you to cater for unexpected guests, to produce meals at a moment's notice, or to plan ahead for different eventualities. When preparing a meal, it is little extra trouble to make double the quantity and to freeze half of it, to serve on a day when you have little time, or when you haven't been able to get to the shops.

Other advantages, however, are more debatable. By buying in bulk you can certainly save money, but quality rather than quantity must be the first consideration. Half a lamb, for instance, will be a bargain only if you eat the fatty cuts as well as the lean ones.

A deep freeze can also mean fewer trips to the shops, which, if you are pressed for time or lack mobility, can be a real benefit. But a weekly run out in the car to the freezer centre to stock up on maxi-packs of meat and fish, or giant bags of vegetables, cannot compare with the imaginative exercise of seeking out and selecting the best fresh foods in season. To the French, our let's-get-it-over-with attitude to shopping for food must be incomprehensible. Buying should be far more creative than that.

Before you buy either a freezer or fridge-freezer, give thought to how you are going to use it. The size and type you choose should be ideally suited to your considered needs.

If you are likely to want to freeze foods in great bulk, and if you have the floor space for one, a chest freezer is clearly preferable. Because cold air is heavier than warm, there is little loss of cold when the chest lid is open, which means less frost formation and economical use of electricity. But the obvious drawback of a chest, apart from its sheer size, is that it can be difficult to reach foods on its floor, a problem which can be largely overcome by using easy-to-remove baskets, bags and cartons.

An upright freezer affords good visibility and accessibility, but cold air tends to spill out when the door is open, with warm air being drawn in to take its place, depositing its moisture and causing frost formation. This problem can be minimised if you close the door immediately.

Some upright freezers are fan-assisted and feature automatic defrost.

The dishwasher

The British have been slow to take to these, and spend an average of 10 hours a week washing-up by hand, when they could save perhaps three of those hours by using a machine. But it is from the hygiene point of view, more even than as a time-saver, that a dishwasher is so beneficial: no soiled, damp drying cloths are involved, and far higher water temperatures are possible. Provided it is used sensibly, it will get everything miraculously clean.

Kitchen knives

As any good chef will tell you, a selection of sharp knives is more essential than any number of gadgets for cutting and chopping. Knives must be used with skill, of course, and the best are expensive, but they prove indispensable, will last for years, and, if they are of the right weight, and perfectly balanced and sharp, they will be a joy to use.

The best knives are carbon steel or stainless steel and are taper ground, made in one piece from bar steel. Cheaper ones are hollow ground, cut from thin strips of stainless steel. Cheaper knives are often very sharp, but usually lack strength and the weight which makes for pleasing balance.

It is not always easy to recognise a good knife. Sabatier have traditionally been thought of as *the* knife-makers, but now knives bearing that hallowed name are produced in different factories to somewhat varying standards. Seek out a reputable kitchen shop and a knowledgeable sales person to advise you. Start off with at least three good basic knives: a small, sharp paring knife; a larger, wider cook's knife for slicing and cutting; and a more robust, larger-yet cook's knife to bear the brunt of chopping, from the coarsest to the finest textures.

Lavish care and attention on your knives. Keep them sharp. Use a fine sharpening steel or oilstone for the best result. More sophisticated sharpeners, although easier to use, tend to be too fierce and quickly wear down the blade.

Chop on a softish surface such as wood or polypropylene to prevent blunting and wearing of your knives. And never leave them to soak or heap them in the sink with the other cutlery. Wash and dry immediately, and keep these lethal tools out of the reach of children.

Food processors

These fast, versatile appliances are increasingly being seen more as an essential than as either luxury or glorified cook's toy. Interchangeable blades and discs will slice, chop, shred, grate, mix, whisk, purée, mince . . . Different models offer different features, some as standard, others as extras. They are particularly useful for home-made soups, shredding and grating vegetables for salads, and for mincing lean meat for burgers etc. To a certain extent they do the work of more traditional food mixers and blenders. A processor entails a lot of washing-up, sometimes out of all proportion to the job it has done, and for small quantities, it may be easier to resort to the following old-fashioned utensils.

* *Mezzaluna* or *hachoir* – excellent for chopping everything from parsley to meat
* Rotary vegetable shredder
* Ricer with a flat grid for shredding potatoes, apples, parsnips, etc. to make purées
* Mandoline for slicing vegetables and fruit
* Box grater
* Cheese slicer
* Mincer
* Hardwood chopping-board (teak, beech or elm) plus two marble or polypropylene boards, one for cutting raw food, the other for cooked foods and pastry-making

Pots and pans

For everyday cooking, inexpensive, easy-to-clean aluminium saucepans are fine, but for the healthy diet, where braising and simmering techniques largely replace frying, heavier-based, more solid types with non-stick surfaces for minimal fat-frying and searing, are essential. Copper, iron and heavy aluminium are all good heat conductors. Suggestions include an ena-melled cast-iron casserole pot for slow, moisture-retaining cooking; it can be used in the oven or on the hob and taken to the table for serving. Do not leave food in a cast-iron pot, as oxidation may take place, and never boil or steam green vegetables in cast-iron or copper pans, as some vitamin C will be destroyed. The attractive, thick glass saucepans and frying-pans are slow conductors, and need gentle heating and a low burner but are cheap and suitable for braising and simmering.

RULE OF THUMB

Be scrupulous about kitchen hygiene. Bear in mind that bacteria love warmth and moisture. Don't leave food to keep warm over a low heat for long periods. Avoid undercooking, particularly of poultry. Beware of cross-contamination, which is a major cause of food poisoning. Store cooked and uncooked high protein foods such as meat and poultry, prime candidates to host bacteria, on separate shelves.

Woks

This traditional Chinese pan is bowl-shaped with twin handles. Iron woks are the most authentic and demand care and attention, as they will rust if not in regular use, and initially they must be seasoned: stand the wok over a high heat, brush lightly with oil, wipe off with kitchen roll, and then oil and wipe twice more. Woks are finding widespread favour here and we have seen the introduction of several variations on the theme. You can also buy versions in steel and in aluminium with a non-stick coating (not judged an advantage). The classic wok is fine for a gas stove, but its rounded base cannot be used on an electric hob without a special stand to prevent it from tilting and spinning. Flat-bottomed woks have been introduced and represent only a partially-satisfactory design solution, since the beauty of the round-bottomed version is that it enables you to heat a very little oil for stir-frying. Other modifications include a single long handle on some models, and a plug-in facility. The electric wok is no great advance, but a heat-proof, frying-pan-type handle has its advantages, since metal lugs can get too hot to handle without a cloth or oven-glove.

The sheer size of a wok makes it specially useful, and its depth and its shape enable you to toss food as you fry. Stir-fried foods should be lightly cooked, so as to retain colour and texture. A wok can also be used for steaming and will accommodate a whole fish (see recipe page 113). Bamboo steamers designed to sit inside the wok are available from Chinese supermarkets. Alternatively, put the food to be steamed on a plate and stand it on a bamboo trivet in the wok and put the lid on.

Steamers

There are a number of different steamers on the market, ranging from the cheap, simple metal basket type to expensive plug-in appliances.

Apart from the bamboo type to use with a wok, Chinese stores also sell metal steamers which stack in tiers over a base pan: one or two perforated containers are set on the base, and food is placed on a heatproof dish or on muslin.

The usual Western-style steamer is similar both in appearance and in use: water is boiled in the base compartment, with one, two or three perforated containers stacked on top, and with a lid over all.

You can now buy a plug-in steamer, but these are expensive, and an alarm which sounds if the water boils away is the only real advantage.

In fact, for its delightful simplicity, we would sooner commend the cheapest steamer. The Japanese basket type is made of overlapping metal plates which allow it to expand or contract to fit in saucepans of different sizes. It won't accommodate a whole salmon, but is fine for a few servings of green vegetable.

A metal colander inside a saucepan works on the same principle as most steamers, and will do the job well enough at a pinch.

Pressure-cookers

Technology has rather overtaken the old-fashioned pressure-cooker, but it remains a good investment as it saves much time and fuel, when used for cooking the lentils, beans and other pulses which play an important part in a healthy diet. The latest models are more sophisticated, easier to use, and give you better control.

Additional implements

The following tools, gadgets and devices will prove invaluable in a well-run kitchen:

Glass fruit squeezer
Self-cleaning garlic press
Drum sieve
Pestle and mortar for grinding spices, crushing herbs
Peppermill
Wooden spoons and spatulas
Clay cooking-pots for fat-free oven cooking
Burger press for lean hamburgers
Whisks
Kebab skewers for grilling
Hinged grill rack to ''sandwich'' and turn meat and fish
Gravy separator
Serving tongs

Scales for (a) large and (b) minute quantities
Set of measuring spoons
Fridge thermometer

Minute timer
Measuring jug

Deep roasting-pan with lid for minimal fat
  pot-roasting
Large salad bowl
Fish kettle (expensive but essential for a More
  Fish, Less Meat plan)

Hygiene in the kitchen

Hygiene is high priority in the mass production and storage of food, and the major retailers are justly proud of their reputation for selling safe products, in marked contrast to the rising incidence of food poisoning in restaurants, hotels, hospitals and institutions.

An ironic consequence of this is that we, the public, have become rather complacent, and take it increasingly for granted that food poisoning is something which happens elsewhere than in the home, which may afflict us abroad, or be a slight hazard with seafood, but which need not unduly concern us in our everyday shopping, storage and preparation.

If we do worry about food, we are likely to be more preoccupied with chemical additives than with the dangers in our own homes – and yet

Always wash-up and clear away as you go. And banish pot plants and household pets form the kitchen

our very ignorance of correct kitchen practice is a contributing factor in their increasing use.

Once again, the information gap between generations, and the rapid developments in kitchen technology, are to blame. We may have failed to assimilate old rules or adequately to understand new ones. Techniques like freezing and slow-cooking are frequently misapplied, and there is a modern tendency simply to throw everything in the fridge, on the vague assumption that "cold" equals "safe". The result has been an increase in certain types of food poisoning, notably salmonella, and this has provided the food technologists, who refer to "customer abuse syndrome", with yet more excuse for piling in the preservatives. We are no longer, it seems, to be trusted.

Food: handle with care

Scrupulous handling and proper storing of food is essential to prevent its contamination by harmful bacteria, the most common being salmonellae, staphylococci and clostridia.

Salmonellae are found in the intestinal canal of certain animals, and are common in poultry and farm livestock. They can remain active in the soil for a year, and in dry dust on floors and tables for long periods, although they need moisture to multiply.

Heat is used to kill these bacteria (at 55°C, 131°F they survive for an hour; at 60°F, 140°F they are destroyed within 15 to 20 minutes). Like other micro-organisms, salmonellae survive cold better than they do heat, and will only stop multiplying at around 5°C, 41°F, so check the temperature of your fridge.

Over recent years there has been an alarming increase in recorded cases of salmonella poisoning, usually from infected chickens. There were 11,471 reported cases in 1980, 14,700 in 1983, and the numbers are still rising. (Salmonellae are responsible for 80 to 90 per cent of all cases of food poisoning.) Even in deep-frozen poultry, the bacteria are not eliminated but are dormant. Once a bird is thawed and the temperature rises above 5°C, they resume multiplying. It is vital to thaw frozen chickens thoroughly, away from other foods. Never return a partly-thawed bird to the freezer, it's a recipe for disaster.

Staphylococci are frequently found in man, and are also present in animals. One out of two people harbour staphylococci in the nose, throat or on the hands and, although not all are harmful, some types of these bacteria can produce enterotoxin, which infects the intestines, causing vomiting and diarrhoea. It is reckoned that one person in five carries the enterotoxin-producing staphylococci, but the right conditions are necessary (ie, warmth and moisture) for them to multiply and make toxins. Flies can carry staphylococci and infect food. The bacteria may be present in meats and dairy produce. They are resistant to ordinary disinfectants, and to salt and, although heating for 30 minutes at 60°C, 140°F will destroy some types, the toxin-producing variety, once they are given warmth and moisture in which to multiply, become extremely difficult to eliminate, and remain even after 30 minutes' boiling. For this reason, cow's milk is cooled immediately after milking, and most is pasteurised; cheese producers use pasteurised milk, and manufacturers of dried milk powder have to take special care. Ice cream is another potential danger, as the bacteria can survive freezing.

The clostridia group grow in the absence of oxygen. Most infamous of this family is *Clostridium botulinum*, which produces a lethal toxin, fortunately extremely rare today. Some clostridia are destroyed by ordinary cooking temperatures, but others are resistant to heat, particularly *Clostridium perfringens*, which can be found in pigs as well as in vegetables from contaminated soil.

Protein foods are favourite breeding grounds for harmful bacteria, and should be refrigerated, separate from other raw and cooked foods. Take care with all cooked meats and poultry, cooked meat products including gravy and stock, milk, cream, artificial cream, custards and dairy produce, cooked eggs and egg products such as mayonnaise, shellfish and other seafoods, and cooked rice.

Safe practice

TAKE SPECIAL CARE WITH SHOPPING in warm weather. If possible, avoid keeping food in the back of the car or carrying it for long distances on stuffy public transport. Try to carry fish, meat and dairy produce separately, loosely packed, rather than squashed beneath a heavy load.

UNPACK THE MINUTE YOU REACH HOME Meat from the butcher should be placed, unwrapped, straight in the fridge, on a plate, so that air can circulate round it. Meat from supermarkets should also be removed from polystyrene trays which retain warmth. It has to be assumed that butchers maintain a decent standard of hygiene, since it is not a good idea to wash meat until just before cooking, because moisture is a boon to bacteria. However, once you take a fresh chicken from the fridge, wash the inside before cooking. Fresh fish should be kept for no longer than a day or so in the fridge. Wrap in clingfilm to prevent the fish from absorbing other flavours. Sausages can be left wrapped.

BEWARE OF CROSS-CONTAMINATION, a major cause of food poisoning. Cooked and uncooked high protein foods such as meat and poultry (which are, remember, prime candidates to host bacteria), should be stored on separate shelves, because bacteria from raw foods can easily be carried on cooked ones. If the uncooked meat or poultry is stored on a lower shelf, any drips travel towards the salad drawer and can be washed off.

Always wash your hands thoroughly before and after handling raw food, and make sure towels in the kitchen are changed often, or use paper ones.

Do not use the same work surface and knives for cutting cooked and uncooked produce (for instance, when preparing raw meat or fish and, say, ham). Ideally, use separate chopping boards or, if you have a built-in work surface of wood or marble, wash it with a bleach solution after preparing raw food.

AVOID UNDERCOOKING The fact must be faced that sometimes one's tastes conflict with the strict rules of hygiene. Those who like rare beef or lamb should make sure the outside is fiercely browned to stop any surface bacteria penetration. It is not a good idea to cook rolled joints rare, in case they have been contaminated during handling.

Chickens should not be eaten rare because of the risk of salmonella poisoning (undercooked chicken is, anyway, highly unpalatable). And, as we have already said, they must be allowed to thaw out completely before cooking (see hints on freezing, page 207). For a 2.25kg (5lb) bird, allow a minimum cooking time, if using foil, of 2½ hours at gas mark 4, 180°C, 350°F. Remember that the legs will take longer to cook than the breast. Prick with a fork to check that the juices run out clear. It is also advisable to cook any stuffing separately from, rather than inside the chicken, so that it does not inhibit heat penetration.

If the chicken is to be served cold, cool it quickly before you transfer it to the refrigerator. All cooked meats should be put in the fridge as soon as they are properly cool, and within 1½ hours of cooking.

THE HIGHEST RISK OF BACTERIAL GROWTH occurs when food is kept warm on a low heat, or allowed to cool slowly. Bear in mind when heating, the lower the temperature the longer it takes to kill bacteria. In temperatures of between 10°C and 63°C, some will thrive; but above 63°C, over a period of time, most will be destroyed.

Be careful when reheating cooked foods and leftovers. When you prepare croquettes, shepherd's pie or similar dishes from cooked meat, make them up just before you want to cook them (and, of course, the cooked meat should be kept in the fridge until then). Make sure the food is piping hot, right through the centre (the same applies to bought pies, pasties etc). The penalty for safety may be a loss of flavour; use garlic, herbs and spices to compensate.

It is wise to freeze leftover soup and stock for use as needed. If they have to be kept in the fridge, cool them first by plunging the container in a bowl of very cold water – not more than 1½ hours should elapse between cooling and refrigerating. Store covered, boil soup or stock every day, and throw away any remaining after three days.

Do not put the dishes for a cold buffet out long in advance, or you may acquire a reputation you really don't deserve.

If you have opened a can, and have not used all its contents, empty out the remainder and store in a covered container, in order to avoid acid attack.

ALWAYS CLEAR UP AS YOU GO Wash up crockery and utensils the minute you have finished with them. Piled-up dirty dishes are an invitation to bacteria. An automatic dishwasher is the most hygienic way of coping with dirty crockery, and is a boon in busy households. If you wash-up by hand, use the hottest water you can stand.

All detergents have similar constituents, which help to remove dirt and grease by forming an emulsion. They usually contain a water-softening agent (eg, washing soda), and a foaming agent which serves no practical purpose. Detergents do help to remove bacteria, but are not disinfectants. Always rinse off in hot water, not because small residues of detergent are hazardous, but because of their effects on the flavour of food. A washing-up brush is easier to clean than a cloth. Allow to dry in the atmosphere, or if you do use a teatowel, change it daily at least (remember how bugs love moisture).

CLEAN WORK-TOPS AS YOU GO, TOO Many products claim to give extra "power" or "sparkle", but the cheapest and most effective cleanser is bleach. Dilute according to instructions on the bottle, as some brands are more concentrated than others, and rinse off. Store the bottle upright, somewhere well away from food and out of the reach of children, and never transfer bleach to another container. Use it to clean work-tops and cooking surfaces and, undiluted, to disinfect pipes and lavatories. There is really no need for an arsenal of cleansing products for cleaning. Diluted washing-up liquid is usually quite sufficient even for washing the floor, though you may need a stronger powder for stubborn grease and stains. A washable blind is preferable to curtains.

MAKE THE KITCHEN A NO-GO AREA FOR PETS, and always wash their dishes separately, with a cloth reserved for that purpose.

BANISH POT PLANTS from over the work area and from the window sills. The kitchen often does double duty as a living area, and it is tempting to introduce these little touches. But ivies, in particular, attract insects, a source of bacteria.

Hints for foolproof freezing

Considerable cold is required to freeze food (ie, to change it from a fluid or pliable to a solid state). For effective food freezing, the temperature must be lowered to −18°C (0°F).

Freezing inevitably has some effect on foods. Ice crystals form within and between the cells which make up food tissues, and cause some damage and distortion, although this can be kept to a minimum by freezing as quickly as possible and keeping at a constant −18°C.

Food spoilage is caused by the activity of enzymes present in all cells, and by different micro-organisms (bacteria, yeasts and moulds). Most micro-organisms are rendered inactive once the food reaches −10°C (14°F), while at −18°C, enzyme function is retarded.

But food in frozen store does not remain unchanged. Colour, texture and flavour will deteriorate gradually and at a rate dependent on the storage temperature, the particular characteristics of the food and its quality when it was frozen. Because all frozen foods will eventually become unacceptable, it is essential to keep meticulous records or to date-mark everything.

To thaw, food has to pass through the same temperature range, in reverse, as for freezing, but the process can take longer. The smaller the pieces of food and, obviously, the warmer the surroundings, the more quickly they will thaw.

Food which has been taken from the freezer will be every bit as perishable, and sometimes more so, than it was before it was frozen. As soon as the temperature reaches −10°C some spoilage bacteria will resume growing, so once they have been allowed to thaw, it is essential that foods be used, not left around for any length of time, even in the refrigerator.

Compared with other methods of preservation, freezing itself has little effect on the nutritive value of foods. Preliminary blanching and subsequent thawing will account for some nutrient loss, but if the food was in prime condition when it was frozen, and if it has been handled properly at every stage, it will not be significantly less nutritious than fresh food prepared in the same way.

Before using a new deep-freeze, wash it out with a solution of bicarbonate of soda, and rinse and dry it, then switch it on, selecting a moderate setting. A freezer thermometer will be necessary to check that nowhere in the cabinet does the temperature exceed −18°C. Take the first reading after three or four hours, in the centre of the cabinet, and if it is above −18° to −20°C (0° to −4°F), turn the dial to a lower setting. Try the thermometer in different positions to ensure the freezer is cold enough at every level, after which it may be used to store ready-frozen foods.

If you wish to freeze fresh raw or cooked foods, turn the dial to its lowest setting or, if there is one, switch on the fast freeze or super freeze facility (for a maximum load, you should do this an hour or two in advance). Keep the food to be frozen in the refrigerator meanwhile.

As a general guide to freezing capacity, not more than 30g of food per litre (or 2lb/1kg per cu ft) of cabinet space should be frozen per 24 hours. For a full freezing load, leave on fast freeze or on the lowest setting for up to 24 hours; for half load, leave up to 12 hours.

A major headache for freezer owners is the fear that a power cut or break-down will cause the contents to thaw, and it is always wise, when you have a full freezer, to insure its contents. However, so long as the cabinet is fairly well filled and you do not open the door, it will be hours before a thawing temperature is reached. In one test with a 110 litre (4 cu ft) model, it was more than eight hours before the warmest peak reached −5°C (23°F), at which temperature most foods remain frozen.

If you find that the freezer is off and you cannot be sure how long it has been that way, there is some cause for concern. Any food such as shellfish which is highly perishable in its fresh state, in particular, should be treated as suspect. Feel the packet: if it crunches, denoting the presence of ice crystals, it can be re-frozen for use as soon as possible. Re-freezing will have a detrimental effect on its taste, but it won't present a health hazard.

If any foods are fully thawed, the wise course is to throw them away. But if fruit or fruit products have a sweet smell, they can be used in a cooked dish or, again, can be cooled and re-frozen for early consumption. Ice-cream, once it is thawed, cannot successfully be re-frozen since the texture is impaired.

Packing food for freezing

Once food has been prepared for the freezer, it must be put into a bag, wrapping or container, and as much air as possible must be excluded. When a package contains liquid such as a sauce or syrup, space should be left for expansion to prevent it bursting. Polythene bags and wire closers, foil, cellulose tissue and cartons for freezing are available from supermarkets and freezer shops.

The simplest way to seal a polythene bag is with a twist of covered wire. Alternatively, you can use an iron at its lowest setting. Expel as much air as possible and make a double seam; place a piece of paper above and below the seam and press. Avoid small bags, since over-filling makes it difficult to expel the air. For extra strength, polythene bags with a foil outer coating are available.

The iron can be used directly on bags of cellulose tissue.

Ordinary household foil is rather too flimsy to be suitable as a wrapping for frozen foods, but a heavy-duty version is ideal. Foil-dishes such as are used by Chinese and Indian take-aways are convenient for freezing prepared meals and can be transferred straight to the oven (though not the microwave). If the food to be frozen is acid, use containers with an acid-resistant coating.

Plastic containers usually have really close-fitting lids and are durable and re-usable, so they can repay their initial high cost. Where cartons have tuck-in lids a strip of tape should be placed over the join. Even close-fitting lids are best held in place with tape, although there is no need to use tape to seal the join.

Freezing vegetables

Nearly all vegetables – though not salad leaves – freeze well, and one of the best uses of a freezer is to store fresh produce such as peas, beans and raspberries from the garden or from a grower, when they are abundant and in prime condition. There is far less point in freezing those vegetables which have a long season. Old carrots and potatoes are not recommended for freezing, although small new potatoes, slightly under-boiled, and baby carrots, blanched, skinned and left whole, probably earn their space in the cabinet. Tomatoes for salads should not be frozen, but firm, ripe, small or medium ones will be fine for cooking after freezing, and tomato pulp can be frozen with great success.

Fresh, morning-gathered herbs are also suitable for freezing, washed and wrapped or trimmed, blanched, chopped and made into ice cubes for sauces.

Generally, vegetables should be blanched before they are frozen, although mushrooms, and peppers for early use, are exceptions.

In a large pan, bring water to the boil, adding a teaspoonful of salt for every pint, to aid colour retention. Allow 6 pints of water to every pound of vegetables and stand over a high heat to ensure that it returns to the boil within 60 seconds of adding the vegetables. There is no need to change the water if blanching several batches of the same vegetable and, indeed, more vitamin C should be retained if you do not. After blanching, refresh immediately in ice-cold water. Allow as long for refreshing as for blanching (see below). Drain and pack immediately or, if you want free-flowing vegetables, spread them on a baking tray and put them directly into the freezer in contact with the evaporating coils for about 4-6 hours (for peas) or 6-8 hours (for sprouts), then pack and seal.

Blanched vegetables can be stored at −18°C or below for up to a year, after which they will deteriorate in terms of eating quality.

Recommended blanching time for vegetables to be frozen

1-2 minutes	Cabbage, finely sliced, shelled peas, mange tout, cleaned and cut in 1-2in lengths
2-4 minutes	Asparagus, broad beans, French beans, runner beans, brussels sprouts, cauliflower florets, whole or halved courgettes, peppers (if they are to be stored for some time), spinach, broccoli
4-5 minutes	Artichoke fronds, halved aubergines, small whole or large diced carrots, corn on the cob, any diced root vegetables
5-20 minutes	Beetroots (depending on their size)

Most vegetables can be cooked directly from the frozen state, although corn on the cob should be allowed to thaw, at least partially, in its wrapping before cooking.

Sprigs of herbs can be taken straight from the freezer and rubbed between the hands for a chopped effect.

Freezing fruit

Although a frozen strawberry is a flabby, flavourless poor relation of a fresh one, most fruits can be frozen with varying degrees of

---

success. Oxidation will cause darkening, which can be a problem with light-coloured fruits, but this can be avoided if ascorbic acid (vitamin C), available in tablet or in crystalline form, is added to the water or syrup during preparation, or if, where appropriate (for instance, with apples, rhubarb and gooseberries) the fruit is blanched or stewed.

For best results, fruits should be picked in tip-top condition, in dry weather, should be kept cool, handled with great care and frozen without delay.

Discard any inferior or damaged specimens, and wash only if necessary by drawing through cold water in a colander.

Certain types of fruit need no other preparation and can be packed, sealed and labelled for immediate freezing. As with vegetables, if you want a free-flowing supply, spread the fruit on a metal tray and place in the coldest part of the cabinet to freeze before packing. Blackcurrants, figs, whole lemons or lemon slices (separated by greaseproof paper), raspberries and strawberries can all be frozen by this method.

Some fruits can be frozen in a coating of dry sugar. Allow 4oz caster sugar per 2lb of fruit; mix gently in a bowl so the sugar coats the prepared fruit, and leave for 1½ to 2 hours. The sugar should draw sufficient juice from the fruit to form a protective glaze when frozen, although you may need to add a sprinkling of cold water while mixing. All fruits except apples and pears, peaches and apricots are suitable for freezing by this method. If, when you take the fruit from the freezer, you notice it has formed what looks like mould, don't be alarmed. It is due to crystallisation, presents no danger and will probably disappear on thawing.

Fruits may also be frozen in syrup, which is another means of preventing oxidation. Prepare the syrup by dissolving sugar in boiling water and standing over the heat for a couple of minutes. For a light syrup, allow 4oz caster sugar per pint of water; for a medium syrup allow 12oz; for a heavy syrup, 16oz. Use the weaker syrups for fruits which are subsequently to be cooked; use heavier syrups for dessert fruits. Apple slices for pies etc need only a weak syrup; blackberries, blueberries, red or black cherries, figs, plums and greengages should be immersed in medium to heavy syrup; whole or halved apricots, halved and peeled peaches, mulberries, peeled, halved and cored pears, raspberries, loganberries, strawberries etc require heavy syrup.

As an alternative to syrup, use the sweetened juice of imperfect fruit.

Gooseberries and rhubarb destined for eventual stewing might just as well be stewed before they are frozen since this is a more economical use of freezer space.

Frozen fruit, particularly with the addition of sugar, will keep well for up to a year (pineapple should be eaten within 6 months at the outside, and is not really ideal for freezing). Home growers will, in any case, have a new crop for freezing after 12 months.

If stone fruits are to be kept for more than 6 months, they will develop a strong almond flavour which some people appreciate. Remove the stone if you want to avoid this.

Freezing meat

Many people use their freezers primarily for the storage of meat, and a bulk purchase such as, say, a side of pork or lamb or a quarter of beef, especially if it has been conveniently cut into joints for you, can represent value for money.

But the preparation and cooking of the cheaper cuts, especially from a frozen state, demands time, skill and ingenuity. If you're more resourceful than rich, or if you find it difficult to make regular trips to the shops, you may do very well to invest in a whole or half carcase. However, to be realistic, there are many for whom this will be a false economy, and it is not the only – or indeed the best – way to reduce your weekly food bill.

At the other end of the scale, the bulk purchase of lean cuts of meat for freezing has still less to recommend it. The principal advantages of a deep-freeze in the healthy kitchen are that it enables you to store fresh produce to enjoy out of season, and that it ensures a supply of food for any eventuality. Unless you are likely to have to feed the local rugby team at short notice, there is no need to stock up with trays of fillet steak, and there are better uses to be made of freezer space.

It should also be remembered, when buying raw meat, that domestic freezers have only limited freezing capacity. It may be necessary to divide the meat into two or three batches, to store some in the refrigerator while the first consignment is being frozen. This assumes, probably wrongly, that you will have refrigerator space. Another option is to freeze all the meat at one time, but this will mean the process is far slower and that it will have a greater effect on quality. The third and possibly the best option, if you do want to store quantities of meat, is to buy it ready frozen, or to pay your supplier to do it for you.

Lamb, pork and beef, poultry and game can all be frozen. The maximum recommended storage periods, at −18°C (0°F) are:

Beef	12 months
Diced stewing steak	6 months
Minced meat	2 months
Lamb	12 months
Pork	9 months
Veal	9 months
Offal	2 months
Sausages	6 weeks
Chicken	12 months
Turkey	9 months
Ducks, geese, pigeons	6 months
Giblets	3 months
Fatty types of game, fully matured	6 months
Lean game	9 months

Meat for freezing should be kept cool and clean and should be trimmed of any excess fat. Birds should be prepared in the normal way. It is not a good idea to freeze a stuffed bird. The stuffing itself can quickly develop an unpleasant flavour, and it can inhibit heat penetration to the meat, which is so essential to ensure that it is fit for consumption.

Ideally, joints of meat from the freezer should be allowed to thaw slowly, say for 24 hours, still wrapped, in the refrigerator (allow 8-10 hours per pound). At room temperature, allow 3-4 hours per pound. Once the meat has fully thawed, cook it without delay. If you are in a great hurry, you can roast a joint from the frozen state. It will take about twice the time to cook, will be tougher and paler, but should be acceptable. The important thing is to ensure that it has reached a sufficient temperature at the centre (74°C for beef, 77°C for veal, 85°C for lamb or pork, to give a medium rather than a very well done result). Use a meat thermometer.

Chops and steaks can also be cooked from frozen, although they take only 2 to 3 hours to thaw at room temperature. Use a high heat to seal each side, then turn it down and allow the meat to cook right to the centre.

Frozen chicken should be allowed to thaw in a cool room or in the refrigerator (but not in contact with any other foods). Allow 5-6 hours per pound in the fridge, while, at cool room temperature, a 5lb (2.25kg) bird will take an average 15 hours to defrost completely. It will be ready when the body is pliable, the legs flexible, and the body cavity is free from ice crystals. Cook it without delay and make absolutely sure that it is done before you take it from the oven. If it is to be eaten cold, cool it quickly and transfer it to the refrigerator.

Proportionately less time should be allowed for the thawing of large birds, but even so, a 15lb (7kg) turkey will take three full days to thaw in the refrigerator.

Giblets should always be removed from the bird and wrapped and frozen separately.

Freezing fish

Because freshness is everything when it comes to frozen fish, it is recommended that you do not carry home wet fish to freeze yourself. As little time as possible should have elapsed between catching and freezing, and the best commercially frozen fish is therefore likely to be superior to anything which has had to survive the journey, first to the retailer, then to your kitchen. Both white and oily fish are suitable for freezing, although oily varieties will have a shorter storage life.

Shellfish such as shrimps and prawns, scallops, crabs and lobsters are also suitable for freezing but have a still-shorter storage life.

The recommended maxium storage period at −18°C (0°F) is:

White fish	4 months
Oily fish (trout, salmon etc)	3 months
Scallops	3 months
Crab and lobster (cooked)	2 months
Shrimps (cooked)	2 months

If you have a supply of very fresh fish or shellfish which you wish to freeze, here are some guidelines.

All fish should be prepared according to their planned use. They should be scaled, cleaned, trimmed, and the intestinal cavity should be washed out.

Scallops should be prepared according to the instructions on page 64.

Crabs and lobsters should be cooked.

Shrimps and prawns should be cooked, shelled and de-veined.

Whole fish can be coated in ice. Place it in the coldest part of the cabinet until frozen, then dip it in a pan of nearly-frozen water and return it to the freezer. Repeat once or twice so that it forms a complete glaze which will help to prevent oxidation. Quickly overwrap to protect the ice from chipping, and return to the freezer before it has time to thaw.

Fillets and steaks of fish should be separated by folded greaseproof paper before wrapping and freezing, to enable you to remove the exact number you require.

The texture of white fish fillets will be improved if you place them for 30 seconds in lightly salted water before wrapping and freezing them.

Whole fish should, for preference, be completely thawed at cool room temperature before cooking, but single portions can be cooked gently from frozen.

Freezing prepared dishes

When preparing and cooking a meal for the family, some people make double the quantity and freeze half for later use.

If a prepared dish is to be eaten cold, it should be allowed to thaw overnight in the refrigerator. Reheating will depend on how the food has been packed. Foil dishes can be transferred immediately to a moderate oven. Boil-in-the-bag wrapping allows you to do just that.

Sweet dishes generally store well in the freezer, but savoury ones will tend to become less palatable after about three months.

This is a convenient but not the most enlightened use of a deep freeze, especially when you consider how quickly and easily a meal can be rustled up from store-cupboard and fresh-frozen ingredients.

The following suggestions for meals in minutes are from chef Alasdair Little and others.

Fast food

Everyone has his or her standbys in the cupboard, fridge or deep freeze: tins, pastas, rice, noodles, eggs, potatoes, onions . . . Here are some ideas for meals in minutes made out of whatever is to hand.

TINNED TUNA flaked and mixed in mayonnaise (a good bottle if pushed) with added strong mustard, sliced raw onion, with cooked potatoes.

PARMA HAM, now generally available pre-packed, is good with tomatoes, cucumber, or

---

RULE OF THUMB

When freezer space is limited, it is better used for storing prime ingredients than for made-up dishes. If you keep a supply of frozen fish and vegetables, if you stock your cupboard with good-quality dried, packaged, canned and bottled ingredients, and if you always have to hand such fresh produce as potatoes, onions, tomatoes, garlic, lemons, eggs and cheese, you will be able to whip up a meal in a moment.

---

pears, mangoes or peaches. The proportion of fat is the same as in other hams, but the overall fat content of one or two wafer-thin slices is not great.

EGGS poached on spinach (frozen) with a sprinkling of Parmesan on top. Spanish omelette made with onion, potato and peppers (or, at a pinch, tinned ratatouille), delicious hot or cold.

PASTA tossed with olive oil, garlic and parsley, or with a spoonful of bottled pesto, or with pounded anchovy fillets and chilli.

THAI NOODLES soaked in hot water for 10 minutes then added to a wok in which you have previously fried onion, garlic and a little dried chilli. Turn the noodles and add chopped parsley and rice vinegar. Eat hot or cold.

TINNED CONSOMMÉ heated and poured over a few prawns (from the freezer, thawed) fried in hot oil with spring onions and parsley.

CRACKED WHEAT: soak a few ounces for half an hour then drain and squeeze dry. Mix with chopped cucumber, tomato, spring onions, fresh mint and parsley (or dried mint), black olives, dark olive oil and lemon juice.

RISOTTO is quick to cook. Use available vegetables (onions, peppers, mushrooms, tomatoes), use consommé as the cooking medium. Sprinkle with Parmesan to taste. Or fry a few prawns (frozen, defrosted) with crushed root ginger and chopped spring onion, and fold into boiled rice with a beaten egg.

PICKLED HERRINGS are good with black or rye bread, which keeps much longer than white or brown. Pumpernickel, from delicatessens, is a long-lasting, rich-tasting rye bread.

The healthy kitchen stores

The choice of stores to keep in the larder depends on available space, the kind of cooking you most enjoy, and on the grocery budget. The following items are stores to add interest and variety to a fresh food diet; the most frequently used and replaced items should be the whole grains, pulses, wholemeal pasta, and oils high in polyunsaturates.

FLOUR (wholemeal) The larger the bran particles, the better, can be sieved for baking; white bread flour; flour for thickening (eg cornflour, rice flour, potato flour).

WHOLEMEAL PASTA Spaghetti and macaroni; soup pasta (eg buckwheat noodles, Chinese noodles).

GRAINS Brown rice; basmati rice for curries; Arborio rice for risotto; buckwheat, roasted or unroasted; millet; bulgur; couscous; polenta; semolina.

NUTS Buy whole, unroasted, lightly toast in non-stick, thick-based pan. Hazelnuts (low in fat); walnuts (high in polyunsaturates); peanuts (high in oil, very high in protein); Brazils and pecans (highest in oil); pine kernels; almonds; cashews; dried chestnuts.

OILS Olive oil (cold pressed) for salad dressings and high-temperature cooking; safflower for gentle cooking and salad dressings (highest in polyunsaturates); sunflower, grapeseed and soya oil for most cooking; sesame and walnut oils to give special flavour to salads.

VINEGAR Wine and cider varieties.

SUGAR The only sugar with any nutrient whatsoever (minute traces of minerals) occurs in honey and molasses. Use sparingly different kinds of sugar for cooking, eg castor, raw cane (Demerara), granulated. Less honey than sugar is needed for sweetness, substitute where possible, and try different varieties.

PULSES (dried and canned) Split red lentils; blackeyed beans; chick peas; butter beans; red kidney beans; soya or haricot beans; flageolets; brown or green lentils; dried whole peas.

SEEDS Sunflower; sesame; poppy; mustard; pumpkin; caraway (best lightly roasted).

WHOLE SPICES Peppercorns; juniper berries; cloves; cinnamon sticks; vanilla pods; nutmegs; coriander seeds; cardamom pods; chilli.

GROUND AND POWDERED SPICES Saffron powder; coriander; cumin; turmeric; chilli.

DRIED HERBS Bay leaves; thyme; rosemary; oregano; tarragon; mint; sage.

DRIED GELATINE

DRIED YEAST

DRIED FRUIT Apricots; apple rings; peaches; pears; sultanas; raisins. Boil for a couple of minutes (to remove sulphur dioxide, used as a preservative), drain, replace with fresh water.

SAUCES/FLAVOURINGS Worcestershire sauce; soya; ketchup; pesto (garlic, basil and pine nut sauce, sold in jars); mustard (wholegrain and smooth); tahini (crushed sesame paste, for houmus and to flavour vegetables).

CANNED FOODS Tomatoes; tomato purée; sardines; tuna in brine; anchovy fillets; sweetcorn; fruit and jams without added sugar; vegetables without added colour, salt or sugar; vegetable stock cubes.

HOME-MADE CHUTNEY

D-i-y food

BEANSPROUTS are widely available from supermarkets and greengrocers. They are wonderful for adding bite to winter salads. But if you want to try other types of sprouted seeds, you have to look far and wide to find them.

A simple solution is to sprout your own seeds at home, using either a special kit or an ordinary jam jar. You can experiment with lentils, mustard seeds, alfalfa, mung beans and many more, available from health shops or from nurseries and garden centres (packet seeds have instructions on the back).

Put a tablespoonful of seeds into a sieve and run cold water on them. Sort them and remove any wizened specimens then put the remainder in a jar filled with lukewarm water and leave them to soak overnight somewhere warm, covered with a piece of muslin held in place with a rubber band.

In the morning, strain off the liquid through the muslin, then flush and strain the seeds several times with cold water.

Leave the jar on its side, somewhere dark like the airing-cupboard, and repeat the flushing twice a day. On the third day, transfer jar to a sunny windowsill. You can "harvest" the sprouts when they are an inch or more long and you see leaf-tips developing.

Soak in cold water to get rid of seed husks. Store in a polythene bag in the refrigerator.

YOGHURT is another healthy food which can be made at home. There are two types of yoghurt-maker: the insulated container and the heated tray with pots. They will produce one or two pints of yoghurt, according to their size.

The heated tray type needs electricity to maintain a constant temperature during incubation, but they are not expensive to run (about the same as a 60 watt light bulb). Some manufacturers provide glass jars with lids; others rather tacky plastic pots.

Insulated containers need no electricity and retain heat by the same means as a Thermos flask. The makers include a thermometer and clear instructions. All equipment should be scrupulously sterilised, and milk should be heated to the correct temperature (here the thermometer provided with insulated containers is very useful). You can start your own yoghurt by adding a spoonful of shop-bought, natural live yoghurt or buy a "mother" culture, enough for 48 litres (available from health food shops).

It is, of course, possible to make yoghurt, as farmers' wives have done for centuries, simply by pouring milk (pasteurised) into an earthenware jug, adding a spoonful of live yoghurt and leaving it in the airing-cupboard overnight. But if you like to have a constant supply of natural yoghurt (and it becomes more and more difficult to find on the supermarket shelves among the chocolate, caramel, toffee and other improbable flavours), if you want a full-proof method and clear instructions, it may be worth investing in a yoghurt-maker.

We tried both types and, on the whole, favoured the insulated container as being quicker, but either produces good results and they are not expensive.

A healthy diet should not be viewed as restrictive; rather it is one which makes imaginative use of the great variety and abundance of fresh foods now available in our shops.

Some restraint is necessary, of course, when it comes to adding such ingredients as butter, cream, cheese, eggs, sugar and even salt — but none of these items appears on any Forbidden List, and all can be used in moderation.

The following recipes have been included to show how the rules of healthy eating can be applied in your own kitchen. They would not, as you would see, be out of place in any cookery book written to celebrate the enjoyment of good food.

Soups and starters

COLD GREEN SOUP
"An elegant and enlightened soup" (Elisabeth Lambert Ortiz). Serves 6.

2 pints (1.1 litre) chicken stock
12oz (350g) chopped raw green beans
12oz (350g) chopped raw courgettes
12oz (350g) chopped cos lettuce
8oz (225g) peas (if frozen, thoroughly defrosted)
4oz (110g) chopped celery
2oz (50g) chopped shallots or spring onions
1oz (25g) chopped parsley, preferably flat-leaved
Salt, freshly ground black pepper
Garnish: 6 slices unpeeled cucumber or 6 slices hard-boiled egg or parsley and chervil

Combine the stock and the prepared vegetables, including the ounce of parsley, in a large saucepan. Simmer, partially covered, for 8-10 minutes or until vegetables are tender.

Remove the solids from the soup and purée them in a blender or food processor. Return the purée to the stock, mix well and season to taste.

PART FIVE

RECIPES FOR ENLIGHTENED EATING

Cool the soup quickly before chilling in the fridge for at least 2 hours. Serve garnished with cucumber or hard-boiled egg, or sprinkled with finely chopped parsley and chervil.

CELERIAC, ORANGE AND WATERCRESS SOUP
This recipe from Victoria Orr-Ewing makes an unusual and refreshing soup to serve 6

2 medium celeriacs, peeled and chopped
2 medium potatoes, peeled and diced
2 pints (1.1 litre) chicken stock plus a little milk (vegetarians can use 1 pint water, 1 pint milk)
Grated zest of an orange
1 bunch watercress
Salt, freshly ground black pepper, paprika

Cook celeriac and potatoes slowly in half the measured liquid. Add the orange zest halfway through cooking. When vegetables are soft but not mushy, strain and reserve the liquid.

Mash the vegetables or, for a smoother texture, put them in a blender or food processor. Return the purée to the stock with the remaining liquid; season with salt, pepper and paprika to taste. Heat through but do not allow to boil.

Trim off thick stalks of watercress; roughly chop leaves and thin stalks and add to the soup just before serving.

FISHERMAN'S CLAM CHOWDER

This is Anton Mosimann's delicate version of a hearty soup. If clams are not available, he says, you could use a piece of monkfish or a small sole. Serves 4

1oz (25g) carrot
2oz (50g) celeriac
4oz (110g) potato
1oz (25g) onion
1oz (25g) leek
1oz (25g) green pepper
24 cherrystone clams
1¼ pints (700ml) fish stock
2 tomatoes, peeled, seeded and diced
1 clove garlic, peeled and crushed
1 small bay leaf
1 tsp chopped fresh thyme
1 tsp chopped fresh parsley
Salt, freshly ground black pepper

Peel carrot, celeriac, potato and onion. Trim leek and seed peppers. Cut all in small dice.

Scrub the clams and place in a large saucepan with the stock. Cover and simmer until the clams open.

Remove from the stock and set aside to cool. Strain the stock through muslin or a fine sieve and reserve.

Remove hard white tendon from the clams and chop flesh.

Sauté the onion, leek, carrot, celeriac and garlic in a non-stick pan without browning. Add the bay leaf, green pepper, potato and reserved stock and simmer for 5 minutes.

Add the clams and tomatoes and simmer for a further five minutes. Remove bay leaf.

Add herbs and season to taste.

SMOKED MACKEREL PATÉ

Delicious with brown toast or freshly baked bread and with a salad made from lettuce, orange and shallot. Serves 6.

2 onions
1-2 cloves garlic
1oz (25g) butter
1 tbsp walnut oil
4 fillets smoked mackerel
Large carton ewe's milk yoghurt or fromage frais
Bunch of parsley, trimmed and finely chopped
Juice of 2 medium lemons
3-4 shakes Tabasco
3oz (85g) fresh breadcrumbs
Freshly ground black pepper
Garnish: parsley sprigs, carrot and lemon slices

Chop the onion and garlic and sauté in the butter. Add the walnut oil and cook gently until onions are translucent. Remove from the heat.

Skin the mackerel fillets and remove any bones. Cut into large chunks and put all the ingredients into a food processor: whizz for about 15 seconds. Check the texture, which should be a little loose, not a purée.

Spoon the pâté into a serving bowl or into ramekins. Chill in the fridge for a few hours.

Decorate with sprigs of parsley and rounds of carrot and lemon.

BULGUR SALAD

6oz (170g) bulgur (fine grade)
4 tbsp olive oil
Juice of 2 large or 3 small lemons
Salt, freshly ground black pepper
Half a cucumber, peeled and diced
4 cherry tomatoes, chopped
Large bunches of parsley and mint, finely chopped

Wash the bulgur (cracked wheat) thoroughly in a fine sieve, then soak for 15 minutes in plenty of cold water so that it softens. Drain in the sieve, pressing down with the back of a wooden spoon to squeeze out as much water as possible.

Make a dressing with the olive oil and lemon juice, salt and pepper, and mix with the bulgur. Leave to stand until it is absorbed.

Just before serving, mix in the cucumber, tomatoes and chopped parsley and mint.

MULTI-COLOURED SALAD OF CHICKEN LIVERS AND HEARTS

Brian Turner serves this showy and appetising salad in London's Capital Hotel Restaurant. Since chicken hearts are not readily available, you will need to find a good butcher who will reserve them for you when he's cleaning chickens (or simply omit them). Serves 4

2oz (50g) carrot
2oz (50g) celeriac
2oz (50g) cooked beetroot
4 leaves Webb's lettuce
8 chicken hearts (optional)
4 chicken livers
1oz (25g) butter
For the vinaigrette: 2 fl oz (50ml) walnut oil, 1 tbsp wine vinegar, salt, freshly ground black pepper, ½oz (15g) chopped shallot

First make the vinaigrette dressing, combining the oil and vinegar then adding the seasoning, followed by the shallots.

Cut the carrots, celeriac, beetroot and lettuce into very thin strips, keeping them separate.

Sauté the hearts and the livers quickly in hot

butter taking care not to overcook (the insides should be pink).

Mix half the carrots, celeriac and lettuce with some vinaigrette and arrange the mixture on individual plates. Place the livers and hearts on top of this.

Toss the remainder of the carrots, celeriac and lettuce in the rest of the vinaigrette and arrange carefully over the livers. Sprinkle the beetroot on top.

WARM SCALLOPS AND AVOCADO SALAD

"Scallops go extremely well with most white fish, and surprisingly well with chicken and veal, and are super in salads" (Richard Smith). Serves 4

12 scallops
Mixture of salad leaves (lettuce, endive, mâche)
1 ripe avocado
½ bottle dry white wine or a little clarified butter
Vinaigrette made with green herb mustard

Prepare the scallops (see page 64). Cut them in thick slices.

Wash, trim and arrange the salad leaves on individual plates. Peel the avocado and arrange thin slices in a fan shape on each plate.

Either poach the scallops gently in a mixture of water and white wine, or shallow fry them in clarified butter, and add them, still warm, to the salad. Dress with vinaigrette and serve.

Variation: a spoonful of mayonnaise mixed with white crabmeat makes an interesting addition to this dish.

SEAFOOD SALAD SAUCE VIERGE

Brian Turner uses scallops, oysters, king prawns or langoustine and mussels, steamed over fresh coriander, for this lavish salad. We suggest making it with slightly cheaper ingredients – it's still sumptuous. Serves 6-8

Fish and shellfish:
You will need about 2lb (900g) mixed fish, eg:
1 pint (200ml) mussels
8oz (225g) squid
8oz (225g) firm white fish (sole, plaice, cod)
3 scallops
4oz (110g) peeled prawns
For the sauce vierge:
5 fl oz (12ml) olive oil
2 tbsp white wine vinegar
Salt, freshly ground black pepper
1oz (25g) chopped shallots
1 carrot, peeled, cut into matchsticks, blanched
1 courgette, cut into matchsticks, blanched
12 black olives

2 tsp coriander seeds, crushed
1 bunch parsley, chopped
For the salad: *a selection of leaves of varying colours and good texture, for instance, lettuce, endive, radicchio, chicory, young spinach, mâche.*

First make the sauce by whisking together the oil and vinegar, salt and pepper. Add the shallots, carrots, courgettes, olives and crushed coriander and chopped parsley.

Prepare the mussels, squid and scallops (see page 64). Cut the white fish in strips or chunks. Poach the mussels, remove them from their shells and add them, still warm, to the sauce. Slice the scallops. Poach the squid, white fish and scallops and add to the sauce. Add the prawns.

Arrange the salad leaves on individual plates and spoon on the dressed fish.

Fish and shellfish

BAKED COD WITH OYSTER MUSHROOMS
Serves 6

1½lb (675g) cod fillets (or other white fish)
4 tbsp wholemeal flour
Freshly ground black pepper
4oz (110g) natural yoghurt
4oz (110g) fromage frais
6 spring onions, chopped
2oz (50g) butter
8oz (225g) oyster mushrooms (or ordinary mushrooms), sliced
1 tbsp chopped dill
2 tbsp chopped parsley
2oz (50g) breadcrumbs
2oz (50g) grated Parmesan

Preheat oven to gas mark 5, 375°F, 190°C.

Wash and dry the fish fillets and coat with a dusting of flour.

Mix together the yoghurt and *fromage frais.*

Cook the spring onions until soft and golden in 1½oz (40g) of the butter. Add the mushrooms and cook for a few minutes.

Put half the mushroom mixture into a baking dish and sprinkle with half the chopped dill and parsley. Lay the fish on top, followed by another layer of mushroom mixture and another sprinkling of herbs, then top with a layer of yoghurt mixture.

Top with the breadcrumbs mixed with Parmesan and dot with the remaining butter. Bake for 20-25 minutes.

CHINESE STEAMED SEA BASS

Steaming coaxes out the flavour of this splendid fish. You can, if you wish, substitute grey mullet or sea bream. Serves 6

1 sea bass weighing approx 3lb (1.5kg)
1 medium carrot
10-12 spring onions
Knob fresh ginger root
Large pinch salt
Large pinch sugar
6 tbsp corn oil
Light soya sauce

Scale and gut the fish (the fishmonger will do this on request) but leave the head on.

Prepare the vegetables: cut the carrots into julienne; chop the onions into 2in lengths then cut them into fine strands. Peel ginger and cut it into wafer-thin slivers, then into threads.

Place the fish on a heatproof dish to fit inside a bamboo steamer in a wok, or in a conventional stove-top or plug-in steamer. Strew the carrot strips on top, cover with the lid and steam over a high heat for 10-12 minutes or until the fish is cooked (the flesh should be flaky but still firm).

Remove lid and keep fish warm over a very low heat. Mop up any excess water with kitchen towel; sprinkle bass with salt and sugar.

Arrange the strands of spring onion and ginger on top. Heat the oil in a small pan until it reaches smoking point. Carefully spoon it over the bass, sprinkle with a little soya sauce and transfer the plate to the table to serve.

SMOKED HADDOCK WITH BABY TURNIPS AND RADISHES

For this cold dish, the haddock is marinated rather than cooked – a wonderful way to bring out the flavour of traditionally smoked fish. No need to add any salt. Serves 4

Bunch of radishes
1½lb (675g) baby turnips
1lb (450g) smoked haddock
Juice of 3 lemons
3 tbsp olive oil
Few sprigs fresh dill
Freshly ground black pepper

Make deep criss-cross cuts in the tops of the trimmed radishes and leave in iced water to "blossom".

Peel the turnips and slice them finely; blanch in boiling water for a couple of minutes then refresh in cold water.

Cut the haddock in small slices and place on a dish. Arrange the turnips and radish "flowers" around the fish. Pour the lemon juice and oil over it, sprinkle with some of the dill, finely chopped, and leave to marinate for one hour.

Before serving, season with coarsely ground black pepper and garnish with the remaining sprigs of dill.

BAKED MONKFISH WITH COURGETTE CRUST

"A marvellous example of cooking without butter or animal fat. You need a little olive oil for flavour, or, if you like, use safflower oil" (Glynn Christian). Serves 4

1 monkfish tail, trimmed, with all membranes removed
4-6oz (110-170g) mixture of green or red pepper, celery and carrot cut in matchsticks
Juice of onion, garlic or fresh ginger root
4oz (110g) courgette, grated
Salt, freshly ground black pepper
Olive oil
Lime or lemon juice (if liked)

Preheat oven to gas mark 5, 375°F, 190°C.

Blanch the matchsticks of mixed vegetables for a few minutes in boiling water. Drain. Flavour them lightly with the juice of onion, garlic or green ginger root, produced by pressing in a garlic crusher.

Make a bed of the blanched vegetables in a baking dish and place the monkfish on top. Season with salt and pepper and smear with a little olive oil.

Coarsely grate the courgettes; flavour them lightly with more garlic, ginger or onion juice, and, if you wish, a squeeze of lemon or lime juice. Shape the courgette mixture over the fish to form a coating and bake for about 25 minutes or until the fish is cooked through.

RED MULLET A LA GRECQUE

Although nothing under the Greek sun quite compares with red mullet cooked in the open air over charcoal, this dish will bring back holiday memories on a grey day. Serves 4

4 red mullet, about 8oz (225g) each
4 tbsp virgin olive oil
Salt, freshly ground black pepper
A few sprigs of fresh thyme
Lemon wedges

The mullet should be cleaned and gutted, with liver left intact (the fishmonger will do this for you if you prefer).

Preheat oven to gas mark 4, 350°F, 180°C.

Cut four rectangles of foil large enough to wrap a fish.

Wash and dry the mullet and place on the foil. Brush with olive oil, sprinkle with salt and pepper, then put a few sprigs of thyme on each fish and fold the foil, sealing the seams to make secure parcels.

Place the parcels in a roasting tin and bake for about 20 minutes.

Serve garnished with wedges of lemon, and accompany with a Greek salad.

Meat, poultry and game

CHICKEN SUPREMES WITH CELERIAC AND GRAPES IN SPINACH LEAF PARCELS

"Pretty colours and contrasting textures make these the epitome of modern eating, fat-free and exciting" (Glynn Christian). Serves 4

4 chicken supremes (or turkey escalopes),
*   weighing 4-6oz (110-170g) each*
2 tbsp dry white vermouth
12 large fresh spinach leaves
3oz (85g) grated raw celeriac
8oz (225g) seedless muscatel grapes
1 fresh lime
Small carton natural yoghurt

Skin the chicken breasts and cut away any pieces of wing bone still attached. Brush the breasts with vermouth.

Blanch the spinach leaves in boiling water for about 30 seconds, then refresh with cold water.

Blanch the celeriac unless you prefer it crunchy.

Cut the grapes in half.

Place the spinach leaves in slightly over-lapping pairs on a board, smooth side down. Arrange a bed of celeriac in the centre of each pair and grate lime zest over. Put a few grapes on top, and finally the chicken breast, smooth side down.

Cover each portion with a spinach leaf and fold and tuck it round to make a neat parcel. Arrange the parcels in a non-stick, shallow tin, cover and steam for 20-30 minutes. The easiest way to do this it to put a roasting pan of boiling water on top of the stove, with a rack inside it on which to set the tin. Cover the roasting pan with a dome of foil and make sure the water is kept at a low boil.

Serve with a dollop of yoghurt into which you have mixed the juice of the lime.

BRAISED GAME WITH RASPBERRIES

"The slightly tart sweetness of raspberries makes them a natural partner for game and the colour lends a cheerful note" (Lynda Brown). The quantities given are per person.

1 small game bird (teal, woodcock, snipe, quail)
*   for each person*
Butter or oil for frying
1 tbsp raspberries (frozen are fine) plus a few for
*   decoration*
1 tbsp brandy
2-3 tbsp concentrated game stock
Few drops of raspberry vinegar

Brown the birds slowly and evenly in a heavy casserole. Remove from the pan and drain off all the fat.

Lightly stuff the cavities with the raspberries, return the birds to the pan and pour over the brandy. Cook for a minute or two over a fierce heat until the brandy is mostly evaporated.

Turn down to the lowest heat possible, moisten with stock, cover with greaseproof paper and jam the lid on tight. Cook for about 35-45 minutes (depending on the birds) until the juices run clear.

Transfer the birds to a serving dish, garnish with the extra raspberries.

To complete the sauce, remove any surface fat, add a few drops of raspberry vinegar, spoon over the birds and serve. Plain rice is all the accompaniment needed.

RABBIT WITH FENNEL IN YOGHURT SAUCE

"I suppose this could be called a *blanquette*, for everything is pale, but it is far better than a classic *blanquette*" (Glynn Christian). Serves 4

1lb (450g) diced rabbit meat
2oz (50g) butter
8oz (225g) fennel bulb, thinly sliced (reserve the
*   green fronds)*
2 cloves garlic, crushed
5 fl oz (150ml) dry white wine
4 tbsp dry white vermouth
Salt, freshly grated black pepper
Strained Greek yoghurt

Melt the butter and stir in the fennel and garlic. Add the rabbit and stir until well covered in butter. Do not brown.

Pour in the wine and the vermouth, season lightly and simmer, covered, until meat is tender (about 45 minutes).

Remove from the heat and stir in enough yoghurt to make a thick white sauce.

Chop the fennel fronds and scatter on top. Serve with jacket potatoes.

VENISON STEAK WITH MUSHROOMS AND POLENTA

A marinated game recipe, typical of the Italian Aosta Valley, from Antonio Carluccio. "It is traditional to serve the venison with polenta, which turns it into a princely dish.'' Venison is now farmed, so more easily obtainable. If you can find wild mushrooms, so much the better.

Four ½in (1cm) thick slices from a venison leg or
    fillet, weighing a total of 1¼lb (600g)
Flour for dusting
For the marinade:
2 pints (1 litre) good red wine
1 small chopped onion
5 bay leaves
1 sprig rosemary
2 cloves of garlic, chopped
2 carrots, chopped
2 celery stalks, chopped
1 sprig thyme
5 cloves
10 juniper berries
1 tbsp split black peppercorns
For the sauce:
1½oz (45g) butter
1 small onion, sliced
4oz (100g) smoked bacon, chopped
¾lb (350g) mushrooms, sliced

Combine the ingredients for the marinade. Marinate the venison for three days.

Take the meat from the marinade, and dry with a cloth. Reserve the liquid.

Lightly dust the slices with flour and then fry for 5 minutes in the butter until brown on each side, and put aside to keep hot.

In the same butter, fry the sliced onion and the chopped smoked bacon. Add the sliced mushrooms and fry all together for a few minutes until golden, then add 2 glasses of the strained marinade, allow to bubble and reduce briefly.

Add the venison pieces, coat with the sauce. Serve with polenta or a choice of vegetables.

BRAISED BEEF WITH GINGER
Economical cuts of beef can be made to taste luxurious with the aid of exotic ingredients. Serves 6

1½-2lb (675g to 1kg) silverside of beef
1 tbsp olive oil
2 medium onions, sliced
2oz (50g) coarse oatmeal
½ pint (300ml) beef stock
1lb (450g) celery stalks, cut into matchsticks
1 tbsp soya sauce
1 tbsp clear honey
1in (2.5cm) piece fresh ginger root, peeled and
    grated
Salt, freshly ground black pepper

Preheat oven to gas mark 3, 325°F, 170°C.
Heat oil in a warmed, heavy, flameproof casserole and quickly brown the meat on all sides. Remove the meat and brown the onions. Add the oatmeal and stock and mix well. Place the celery matchsticks on top of the onions and set the browned meat on top. Mix together the soya sauce, honey and ginger, and pour over the meat. Season to taste.

Bring to boiling point on top of the stove then cover the casserole and cook in the oven for about 1½ hours or until the meat is tender.

SWEET AND SOUR VEAL KIDNEYS
A New Classic Cuisine dish from Michel and Albert Roux. Serves 4

2 veal kidneys (fat, veins and membranes
    removed), weighing about 18oz (500g) after
    trimming
1 orange
2 lemons
4 tbsp port
1½oz (40g) caster sugar
4oz (110g) cranberries (fresh or frozen)
1 tbsp white wine vinegar
8 fl oz (200ml) veal stock
1 tbsp clarified butter
1 tsp English mustard powder dissolved in ½ tsp
    water
Salt, freshly ground black pepper
1 tbsp butter

Pare off the rind of the orange finely and cut into julienne. Blanch, refresh, drain and keep in a cool place. Using a sharp knife, peel the orange, removing all the pith, cut into segments and keep in a cool place.

Finely pare the rinds of the lemons and cut into julienne. Blanch, refresh, drain and keep cool. Cut the lemons in half. Squeeze them and reserve the juice.

In a small saucepan, heat the port with a quarter of the sugar. When it comes to the boil, add the cranberries and poach for 1 minute. Keep at room temperature.

To make the sauce, boil the vinegar and remaining sugar in a shallow pan and set over a high heat. When the mixture caramelises, add the lemon juice to prevent it from cooking any further. Stir in the orange segments and veal stock. Lower the heat and cook gently for about 15 minutes, until the liquid has a syrupy consistency. Strain and keep warm.

Slice the kidneys thinly. Heat the clarified butter in a shallow pan, and when it is very hot, sauté the kidneys for no more than 1 minute; they should be seared and lightly browned but still bloody. Transfer to a colander and discard the cooking liquid.

Pour off the fat from the pan and deglaze with the port in which the cranberries were cooked. Set over high heat and reduce by half. Pour in the sauce and bring to the boil. Add the kidneys and cranberries, then the mustard. Season to taste with salt and pepper and stir in 1 tbsp butter. Take the pan off the heat and serve immediately.

Grilled Calves' Liver with Lime
A wonderfully aromatic and quick-to-make recipe from Pierre Koffman. Serves 2

4 thick slices of calves' liver
1 tbsp caster sugar
2 tbsp wine vinegar
Juice of ½ lemon
Juice of 1 orange
1 cup chicken stock
2 shallots, chopped
1 knob of butter (optional)
1 lime, cut into quarters

To prepare the sauce, put the sugar and vinegar in a heavy saucepan and mix together. Cook until the mixture caramelises.

Add the lemon juice, orange juice, chicken stock and chopped shallots. Boil until the liquid is reduced by half. You can then add a knob of butter if you wish.

Grill the liver slices for about 2 minutes each side, so they remain pink inside.

To serve, pour the sauce over the liver and use the quartered lime as a garnish.

Trippa a Modo Mio (Tripe Prepared My Way)
Italian cookery is notable, amongst other things, for delicious dishes using offal. Here is another traditional recipe from Antonio Carluccio, to give new thoughts on tripe. Serves 6.

2lb (1kg) tripe (different textured cuts including honeycomb)
2 carrots
3 sticks celery
2 cloves garlic
5 tbsp olive oil
2 large ripe tomatoes or 1 medium can peeled plum tomatoes
2 bay leaves
1 sprig rosemary
Salt, freshly ground black pepper
2 dried red chilli peppers
Half a glass of white wine
A cup (200ml) of stock (use a cube if pushed)
2 medium cans of drained borlotti beans

Thoroughly clean the tripe and cut it into slices at least ½in (1cm) thick.

Chop the carrot and celery and slice the garlic finely.

Heat the olive oil in a large saucepan, add the carrots, celery and garlic and fry until they are well coated with oil, then add the tomatoes and their juice, the bay leaves, rosemary, salt and chilli peppers and bring to the boil.

Turn down the heat and simmer for 20 minutes. Add the tripe and the wine, and if necessary some of the stock. The tripe should be covered with liquid while cooking. Simmer for at least an hour.

Drain the borlotti beans and wash them under cold water. Add to the tripe after 45 minutes of simmering and season with salt and pepper.

The tripe should be cooked after 1 hour, but the whole cooking time depends on how cooked the tripe was when you bought it. Test throughout simmering, as overcooked tripe becomes slimy in texture. Serve with some good home-made bread.

Sauces

Sauces do not have to be made with lashings of butter and cream to be delicious. The following are easy to make in a food processor or liquidiser, and give a piquant flavour to a variety of dishes.

Coriander Sauce
Ideal to serve with many dishes, particularly fish, pork and chicken, or use as a dressing for salads. Ground coriander seeds can be used in place of fresh leaves. The quantities of yoghurt or *fromage frais* can be doubled for a more delicate flavour. Or you can use equal amounts of yoghurt and *fromage frais*.

1 large bunch fresh coriander
2 tbsp safflower oil
1 tbsp olive oil
1 tbsp walnut oil
8oz (225g) natural yoghurt or low-fat fromage frais
1 tsp strong Dijon mustard
Freshly ground black pepper

Wash the coriander and trim off the thick stalks. Tear roughly and put in the food processor with all the other ingredients and whizz for about 20 seconds. Taste for seasoning; add more pepper if necessary.

Mustard Sauce
Good with salad dishes and particularly with cold cooked root vegetables. Also with strong-

flavoured fish such as mackerel or herring, or with cold chicken or cold boiled beef.

2-3 tbsp olive oil
2 tbsp strong Dijon mustard
2 tbsp thick yoghurt
Freshly ground black pepper
Sprinkling of thyme

Simply process or liquidise all ingredients together.

CARROT AND CUMIN SAUCE
Ideal with fish and vegetable pâtés and terrines. 3 or 4 cardamom pods may be used, crushed, in place of the cumin.

4 large carrots
1 tsp cumin seeds, crushed
Large pot ewe's milk yoghurt
Freshly ground black pepper
2 tbsp chopped fresh parsley

Peel the carrots and cut in chunks. Mince them in a food processor, then add the other ingredients.

WALNUT AND SESAME SAUCE
Offer as a dip with crudités, or as a sauce to accompany a whole fish, simply baked or steamed and served cold. Serves 6-8

8oz (225g) walnuts
Juice of 3-4 lemons
6-8 tbsp tahini paste
3 cloves garlic, peeled and crushed
Salt, freshly ground black pepper
1 bunch fresh parsley

Either crush the walnuts with pestle and mortar, or use a spice- or coffee-grinder – but don't overdo it, they should be gritty not powdered. Put them in the liquidiser jug with lemon juice and tahini, garlic and seasonings and blend. Adjust the seasoning; add more lemon or tahini if required. Finely chop parsley and fold it in.

CHILLI TOMATO SAUCE

1½lb (675g) tomatoes, peeled, seeded and chopped
2 shallots, peeled and sliced
2 tbsp olive oil
2 large cloves garlic, peeled and crushed
3 green chillies, seeded, cut in fine strips
2 tsp caster sugar
Salt, freshly ground black pepper

Heat the oil and soften the shallots in it. Add the garlic and cook until just golden. Add the tomatoes and chillies, sugar and seasoning,

bring to the boil then lower the heat and simmer for 20 minutes until thickened. Use hot or cold.

YOGHURT AND MINT SAUCE

1 carton natural yoghurt
2 tbsp finely chopped fresh mint
2 tbsp lemon juice
2 tsp sugar
Generous pinch of turmeric powder

Combine the mint, lemon juice and sugar then stir in the yoghurt and turmeric for a cooling sauce to accompany spicy kebabs or curries, tandoori chicken or fish.

Vegetable dishes

WHEAT CASSEROLE
"This makes a wonderfully nutty, rich dish and could convert seasoned meat eaters" (Craig and Anne Sams). Serves 4-6

1 cup whole wheat grains
3 tbsp oil
1 large onion, finely chopped
2 cloves garlic, finely chopped
1lb (450g) mixed vegetables (sweetcorn, peas, diced carrots, broad beans, for varying colours and textures)
1 tbsp tamari soy sauce (naturally fermented, without added colour or flavour)

Wash the whole wheat grains thoroughly then put in a saucepan and cover with 2 cups water. Bring to the boil, turn the heat down as low as it will go, and allow to simmer for 2 hours or until grains are soft.

Heat the oil in a heavy pan and sauté the onion and garlic. Add the vegetables, wheat-grains and any remaining cooking liquid, and soy sauce. Add more liquid, cover and cook on a low heat (or in a moderate oven) for an hour.

WILD RICE RING WITH CREAMED MUSHROOMS
"Wild rice is expensive, but you need only a little and it gives an unforgettable flavour" (Craig and Anne Sams). Serves 4-6

For the mould:
1 cup wild rice
1 cup brown rice
1 onion, chopped
4oz (110g) mushrooms, wiped clean and roughly chopped
2oz (50g) melted butter or a little vegetable oil
1 clove garlic, sliced
½ tsp freshly grated nutmeg
4 tbsp dry sherry

For the filling:
1lb mushrooms, sliced
1 tbsp finely chopped onion
2 tbsp dry white wine
Pinch of paprika
1 tbsp mixed fresh herbs
2 tbsp wholemeal flour
½ pint (300ml) milk or soya milk
¼ tsp cloves, crushed
½ bay leaf

Cook the wild rice and the brown rice separately in salted water until tender but retaining bite.

Preheat oven to gas mark 5, 375°F, 190°C.

Sauté the chopped onion and 4oz of roughly chopped mushrooms for the mould together in a little of the butter or oil.

Mix the cooked rice, garlic, mushroom mixture, butter or oil, nutmeg and sherry together and press into a well-greased ring mould. Set the mould in a pan of hot water and bake for 30 minutes.

While it cooks, prepare the filling. Sauté the mushrooms and onions and add the wine, paprika and mixed herbs.

Make a sauce by melting the butter and gradually stirring in the flour, then cooking for 5 minutes. Gradually stir in the milk, then add the crushed cloves and the bay leaf.

Transfer the white sauce to a double boiler and stand it over a moderate heat for about 15 minutes.

When the rice ring is cooked, loosen the edges gently with a knife and very carefully invert the contents on to a serving dish. Fold the mushroom mixture into the sauce and pile into the rice mould.

CALAMATA OLIVE PÂTÉ WITH OAK SMOKED TOFU

Tofu, now stocked in various forms by many health food shops and delicatessens, is a paste made from soya beans. It makes a useful basis for dips and sauces as it is very low in fat and high in calcium and protein. This recipe and the one that follows are from Alison Leeming, vegetarian cookery writer, who suggests using it as a filling for baked potatoes, or for tomatoes or pastry cases as an hors d'oeuvre.

4oz (110g) Calamata olives (Greek olives
*   preserved in brine and olive oil)*
2oz (50g) capers
2 cloves garlic
1 tsp mixed herbs
3 tbsp olive oil
Juice of ½ lemon
4oz (110g) smoked tofu

Stone the olives and put in a coffee grinder with the capers, garlic and herbs.

Grind and transfer to a blender or food processor with the olive oil and lemon juice. Blend until smooth.

Grate the smoked tofu and stir into the mixture. (To thicken the pâté, a few fresh breadcrumbs can be added.)

GINGER AND SAFFRON TOFU DIP

This is excellent served as a dip with crudités and lightly cooked vegetables.

8oz (225g) silken tofu
3 cloves garlic
2 tbsp tomato purée
2 tbsp olive oil
1 tbsp finely grated fresh ginger
2 tsp French mustard
Pinch of cayenne pepper
5 saffron stamens, plus 4 stamens for garnish
Juice of 1 lemon

Drain the excess liquid from the tofu and put it, with the other ingredients, in a blender or processor. Whizz until quite smooth. Transfer to a bowl and put the four extra saffron stamens on top. As they become wet they will expand to lend a lovely red contrast to the creamy dip.

Serve with an array of raw and lightly cooked vegetables such as asparagus tips, mangetout, baby carrots, miniature sweetcorn, fennel, celery, peppers and cauliflower florets.

BULGUR AND VEGETABLE PILAU

"Experiment with different vegetables according to their availability, but do start with some nice green leaves – spinach, Savoy cabbage or spring greens" (Glynn Christian). Serves 4

5oz (140g) bulgur (cracked wheat)
Oil for frying
3oz (85g) finely chopped onion
1 clove garlic, peeled and crushed
8oz (225g) spinach or cabbage leaves, torn into
*   shreds*
½ tsp salt; freshly ground black pepper
Generous pinch freshly grated nutmeg
8oz (225g) prepared vegetables (sliced
*   courgettes, French beans broken into*
*   pieces, cauliflower florets, sliced leeks,*
*   thinly sliced carrots)*
1 tbsp freshly chopped herbs (parsley, chervil,
*   tarragon, marjoram)*
½ pint (300ml) hot chicken or veal stock
Natural yoghurt

Wash the bulgur in a sieve under the cold tap until the water runs clear.

Heat the oil in a heavy-based pan and gently cook the onion and garlic until they soften. Add the spinach or cabbage leaves, season with salt, pepper and nutmeg, and continue cooking for a minute or two until leaves are limp. Add the remaining vegetables, spreading them evenly over the base of cooked greens, then add the drained bulgur and the herbs in a layer.

Add the stock to the pan, bring to the boil and cook uncovered, over a moderate heat, for 15 minutes. Reduce the heat to its lowest setting and continue cooking for 10-15 minutes or until all the water has been absorbed.

Turn off the heat, cover the pan and let the pilau rest for 10 more minutes.

Put a suitable serving dish over the pan and invert it so that the green vegetable layer is on top with the layers of vegetables and burghul underneath. Drizzle the yoghurt over the top and serve the pilau cut in slices. Hand extra yoghurt separately.

KUTU

A spicy dish from Southern India. Serves 4-6

1½ cups lentils
5 cups water
½ tsp turmeric powder
1½ tbsp vegetable oil
Half a cauliflower
4 small or 2 medium potatoes
8oz (225g) shelled peas (frozen will do but fresh are better)
1 tsp salt
2 tbsp (yes, tablespoons) chilli powder
2 tsp urad dal (a type of split pea)
1 tsp cumin seeds, crushed
¾ tsp black pepper
¼ tsp asafoetida
2 tbsp desiccated coconut

Boil the lentils in the measured water with the turmeric powder and a teaspoonful of the vegetable oil until soft.

Divide the cauliflower into florets, cut potatoes into chunks and add both to the cooked lentils. Add the peas, salt and chilli powder and cook until the vegetables are soft.

Fry the urad dal in the remaining oil until golden brown. Add the cumin, black pepper, asafoetida and coconut and cook all together until the coconut is golden brown. Stir this mixture thoroughly into the lentils and serve.

MOREKADI

This dish and kutu above would both go well with Glynn Christian's bulgur pilau for a vegetarian feast. Serves 4 as a side dish.

8oz (225g) okra
Vegetable oil
Large pot of natural yoghurt
6 fresh green chillies, chopped
1 tbsp coriander seeds
2 tbsp desiccated coconut
1 tsp mustard seeds
Salt

Wash the okra under cold running water and scrape the ribs with a knife. Dry them, top and tail them and fry them with the mustard seeds in a little oil until soft (about 10 minutes).

Put the yoghurt and chillies, coriander seeds, coconut and salt in a liquidiser or processor and blend until smooth.

Pour the yoghurt mixture into a pan and add the okra; bring to the boil, stirring once, and remove from the heat to serve.

CUSTARD SQUASH IN TOMATO SAUCE
Serves 4 as a side dish

1 onion, chopped
1 tbsp vegetable oil for frying
1lb (450g) tomatoes, peeled, seeded and chopped
1 clove garlic, crushed
1 tbsp tomato purée
1 tbsp fresh basil or mint
Salt, freshly ground black pepper
12oz (350g) custard squash, peeled and sliced

Fry the onion until soft. Add the tomatoes, garlic, tomato purée, basil or mint and seasoning. Simmer for 5 minutes. Add the squash and cook, covered, until just tender.

Puddings

MANGO MOUSSE
Elisabeth Lambert Ortiz suggests serving this light, refreshing mousse with a garnish of strawberries or raspberries in season. Serves 6

2lb (900g) mangoes
3 fl oz (75ml) cold water
1 tbsp gelatine
2oz (50g) sugar (or less)
2 tbsp lime juice (or lemon will do)

Pour the water into a small saucepan and sprinkle the gelatine over it. Let it soften, then dissolve it, stirring, over a low heat. Set aside to cool.

Peel the mangoes, chop the pulp from the seeds and purée it in a blender or food processor with the sugar, lime or lemon juice and the gelatine.

Pour the mixture into a large bowl and chill in the fridge until syrupy and almost set. Beat it with a whisk until light and fluffy.

MIXED APPLE FOOL
Decorate this fool with colourful fruit such as kumquats. Serves 4

8oz (225g) Bramley apples
8oz (225g) Discovery or Cox's apples
5 fl oz (140ml) natural yoghurt
1oz (25g) light brown sugar
2 tbsp clear honey
4 level tsp powdered gelatine

Peel and core the apples and slice them roughly. Cook gently in a very little water (about a cupful) until they are fairly mushy and thick (about 15 minutes). Sieve the apples to make a purée, add the yoghurt, and sweeten with sugar and honey.

Sprinkle the gelatine over 6 tbsp water in a cup and leave to soften. Stir gelatine into the hot apple purée until dissolved. Divide the mixture between four glasses and chill.

DRIED FIGS IN WINE
Lynda Brown's quick, fibreful and delicious store cupboard recipe.

3-4 small dried figs per person
Red wine

Put the figs in a bowl and cover with boiling water. Leave to soften for 5 minutes, then drain.

Arrange the figs in a pan and pour in enough red wine to cover them completely. (The wine can be diluted with 1/3 water if preferred.) Poach gently for about 30 minutes, almost covering with a lid, until the figs are very soft. Leave to stand overnight, or longer.

To serve, pinch each fig to restore its shape, and heat wine and figs gently to boiling point. Transfer the figs to warmed serving dishes, pour over the sauce. Can be served hot or cold.

BANANAS POACHED IN ORANGE AND CARDAMOM SAUCE
Lynda Brown.

Half a large ripe banana per person
Seeds from 4 or more cardamom pods
Concentrated orange juice

Peel the bananas, halve lengthways, cut each half in two.

Crush the cardamom seeds in a pestle and mortar or grinder.

Put the bananas and ground cardamom in a small pan, barely cover with orange juice diluted with 2-3 tablespoons of water. Poach very gently for about 5 minutes until the bananas are soft, and have turned a brilliant marigold orange-yellow.

Serve immediately, spooning over the sauce. No additional sugar is needed.

LIME CREAM
Serves 4

Large carton strained Greek yoghurt
Zest and juice of 1 lime
1 tbsp clear honey, or to taste
A few drops vanilla essence
1 kiwi fruit
Langue de chat biscuits (optional)

Simply combine the yoghurt, lime juice and zest, honey and vanilla essence. Spoon into individual dishes and chill very slightly. Top each dish with a slice of kiwi fruit. Hand *langue de chat* biscuits separately if desired.

SUMMER PUDDING
This is usually made with soft summer fruits, but an autumn version might include greengages, damsons, plums and blackberries.
Serves 6

2lb (900g) mixed fruits (choose three or four of
*   the following: redcurrants, blackcurrants,*
*   raspberries, peaches, nectarines,*
*   gooseberries, loganberries)*
4 tbsp clear honey
Small wholemeal loaf, sliced

Put currants and gooseberries, if you're using them, in a large pan with a little water and the honey and simmer for about 5 minutes. Add the berries, and any larger fruit, peeled and sliced. Cover with a tight-fitting lid and turn off the heat. Leave the fruit to render its juices.

Line a 2 pint (1 litre) pudding basin with slices of the bread with crusts removed. Spoon in the juicy fruit mixture and cover closely with a top layer of bread.

Choose a small plate which will fit into the bowl, invert it over the pudding and put some weight such as a jar or tin on top.

Leave in the fridge overnight to allow the juices to seep into the bread.

To serve, remove the plate and invert the bowl on to a dish. Accompany the pudding with a little whipped cream for a rare treat.

PART SIX

DIETS FOR SPECIAL NEEDS

Babies

From three to six months, to until a year to 18 months, babies are gradually introduced to solid foods. The most suitable foods to begin with are vegetable and fruit juices, with baby cereals in moderate amounts. It is best to avoid eggs and cow's milk until after six months. There is a lot to be said for giving even young infants the taste for fresh, natural foods, rather than relying solely on tinned baby products. A mouli, sieve or liquidiser is an essential tool for preparing baby foods. Do not add sugar or salt to the food and be scrupulous about hygiene.

Young children

Children have higher energy and nutrient needs in relation to their size than adults, so it is natural that they always seem to be hungry. Do not be tempted to provide them with a store of sweets and convenience snack foods. But remember that they need to eat more frequently than adults, though with smaller portions, and that they should enjoy a varied diet to supply the nutrients needed for growth. Include cereals, especially wholegrain varieties, fresh fruit and vegetables of all kinds, poultry, fish, lean meat and occasionally liver, and dairy products such as cheese, milk, yoghurt and eggs. For snacks, provide nuts, fresh and dried fruits, sandwiches or raw vegetables with dips, and discourage the consumption of sugary products and crisps.

Adolescents

During adolescence, food is often consumed in vast quantities in an attempt to fill a seemingly bottomless pit. Regular exercise and well-balanced meals should help to avoid over-weight which can cause so much embarrass-ment and misery at school as well as being the forerunner of later potential ill-health. Head-strong teenagers, subject to peer pressure, and probably more concerned with being slim and fashionable than with general good health, are inclined to follow faddy diets. If a firm line is taken at home, if a variety of fresh foods is available at family meal times, and if there are tight controls on irregular snacks and on the consumption of sugary and high-fat foods, a standard will at least be set, even if — as is probable — this is ignored outside the house. Nutrients of particular importance in adolescence are calcium, iron and vitamin D. Young girls in particular, after the onset of menstruation, should ensure that their diet supplies adequate iron.

Pregnancy

Although there is no need to follow a special diet during pregnancy, the wide range of nutrients derived from a varied, healthy regime are crucial for the growth of the developing baby, as well as for the continuing health of the mother. A pint of milk a day is considered sufficient to supply the additional protein and calcium necessary (if you don't like milk on its own, take it in soups, custard, yoghurt or cheese). If the diet does not supply sufficient iron and folic acid (see page 31), supplements may be recommended by doctors. Supplements of vitamins A, C, D and calcium may also be recommended, and should be taken only on medical advice. Constipation, a common complaint in pregnancy, can generally be avoided by eating plenty of wholegrain and other high-fibre foods and drinking about two litres of water a day. It is advisable to give up smoking and to cut right down on alcohol or avoid it altogether. Coffee should also be drunk only in moderation — an American study has shown that excessive caffeine intake can be associated with complications in pregnancy. Exercise, as long as it is not too strenuous, it usually encouraged. There is no need to increase greatly your total kilocalorie intake —

"eating for two" is inadvisable, though it is important to enjoy a diet rich in protein, vitamin and mineral nutrients. See page 12 for energy requirements of pregnant and lactating women.

The elderly

Elderly people, particularly those living alone, can all too easily lose the motivation to prepare meals for themselves. Appetite and energy requirements generally decrease, but nutrients are as important for this age group as for any other. The sense of thirst, too, can become less urgent, yet water is still vital to the maintenance of bodily functions. Active and contented elderly people may have no diet problems, but for the sick and the housebound, those on medication or suffering from loneliness and bereavement, eating can become an intolerable chore, and encouragement may be needed to return to a normal eating and living pattern.

There is no need in old age for any drastic alterations to a diet which has been habitually enjoyed. The consumption of salt, sugar and fats need not be drastically reduced (and it's not a good idea at this time of life to substitute skimmed milk for whole milk). Nor should intake of fibre be drastically increased, since too much fibre can interfere with calcium absorption and may cause problems with digestion. A moderate increase in fibre, however, is desirable, and this might involve a switch to wholemeal bread and the consumption of more fresh fruit and vegetables.

Eating patterns may change with age, and smaller meals, taken more frequently, may better suit the individual's appetite. It is not a good idea to go for long periods without food, and continuing loss of appetite should be a matter of concern. But even a fairly restricted diet, balanced over the week, can provide efficient nutrients, so that supplements, except for specific medical reasons, should not be necessary. Taking exercise, going out and about and enjoying the company of others, can help to promote appetite, ensuring that food is a pleasure and the body receives what it requires.

Slimming

Many people, especially women, feel guilty about overweight yet are unable to act positively to solve the problem. Instant, drastic diets hold a fateful attraction, and of course it is possible to lose weight by eating nothing but apples or grapefruit or, for that matter, nothing but bread and water; the result, however, is more harmful than beneficial. Crash diets, unless very carefully formulated, invariably mean loss of valuable nutrients, and the moment the diet is abandoned, a return to former eating habits ensures the return of the extra pounds.

Start a slimming programme with a visit to the doctor, to establish the degree of overweight (if any), and to seek advice as to how and for how long you may need to diet.

In most cases, overweight is the result of an intake of kilocalories over and above energy requirements. The week's food intake should be scrutinised in the light of a knowledge of healthy eating. Do fats, sugar or alcohol supply too many kilocalories? Is your intake of filling fresh raw foods, wholegrains, vegetables and pulses too low? Do you rely heavily on fast foods and fat-rich takeaways? If you can answer an honest "no" to these questions, you must make the choice between taking more exercise without increasing calorie consumption, or reducing your energy intake. The first option does not have to involve drastic action: a brisk walk instead of using the car or public transport for local journeys, walking upstairs instead of taking the lift, and performing simple exercises every day will make some small difference. To reduce energy intake, you might find it easier to remove yourself from the worst sources of temptation. It is difficult to cut down when eating with others who have no need to slim, but if you can eat smaller portions, more often, this will help to assuage hunger pangs. And however strict you are with yourself, remember that a gradual weight loss is more easily achieved, healthier and more lasting.

One pound of body fat is equal to 3500 kcal. By cutting daily energy intake from 2500 kcal, in the case of a young, sedentary male, to just 2000 kcal per day, a deficit of 3500 kcal could be achieved over a week, resulting in the loss of one pound of fat. It makes sense to aim for a loss of one or two pounds a week. If you lose any faster, you are more likely to regain the weight.

People who have no wish or need to diet are often unsympathetic to slimmers, so if you find a lack of support or antagonism at home, join a slimming group or find a friend with similar problems for mutual encouragement.

Vegetarianism

A growing number of people in this country (an estimated 1.5 million) have decided to eliminate meat, fish and animal products from their diet. People have their own reasons for becoming vegetarians. Some believe, simply, that it is wrong to kill animals, others see it as a gesture towards solving desperate food shortages in the Third World, while yet others find that, on a vegetarian diet, they feel better. Whatever the motivation, the vegetarian way of life is attracting more converts. If you are thinking of making a radical change in your diet, give some thought to how this may be best done. Any abrupt change of eating habits is disturbing to the body, as many travellers find on holidays abroad. The Vegetarian Society recommends a gradual transition to vegetarianism by, for instance, making one day of the week a vegetarian day, then increasing the number of days until you are accomplished at shopping for and cooking vegetarian foods, and your body has had time to adjust. Alternatively, cut out first red meat then poultry and finally fish, again over a period of weeks.

Vegetarians must pay extra attention to nutrition to obtain all the necessary nutrients. It is a common mistake among those who will eat them, to consume a higher proportion of dairy products as a substitute for meat, which creates an imbalance in the diet. Make sure you eat a good proportion of different nuts, wholegrains, a wide range of cooked and raw fresh vegetables, and fresh and dried fruit. Essential amino acids, constituents of protein, can be obtained by eating complementary foods such as milk, cheese, eggs, nuts, pulses and grains (simple mixed protein dishes include cheese sandwiches, baked beans on toast, porridge with milk, baked jacket potatoes with cottage cheese . . .).

If you consider adopting a vegan diet, which excludes dairy produce, you will clearly need to obtain further information. (A book list can be had from the Vegan Society, address below.)

Vegetarians must ensure in particular that they consume enough iron and calcium. Although meat, particularly liver, is the best source of iron, it is also found in many vegetables (see pages 24-27). Its absorption is related to vitamin C so plenty of fresh fruit and green vegetables should be eaten.

Apart from the many excellent books available on vegetarianism, the best sources of information are The Vegetarian Society, of the UK Ltd, 53 Marloes Road, Kensington, London W8 6LA, and the Vegan Society, 47 Highlands Road, Leatherhead, Surrey.

Diets in illness

Infections and fevers The golden rule, for minor infections such as colds and flu, is to take plenty of liquids such as clear soups, freshly pressed lemon and orange juice diluted with water, weak tea or herbal teas and warm drinks made with yeast or meat extracts. In cases of severe vomiting or diarrhoea, salt and glucose must be replenished once liquids can be kept down. Supply these with beef or vegetable extracts and with glucose drinks. Do not take drinks too hot or too cold or you may provoke intestinal reaction. Progress gradually from a liquid to a more solid diet, with small portions of porridge, toast, plain biscuits, delicate sandwiches, clear soup with a little fine pasta, and fruit mousses. Avoid strongly flavoured, highly spiced or fried foods.

Convalescence Apart from special diets advised by doctors in particular circumstances, convalescent food should generally be light, attractive in presentation and small in portion, to be taken frequently. There is no need to serve bland food, but avoid fried dishes and strong, pungent flavours. When nursing a convalescent, consult the patient as to preferences in order to revive appetite.

Arthritis Rheumatoid arthritis can occur at a relatively early age, particularly in women, and usually affects the small joints of the hands and feet, causing pain, stiffness and swelling. Although the medical profession does not yet agree that diet plays a definite part in the management of the disease, people with a food allergy who are following an exclusion diet often find that arthritic symptoms show a marked improvement. It does, however, take a long time and much patience to establish whether you have a true food allergy, and this should only be done in consultation with your doctor. There is no magic diet that will improve all the many different kinds of arthritis, or that will account for individual differences, but undoubtedly conventional treatment (taking aspirin, or synthetic variations of cortisones, and steroids) has unpleasant side effects, and it might well be worth trying alternatives. Homoeopathy, acupuncture, the manipulations of osteopaths and chiropractors, herbal remedies and even copper bracelets all have their supporters who have found relief from pain with these methods, despite scepticism from some conventional doctors. (Manipulatory techniques, however, can be dangerous if inflammation is present.) Alternatives to conventional treatment may work for you, but beware of practitioners who charge fees and insist on unnecessarily frequent visits. It is always best to consult your doctor first.

Degenerative arthritis (osteoarthritis) is associated with the ageing process, and the affected joints are those which bear the most weight — knees, hips, ankles, spine. Understandably, as it is painful to move, sufferers are often over-weight. In such cases, losing weight helps considerably to reduce the burden, but it has also been found to clear up the symptoms completely.

Arthritis Care, 6 Grosvenor Crescent, London SW1X 7ER, is an organisation which gives support, help and information on all aspects of coping with arthritis. It has over 300 branches. A fact sheet on diet is available (enclose sae).

Ulcers A healthy, varied diet is the best treatment for a peptic ulcer. Pay particular attention to wholegrain foods, eat small, bland meals often, and avoid stimulants such as alcohol, strong tea and coffee, very hot or cold foods and anything rich in fat and cream. Cut out sugary foods and drink plenty of liquids between meals. Do not overload the digestive system with too-substantial meals, and do not have your last meal too late in the day. A warm, milky drink before you go to bed helps to prevent pain during the night and encourages a good rest.

Coeliac disease Sufferers experience allergic reactions to gluten, the protein in grains such as wheat, rye and barley (maize products and rice do not contain gluten). The result is intestinal damage and difficulty in absorbing food, and patients must adopt a permanent gluten-free diet. Informative labelling is not always sufficient to signal that a product contains gluten, but major retailers will usually provide details of gluten-free products on request. Avoid manufactured dishes such as pizza, pasta, cakes and puddings; in home cooking substitute wheatstarch, cornflour, soya flour, arrowroot, ground rice and potato flour for ordinary flour. The Coeliac Society of Great Britain and Northern Ireland (PO Box 181, London NW2 2QY) offer advice, information and recipes: write to them enclosing sae. Or ask your doctor or health visitor to put you in touch with a dietician.

Hyperactivity in children (hyperkinesis) This is a difficult and rare condition, not least because it can be a problem to obtain a correct diag-nosis. Noticeable symptoms include excessive activity, difficulty in containing frustration and short attention span, but these can equally be due to psychological or physiological disturb-ances, or to a combination of the two. Contrary to popular belief, if a child fails to sleep at night, this is not a symptom of hyperactivity but is usually due to insufficient exercise during the day. The role of food allergy in hyperactivity is still doubtful. A recent study has found that with adults who *believe* they have a food allergy,

only about one per cent actually do show intolerance, and it is very difficult to detect in children.

Various therapies have been used for hyper-activity – psychotherapy, behaviour modifica-tion, educational techniques – but dietary manipulation in particular has received the greatest public interest.

The Feingold diet, initiated by the American Dr Feingold, attempted to pinpoint the root problem as being sensitivity to certain food additives: artificial colours (the azo dyes), artificial flavours, monosodium glutamate (MSG), the preservatives BHA and BHT, and sodium benzoate (see also pages 86-87). Test results from Dr Feingold's techniques have been far from conclusive, with about 10 per cent of young children showing definite improvement, but many parents have found the regime beneficial. Some doctors are concerned that strict adherence to the Feingold diet over a period of time could result in nutritional deficiencies. However, no harm comes from providing a balanced, home-prepared, varied diet, free from additives, as a first step to help a hyperactive child. For further information contact Sally Bunday, Hyperactive Children's Support Group, 59 Meadowside, Angmering, Littlehampton, West Sussex BN16 4BW, enclosing large, self-addressed envelope and two first-class stamps.

Food allergies The number of people who experience adverse reactions to certain food is unknown, but a group of doctors, "clinical ecologists", believe that many illnesses and behaviour disturbances are related to diet. They contend that intolerance to particular foods is responsible for such afflictions as eczema, asthma, migraines, rheumatoid arthritis, and other difficult-to-attribute symptoms such as excessive fatigue, weight fluctuation and back pain. In their opinion, environmental changes from the increasing use of insecticides, ferti-lisers, and some food additives are also likely to result in food allergies. Diagnosis and treatment consist of tracking down those substances which cause a toxic reaction, followed by an elimination diet and changes in eating habits.

Clinical ecologists claim a 60-80 per cent success rate in overcoming symptoms of certain illnesses – a claim treated with some scepticism by some conventional practitioners. While research is as yet insufficient for conclusive evidence, clinical ecologists have at least opened up an important new area of discussion and they have treated successfully a number of patients. For more information, contact the

British Society for Clinical Ecology, The Burgh Wood Clinic, 34 Brighton Road, Banstead, Surrey SM7 8XP, or the Royal Liverpool Hospital, Prescot Street, Liverpool L7 8XP.

Diabetes At least one million people in Britain suffer from diabetes, the body's inability to regulate blood sugar levels due to a lack of absence of insulin. Some patients need insulin treatment, by injections or oral drops, and practically all sufferers need to change their diet to help keep the blood sugar level from falling too low or rising too high. In 1982, the British Diabetic Association revised traditional dietary recommendations. Their main conclusions were that every diabetic should be given an estimate of total energy (kilocalorie) requirements for his or her circumstances; that fats should be reduced to 35 per cent of all energy intake, with the higher proportion of these to be polyunsaturated; that at least half of total kilocalorie should come from carbohydrates, with the emphasis on fibre-rich foods; and that regular physical exercise be recommended.

Most diabetics are referred by their doctors to a dietician at a local hospital or nearby health clinic, where individual diets can be worked out. In broad terms, diabetics will probably follow most of the principles of the enlightened eating regime. For further information, leaflets and cookery books, write to the British Diabetic Association, 10 Queen Anne Street, London W1M 0BD.

Recovering from heart disease Heart disease is taken generally to mean any abnormal condition of the heart, ranging from its poor functioning due to high blood pressure, to diseases of the arteries. Fortunately, there are now treatments which cure or improve many forms of heart disease. It is also known that you can help your heart by watching your weight, taking regular, moderate exercise, giving up smoking, cutting down your alcohol intake, and eating the right foods. Diet can play a key role in heart disease, particularly in sufferers of coronary artery disease whose blood cholesterol is high. Specific and quantified dietary recommendations are not usually given nowadays, but most doctors will advise that you follow the low fat, low sugar, high fibre, fresh food guidelines detailed in this book.

For further information contact The Chest, Heart and Stroke Association, Tavistock House North, Tavistock Square, London WC1 9JE, who have a counselling service. The British Heart Foundation, 102, Gloucester Place, London W1, is bringing out a diet book in 1986-7.

INDEX

INDEX

ACKNOWLEDGEMENTS

These books have provided inspiration in thinking of healthy recipes which make you want to cook and eat, as well as just read. Any selection is bound to be personal, but, apart from Elizabeth David, Jane Grigson and Arabella Boxer who will probably be the mainstay of any collection of cookery books however small, here are my particular favourites:

The Sunday Times Complete Cookery Book, presented by Arabella Boxer (Weidenfeld and Nicolson). A source of techniques, invaluable for initial ideas on what to cook.

A New Book of Middle Eastern Food by Claudia Roden (Viking). Some of the best ways of using fresh ingredients without spending hours in the kitchen.

Mediterranean Seafood by Alan Davidson. A scholar who loves and knows about all varieties of fish – and scours the world for wonderful fish recipes.

A Cook's Tour of Britain by the WI and Michael Smith (Collins Willow). Not always low in fat, but a reminder of how good our own national dishes can be.

Delicatessen Cookbook by Glynn Christian (Macdonald). An eclectic writer of impeccable taste, excellent ideas on pasta, pulses, grains, breads, pâtés and terrines and a reliable guide to unfamiliar foods.

Fresh Thoughts on Food by Lynda Brown (Chatto & Windus). A relatively new and unconventional food writer, concentrating on lighter healthy dishes.

Caribbean Cookery by Elisabeth Lambert Ortiz (Penguin). An always stimulating writer who gives down to earth guidance on exotic foods.

An Invitation to Italian Cooking by Antonio Carluccio (Pavilion Books). The most wholesome of all cuisines – and most of it is straightforward to cook at home.

The Roux Brothers New Classic Cuisine (Macdonald). A book for experienced cooks but there are some simpler recipes. At the very least, a good read.

New Indian Cookery by Meera Tanega (Fontana). For the lighter style (less ghee, fresh tasting ingredients).

Kenneth Lo for all things Chinese.

Few vegetarian cookery writers really induce non-vegetarians to take the plunge. However, here are some whose recipes I find irresistible:

Eastern Vegetarian Cooking by Madhur Jaffrey (Jonathan Cape).

The Brown Rice Cookbook by Craig and Ann Sams (Thorsons).

Cordon Vert by Colin Spencer (Thorsons).

My warmest thanks to the chefs who gave recipes for this book and to the following cooks and food writers for their enthusiasm and ideas:

Brig Davies, Nicky Hessenberg, Tom Jaine, Jerome Kuehl, Panikos Andreou, Victoria Orr-Ewing.

LIS LEIGH

Cover photograph by Les Wies
All other photographs by Charlie Stebbings
Cartoons by David West
Illustrations by Cooper West and Andrew Farmer